Daniel Oliver, Verney Lovett Cameron

Across Africa

Daniel Oliver, Verney Lovett Cameron

Across Africa

ISBN/EAN: 9783337308933

Printed in Europe, USA, Canada, Australia, Japan

Cover: Foto ©Andreas Hilbeck / pixelio.de

More available books at **www.hansebooks.com**

BY

VERNEY LOVETT CAMERON, C.B., D.C.L.

COMMANDER ROYAL NAVY

GOLD MEDALLIST ROYAL GEOGRAPHICAL SOCIETY, ETC.

IN TWO VOLUMES
VOL. I.

WITH NUMEROUS ILLUSTRATIONS

LONDON
DALDY, ISBISTER & CO.
56, LUDGATE HILL
1877

Dedicated

BY PERMISSION

TO

HER MAJESTY QUEEN VICTORIA

BY HER HUMBLE AND OBEDIENT SERVANT

THE AUTHOR.

PREFACE.

IN placing this book before the public, I am conscious of its shortcomings as a narrative having an unbroken interest for the general reader. As a fact, I never contemplated writing a book of travel; but merely undertook the journey under the circumstances detailed in Chapter I.

To have introduced and enlarged upon personal events, sport, the sayings and doings of my followers, &c., would have increased the size of this work to an alarming degree; for it must be remembered that the period dealt with extends over three years and five months. Nearly the whole of that time I was on the tramp; and it has been my object to make this a guide by which my footsteps may be traced by those interested in the exploration of Africa, rather than a personal narrative of adventure and travel.

With this purpose I have principally confined

myself to detailing the particulars of my route; the peculiarities of the country; the manners and customs of the natives; the methods under which the detestable traffic in slaves is conducted, and the desolation and destruction that follow in its train; and to showing the prospects of opening up and civilising Africa.

My time has also been much occupied in many ways, and had I not received cordial assistance from willing hands it is possible this attempt would never have seen the light.

The accompanying map, too, has been most carefully prepared from my numerous notes, observations, and sketch-maps, by Mr. Turner of the Royal Geographical Society, and I feel every confidence in putting it forward as a thoroughly reliable guide to my journey from the East to the West Coast of Africa.

V. LOVETT CAMERON.

December, 1876.

CONTENTS OF VOL. I.

CHAPTER I.

PAGE

The Livingstone Search Expedition.—Motives for Volunteering.—Abandonment of the Search.—A New Expedition decided upon.—Selected for the Command.—Departure from England.—Arrival at Aden.—Zanzibar.—Fitting out.—Disadvantages of having arrived with Sir B. Frere's Mission.—Difficulties in obtaining Men.—Ordered to push on.—Ill-advised Haste.—The Start from Zanzibar.—Bagamoyo.—The French Mission.—A Balooch Commander-in-Chief.—Kaoli.—A Banquet.—A Fire.—Paying Pagazi.—An Arab Festival 1

CHAPTER II.

Parting Visit to Zanzibar.—Completing Equipment.—French Charlie's Store.—Farewell Dinners.—Our First Campaign.—A Fracas.—Upholding our Dignity.—The Father pleads for his Son.—Shamba Gonèra.—Visit from Dr. Kirk.—Our first Touch of Fever.—A new Volunteer.—Start for Kikoka.—The March.—Alligator-Shooting.—Deserters 22

CHAPTER III.

Leaving Kikoka.—Form of Camp.—Mode of Hut Building.—Foraging for Provisions.—A " Short Cut."—Bombay as a Guide.—A luckless Cruise.—A needless Scare.—Levy of Mhongo.—Msuwah.—Fortified Villages.—An Artful Dodger.—An Arab Caravan.—Offerings to Spirits.—Baobab-trees.—Kisémo.—The Lugerengeri.—The Kungwa Hills.—Simbawéni.—Its Queen.—Rumoured Terrors of the Makata Swamp.—Lazy Porters.—Honour amongst Deserters . 37

CHAPTER IV.

The Makata Swamp.—Mud Traps.—The Makata River.—A Native Bridge.—Transporting Donkeys.—Rehenneko.—Laid up.—A Strike among the Men.—Routine in Camp.—Visitors.—A swaggering Half-Caste.—News from Murphy.—His Arrival.—Death of Moffat.—Organizing the fresh Arrivals.—The Strength of the Expedition.—Women and Slaves.—Losses by Death and Desertion.—Armament.—Our Dogs and Donkeys.—Ready 61

CHAPTER V.

Our Porter's Vanity.—A Rocky Gorge.—Camping on a Slope.—An Impudent Beggar.—Mirambo—Monster Trees.—Wife-Beating.—Its Remedy.—A Blunder and its Consequences.—Fortune Seekers.—Several Caravans join us.—An Elephant-Hunter.—A Distressing Sight.—A Terekesa.—A Dry Country.—Death from Exhaustion.—Water once again.—Strange Doctrine of a "True Believer."—Tembé Huts.—The Wadirigo.—A Warlike Race.—Their Arms.—Harvesting.—Bitter Waters.—The Marenga Mkali.—Sharp-Eyed Wagogo 75

CHAPTER VI.

Entry into Ugogo.—Character of the Wagogo.—Defeat of an Arab Expedition.—Ugogo.—Water Supply.—A Wake.—Wanyamwési and their Ingratitude.—The 'Wagogo.—Extraordinary Earrings.—Fantastic Coiffures.—Personal Adornment.—A Struggle for Precedence.—Curiously formed Trees and Excrescences.—Astonishing the Natives.—Adopted Fathers.—A Thieving Tribe.—Bombay in a Fog.—A Chilly Morning.—Manufacture of Salt.—Smallpox . . . 92

CHAPTER VII.

Kanyenyé.—A veritable Methuselah.—Harsh-tongued People.—A drunken Official.—Laziness of our Pagazi.—A Fancy for Goggles.—A little Visitor.—Sambo shot.—A Thick Head.—Retributive Justice.—Fines for shedding Blood.—Hyænas.—A Rain-Spirit.—Pigeon-Shooting.—Witchcraft.—The Penalty of Failure.—Wizards roasted alive.—Usekhé.—Obsequies of a Chief.—The Wahumba.—Cost of Provisions.—Admiring Spectators.—Immense Tusks.—A distressed British Subject.—Expenditure in Mhongo . . . 107

CONTENTS.   xi

CHAPTER VIII.

PAGE

The Mgunda Mkali.—A serious Misunderstanding.—Restoration of Peace.—Rejoicing in the Village.—The Mabunguru Nullah.—An unexpected Chase.—Native Farming.—An intelligent and industrious People.—Jiwé la Singa.—Complimentary Beggars. Moonstruck Askari.—Hatred of Snakes.—Pitfalls.—A Dry March.—Burnt-up Country.—A Hunter's Paradise.—A well-fortified Village and well-dressed Chief.—Discovery of a Den of Thieves.—A Haunted Well.—An Attack by Ruga-Ruga 127

CHAPTER IX.

Unyanyembé.—Morning Calls.—Excessive Hospitality.—The Fighting Mirambo.—The Origin of the Struggle.—The Garrison of Unyanyembé.—Atrocities.—Kidnapping our Pagazi.—A Letter from Sir S. Baker.—Communication with Mtésa.—A difficulty in his Conversion to Mohammedanism.—Gross Outrage upon a Pagazi.—Mutiny amongst the Askari.—The Unpleasantness of the Situation.—Our Troubles and Worries.—Fever and Blindness.—Desertion of Pagazi.—Consequent Expense.—Kindness of the Arabs.—An Auction.—Public Sale of Slaves.—The Death of Livingstone . . . 147

CHAPTER X.

Arrival and Reception of Livingstone's Body.—Some Particulars of his Death.—The Future of the Expedition.—Its partial Abandonment. — Murphy resigns. — Dillon compelled to turn back. — The *Personnel* of my Expedition.—Parting from Dillon.—I go forward alone.—Troubles of Transport.—I throw away Preserved Provisions.—A Native Plea for Slavery.—The Death of Dr. Dillon.—A Sad Blow.—Kasékerah.—Offended Dignity of Askari.—Shirking their Work.—Determined Deserters.—A pleasant March.—Village Clubs.—A Visit to Murphy.—The Manner of transporting Livingstone's Body.—Capture of a Thief.—I reduce my Kit.—A dirty and drunken Chief.—Muscat Donkeys.—The Road blocked . . 167

CHAPTER XI.

Driven back to Hisinéné.—A miserable Christmas.—Superstitions regarding Snakes.—Customs of the People.—Dancing.—Cooking Arrangements.—Storing Corn.—Their Huts.—Food.—Curing.—Provisions.—Cloth-making.—Grinding Corn.—Tribal Marks.—Hair-dressing.—Warned against Mirambo.—A Spy shot.—On the Road again.—A hospitable old Lady.—Missing the Way.—Sack-making. —An Elopement.—Disordered State of the Country.—The South Ngombé.—A Day's Shooting.—A Hunter's Story 187

CHAPTER XII.

Ugara.—A ludicrous Sight.—Mirambo's Head-quarters.—Destruction and Desolation.—The Havoc of the Slave-trade.—A Field for England's Labours.—Leo surprises the Natives.—Leg Ornaments.— Liowa.—My Pets.—A lawless Set of Ruffians.—Heavy Rains.—Bee-nesting.—A Stampede.—Lost in Jungle.—A Panic.—Rocky Residences.—An Attempt at Extortion.—I give a Lecture on Hospitality. —Its good Effect.—Nothing to eat.—Jasmin dies.—Tameness of my Goat.—Unfriendly Villages.—A Buffalo Charge 205

CHAPTER XIII.

Floating Islands.—Their Origin and Growth.—Crossing the Sindi.— Uvinza.—A Cordial Reception.—Strange Economy.—A Boy Chief. —Curious Visitors.—Ceremonious Salutation.—Tattooing.—Ugaga. —Approach of Mirambo.—On our Defence.—Destruction of several Villages.—Ferry Charges.—A Host of Claimants.—The Malagarazi Ferry.—Sambo's Cookery.—Salt-making.—A considerable Trade.— Liquid Snuff.—A Droll Sight.—My faithful Leo dies.—A Wild Beast in Camp.—Sighting Tanganyika.—Arrival at Kawélé . . 222

CHAPTER XIV.

Recovery of Livingstone's Papers.—Robbery of my Stores.—Punishment of a Thief.—Difficulty in sending the Journals to the East Coast.—The Traders of Kawélé.—The Native Dress and Ornaments.—Their Markets.—Warundi Body-Colouring.—Products of the district.—Their Currency.—Hiring Boats.—Curious Mode of Payment.—Fitting out.—I am thought "unlucky."—My Guides desert me.—"Negro Melodists."—Sailing away on the Tanganyika.—Devils' Dwellings.—Propitiating the Spirits.—Slave-Hunters 240

CHAPTER XV.

Profitable Slave-Buying.—Street Acrobats.—War-Paint.—A bad Night.—Cowardly Boats' Crews.—Kabogo.—A public Entertainment.—Stealing Men's Brains.—Coal.—A Honey Demon.—A

CONTENTS. xiii

PAGE

Plague of Frogs.—Enlargement of the Lake.—Massi Kambi.—An Optical Illusion.—Many Devils.—One of my Men shoots himself. —Doctors differ.—Curious Hair-Oil.—The Chief of Makukira.— His Dress.—Wives.—Dolls.—Infantine Taste for Drink.—Cotton Manufacture.—Spread of the Slave-trade.—The Watuta.—Customs and Dress.—Twins 257

CHAPTER XVI.

The Art of Pottery.—My Men grow Bolder.—Akalunga.—The Chief.—A Native Notion of Portugal.—Granaries.—Strange Mutilation by Women.—Ornaments.—The Luwaziwa.—Gorillas.—Hillside Cultivation.—Spiders.—Mosquitoes, Boils, and Sore Feet.—A Strike. — Hot-water Spring. — Waguhha Hair-dressing. — Idols. — The Lukuga.—Return to Ujiji.—Letters from Home.—My Men indulge freely. — Arab Opinion of the Lualaba.—Fear of Opposition Traders.—Bombay's Jealousy.—Cost of cutting the Sod in the Lukuga.—I give Readings.—Arson.—Domestic Jars.—More Orgies. —Off again 288

CHAPTER XVII.

Hopeful prospects.—Ruanda.—Copper.—Bombay's Ingenuity.—An Accident.—Last view of Tanganyika.—Dishonest fellow Travellers. —Mókéto.—A brutal Slave-dealer.—Dress and Ornaments.—Weapons.—Fish-dealers.—River-side Scenery.—Game.—Skulking Carriers. — Bowl-making. — Indiarubber. — A trying March. — Fetish Huts.—A Good Samaritan.—My Men want to turn back.—" Making Brothers."—An Artist in Oils.—Fearful Imprecations.—Musical Instruments. — Mrs. Pakwanywa.—Perforation of Upper Lips.— Dress.—Tattooing.—Charms.—A Hot Stream.—A Mixed Caravan . 317

CHAPTER XVIII.

Pakhûndi.—Foundries.—Dust and Ashes.—Slave gagging.—Freedmen the Harshest Masters.—Salutations.—Disobliging People.— Hair, Dress, Tattooing. — Naked People. — Natural Stomachers.— Building Operations. — No Ventilation. — Uvinza. — Clay Idols.— Carving. — Arms. — The Arabs' Kirangosi. — His Impertinence. — Climbing Oil-palms.—My Showman.—The Bambarré Mountains. —Magnificent Trees.—A dark Ravine.—Manyuéma.—Dress and Arms.—The Women.—Economy in Clothing.—Livingstone's Influence.—An Enlightened Chief.—Dwarfs.—Musical Instruments.— Fearful Cannibals.—Dancing.—No Shooting allowed . . . 339

CHAPTER XIX.

The Luama.—Fisherwomen.—Shooting Hippopotami. — Open-air Granaries.—Iron.—A Burning Country.—Shameful Behaviour of Traders.—A Suspension Bridge.—The Natives turn upon the Traders. — Contemplated Attack on the Caravan. — Two Chiefs treacherously shot.—Villages burned.—Women and Children captured.—I plead for Peace.—Influence as an Englishman.—A Palaver. —The Captives are liberated.—My Views are not appreciated.— Foundries. — Smithies. — Manyara Dress. — A Drum-Major. — The Slaving System.—The Mighty Lualaba.—Going with the Stream.— Nyangwé is reached 361

ILLUSTRATIONS TO VOL. I.

Map, showing Author's Route . . *In Pocket at end of Volume.*

FULL-PAGE PLATES AND FACSIMILES

Looking back over Makata Swamp . . . . *Frontispiece*
Paper of Recommendation issued by Khedive (*facsimile*). *To face p.* 6
Camp at Msuwah 46
Letter from Jacob Wainwright reporting Death of Dr.
 Livingstone (*facsimile*) 165
Kwiharah 171
Soko at Kawélé 244
Village of Kitata, Tanganyika Lake 274
Rawlinson Mountains 289
Camp at Mékéto 323
Crossing the Lugungwa River 327
Village in Manyuéma 352
Pot-Pourri 357
Crossing the Luama River 362
Waiting for Canoes 376
Nyangwé 378

SMALLER WOODCUTS.

	PAGE		PAGE
Steamer Point, Aden	7	Camp	64
Dhows	21	Riding Donkeys	73
View in Bagamoyo	25	African Fireplace	74
Camp at Shamba Gonèra . .	30	Tembé	87
Loaded Donkey and Pagazi .	36	Earthen Pot, Ugogo	91
Bombay and Two Chums . .	40	Arms and Ornaments . . .	97
Return of the Deserter . . .	59	Ziwa, near Mpanga Sanga . .	103
Flowers	60	View in Ugogo	105

ILLUSTRATIONS.

	PAGE		PAGE
Heads	106	Heads of Waguhha and other Lake Tribes	303
Rocky Hills in Usekhé	114		
Camp, Usekhé	115	Entrance to Lukuga, or Marie Alexandrovna	305
Enormous Sycamores	119		
Rocks, Usekhé	126	Bow-stands of Waguhha	314
Halting-place near a Pond	131	Bay in Kavira Island	316
Village in Unyanyembé	146	Head of Uguhha Woman	318
Plan of House at Kwiharah	148	A "Handa"	319
A Good Cook : price Two Hundred Dollars	165	Whistle, Hatchet, and Pillow	323
		Dress and Tattooing of Woman of Uguhha	325
Manner of fettering Slaves	166		
Plan of Dr. Dillon's Route	175	Mrua Fishmonger	326
Drums	186	Drum and Idol	329
Zebra	189	Idols	330
Ants' Nest	204	Women of Ubûdjwa	336
Buffalo charging Caravan	221	Charms	337
Crossing the Malagarazi	229	Carved Stick	338
Crossing the Rusugi	235	Huts in Uhiya	346
Arms	239	Heads of Men of Manyuéma	353
Ujiji Pottery	256	People of Manyuéma	354
Camp on Spit	267	Women going Fishing	359
An Inhabitant of Massi Kambi	270	Sambo	360
Brother Rocks	274	Karungu	366
Watuta Woman	286	Hills on Road to Manyara	370
Tanganyika Fishes	287	Coming to Market	375
Tembo Bwana	291	Nyangwé from the River	378
King Miriro and his Granary	293	Market Women, Nyangwé	379

CHAPTER I.

THE LIVINGSTONE SEARCH EXPEDITION.—MOTIVES FOR VOLUNTEERING.—ABANDONMENT OF THE SEARCH.—A NEW EXPEDITION DECIDED UPON.—SELECTED FOR THE COMMAND.—DEPARTURE FROM ENGLAND.—ARRIVAL AT ADEN.—ZANZIBAR.—FITTING OUT.—DISADVANTAGES OF HAVING ARRIVED WITH SIR B. FRERE'S MISSION.—DIFFICULTIES IN OBTAINING MEN.—ORDERED TO PUSH ON.—ILL-ADVISED HASTE.—THE START FROM ZANZIBAR.—BAGAMOYO.—THE FRENCH MISSION.—A BALOOCH COMMANDER-IN-CHIEF.—KAOLI.—A BANQUET.—A FIRE.—PAYING PAGAZI.—AN ARAB FESTIVAL.

1872.

LONG ago, when serving as senior lieutenant of H.M.S. *Star* on the East Coast of Africa, I had full opportunity of seeing some of the cruelties and atrocities connected with the slave-trade; and the sufferings which I witnessed on board the dhows—such as have been so graphically described by Captain G. L. Sulivan, R.N., in "Dhow-Chasing in Zanzibar Waters"—awoke in me a strong desire to take some further part in the suppression of the inhuman traffic.

I soon became convinced that unless it could be attacked at its source in the interior of the continent all attempts at its suppression on the coast would be but a poor palliation of the fearful evil.

I am, however, far from laying claim to having been actuated solely by purely philan-

1872. thropic motives, as some time previously my aspirations for travel and discovery had been excited by reading papers descriptive of the expedition of Burton and Speke in Somáli land. And I became still more anxious to undertake some exploration in Africa on hearing that Arab merchants from Zanzibar had reached the West Coast; for I felt convinced that what had been accomplished by an Arab trader was equally possible to an English naval officer.

After the *Star* was put out of commission I was appointed to the Steam Reserve at Sheerness, and my efforts to obtain more active employment being ineffectual, I volunteered my services to the Royal Geographical Society to go in search of Dr. Livingstone and render him any assistance possible, it being supposed at that moment that the expedition under Mr. Stanley had failed.

Soon after this subscriptions were opened for the "Livingstone Search Expedition," but it was not my fortune to be selected by the Royal Geographical Society, the command being given to Lieutenant L. S. Dawson, R.N., an officer eminently fitted for the post both by his scientific attainments and physical powers.

Unfortunately when this expedition was about to start from Bagamoyo it was deterred from proceeding further by the news brought to the coast by Mr. Stanley, of the *New York Herald*. This was to the effect that Livingstone had already been relieved and objected to any "slave expedition" being sent to him. In consequence of this unfortunate misapprehension of Dr. Livingstone's despatches Lieutenant Dawson, supposing that his expedition would no longer be required, resigned the command.

Lieutenant Henn, R.N., then took charge with the full intention of proceeding, but was also persuaded to throw it up, though much against his wish.

Upon Oswell Livingstone, a son of the Doctor, the leadership then devolved. But after a time he renounced the idea of proceeding up country to join his father; and thus a most carefully organized expedition, which possessed most, if not all, the requisites for a complete success, was abandoned.

Mr. New, another member, withdrew with Lieutenant Dawson, and the services of a gentleman well versed in African character, having a competent knowledge of Kisuahili, and accustomed to African travel, were thus lost. I may here mention how great was my regret soon after arriving at Loanda to hear of the death of Mr. New. He was a single-minded, brave, and honest man, who devoted himself to the task of bettering the condition of the natives of Africa, and in so doing sacrificed a valuable life.

Although disappointed at my failing to obtain the command of this expedition, I still entertained some hope of leading another and carrying out the project which I had so much at heart, and therefore determined to further prepare myself for the undertaking by studying the Suahili language.

Of the difficulties entailed by such a service I had gained some knowledge from eight months passed in the Red Sea during the Abyssinian war, and nearly three years on the East Coast of Africa, much of which period was spent in open boats. With this experience of work in a hot climate, added to my having suffered severely from fever at Zanzibar, it was not without counting the cost that, as soon as Dawson's expedition was reported to have been broken up, I volunteered to proceed to join Dr. Livingstone, taking with me such instruments and stores as he might require, and offering to place my services unreservedly at his disposal.

This was in June, 1872, but no intention of sending out another expedition to assist our great traveller appeared then to be entertained.

I next drew up a scheme for the exploration of the route to Victoria Nyanza *via* Mounts Kilima Njaro and Kenia and the volcano reported to lie to the north of them—thus passing close to the watershed between the coast rivers and the feeders of the Victoria Nyanza—and after surveying that lake to work my way to the Albert Nyanza or Mwuta Nzigé, and thence through Ulegga to Nyangwé and down the Kongo to the West Coast.

The latter part of this route is now being

attempted by Mr. Stanley, one of the most successful and energetic of African travellers, under the auspices of the *New York Herald* and *Daily Telegraph*.

1872.

In this I was encouraged and assisted by Mr. Clements Markham, C.B., and to his counsel and kindly help in many matters intimately connected with my African travels I am deeply indebted.

The Council of the Geographical Society were, however, of opinion that this scheme, though meeting with the approval of some of its most eminent members, could not be carried out with the funds at their disposal.

It was afterwards decided to utilise the surplus remaining from the subscriptions to the first Livingstone Search Expedition in fitting out another. This was intended to be placed entirely under the orders of Dr. Livingstone for the purpose of supplementing his great discoveries, in the prosecution of which he had on that last journey—extending over a period of nearly seven years and brought to a close only by the national misfortune of his death — patiently and unremittingly toiled, besides having previously devoted twenty years of his life to the cause of the regeneration and civilisation of Africa.

For the new command I had the happiness of being selected, and the Council kindly allowed Mr. W. E. Dillon, assistant surgeon—one of my dearest friends and an old messmate—to accompany me,

November, 1872. for which purpose he resigned an appointment he then held.

He was admirably adapted for the work, and had his life been spared to cross the continent with me would have been of incalculable assistance and comfort in my various difficulties and troubles. His unvarying kindness and tact in his intercourse with the men of the expedition were the greatest help to me during our journey to Unyanyembe, and, indeed, I cannot pay a sufficient testimony of gratitude and honour to his memory.

Dr. Dillon and I left England on the 30th November, 1872—the same day on which Lieutenant Grandy and his brother left Liverpool for the West Coast—in order to join Sir Bartle Frere at Brindisi, hoping to get a passage on board the *Enchantress* with his mission to Zanzibar. But her accommodation was too limited to allow of our being received on board.

Thus we lost the advantage we had anticipated of obtaining some instruction in Arabic and Kisuahili kindly promised by the Secretary of the Legation, the Rev. Percy Badger. Remaining at Brindisi until Sir Bartle Frere's arrival, we then took passage in the P. & O. steamer *Malta* to Alexandria. We accompanied Sir Bartle Frere to Cairo, where he procured a letter from H.H. the Khedive commending us to the care of the Egyptian officials in the Soudan and ordering them to give us every assistance.

الى حامرين ' حكو

حيث ' ان مستر كامرون من ضباط :
ستوجيه ' الى ' افريقيه الوسطى للبحث
روستكت ف الاراضى المجهوله هناك
الى ' حكومه ' المصريه ببذل المبادره
من طرف ' الجميع فى تسهيل و تسهيل
و ' رجا' على تتقضا ه ٨، ١٢٨٩

ed in the service of the said Government, are
to these parts to explore the unknown regions.
and to give them protection on all sides, to

ISMAEL BASHA.

عددن

الى مامورين حكومة الخديوية المصرية بالاقاليم السودانية عموما

حيث ان ستر كامرون من ضباط بحرية دولة انكلترة الخجمة والدكتور ديهلون من معتبرين الدول انكليز
سوف يتوجه الى اوسط افريقيا للبحث والاجتماع على الدكتور ليوينكستون الذي كما توجه سابقا الى ذلك الطرف
وسلك في الاراضي المجهولة هناك فينبغي انه عند مرورهم وصولهم الى اي جهة واي مركز من جهة ان بعد
الى حكومه المصرية بصرف مبادرة من المامورين والحكام والاسماج بمتا علتهم بالاعتذار والوقار والاحترام
من طرف الجميع في تحصيل وتمكين غرضهم ومساعدتهم وما علتهم حسبما يلزم وهذا امرنا عموما نفذ كما يعتمد
وروجى على مقتضاه في ٢٨ معص ١٢٨٩

NOTICE.

TRANSLATION.

To those in Command under the Authority of Egypt in the lands of Soudan.

Whereas Lieut. Cameron, an Officer of the Royal English Navy, and Dr. Dillon, esteemed in the service of the said Government, are proceeding to Central Africa to search for, and to meet with, Dr. Livingstone, who before went to these parts to explore the unknown regions.

All Officers of Egypt, and Kings, and Sheikhs, are required to receive them with honor, and to give them protection on all sides, to assist and help them on their journey as may be required.

This is Our public order to that end issued accordingly.

Dated 28th Haj, 1289.   [L. S.]   ISMAEL BASHA.

True Translation—JOHN KIRK.

ARRIVAL AT ADEN.

This document proved of service with Arabs in the interior, who had all heard both of the Khedive and the Sultan of Turkey, although we never came across any of those for whom it was particularly intended.

December, 1872.

After a short stay at Cairo we went to Suez, and thence by the *Australia* to Aden, where we were very kindly received by the resident, Briga-

STEAMER POINT, ADEN.

dier-General Schneider, Colonel Penn ("steel pen" of Abyssinian fame), and the rest of the garrison; and from Dr. Shepheard, P.M.O., we received a most valuable supply of quinine, a *sine quâ non* in African travel.

Whilst here Dr. Badger obtained for us from a Santon named Alowy ibn Zain el Aidûs a letter

December, recommending us to the care and consideration of
1872. all good Moslems in Africa, and this we found the most useful of all our papers.

Lieutenant Cecil Murphy, R.A., acting commissary of ordnance, here volunteered to accompany the expedition, provided the Government of India would consent to continue his Indian pay and allowances; and this being granted after our departure, he joined us at Zanzibar by the next mail.

Our anticipations that H.M.S. *Briton* would have taken us to Zanzibar were doomed to disappointment, for she had already sailed. We had therefore to await the departure of the mail-steamer *Punjáb*, Captain Hansard, in which we proceeded. Colonel Lewis Pelly, political agent at Muscat, and Kazi Shah Budin, a gentleman appointed by H.H. the Rao of Kutch to accompany Sir Bartle Frere to Zanzibar and to use his influence with the subjects of the Rao in support of the objects of the mission, were our fellow-passengers.

When I arrived at Zanzibar I was laid up with fever which had attacked me a day or two previously, and as Dr. Kirk's house was fully occupied by those who had already gone ashore from the *Enchantress*, Dillon and myself took up our abode in the hitherto untenanted English gaol. There was plenty of room for our stores, and with native bedsteads, chairs, &c., we were soon comfortably housed. However, some old messmates of mine, Lieutenants Fellowes and Stringer, kindly took me off to the *Briton* and looked after me on board until I was tolerably well again.

January, 1873.

When sufficiently recovered to go ashore I rejoined Dillon, who had already laid in some stores, and we at once began to look out for men and donkeys. We also secured the services of Bombay (Mbarak Mombée), the chief of Speke's faithfuls, which at the time we thought of great importance on account of his previous experience.

But he rather presumed on our ignorance, and we soon learned that however useful he might have been in days gone by he was not the best man to consult in fitting out an expedition, not having sufficient readiness and knowledge to advise us as to the most serviceable things with which to supply ourselves. He had besides lost much of the energy he displayed in his journeys with our predecessors in African travel, and was much inclined to trade upon his previous reputation; but the high opinion we had formed of him at first blinded us to his many failings.

The fact of our having arrived on the scene with Sir Bartle Frere caused us to be inseparably connected by the Arabs, Wasuahili and Wamerima, with the mission upon which he was engaged, and this occasioned us numerous vexatious troubles and enormous expense, besides being prejudicial to the interests of the expedition.

In the first place they naturally supposed that we were in the employ of the English Govern-

January, 1873.

ment, and therefore ought to pay twice or three times the ordinary price for men and stores. All who thus defrauded us considered themselves perfectly justified in cheating a Government so rich and liberal as ours has the reputation of being, although they would have had far greater scruples about swindling private individuals.

In the second place, owing to the avowed intention of the mission to abolish the slave-trade, we were thwarted and imposed upon in various underhand ways by the lower classes of the Wasuahili and Wamerima.

In addition to this, our orders being to push on with all despatch and at all hazards, we were obliged to accept the riff-raff and outscourings of the bazaars of Zanzibar and Bagamoyo instead of waiting for regular porters, and also had to pay them double the hire of better men.

This scarcity of porters was owing to the season of the year, as the usual time for the up caravans had long passed, and no down caravans had yet arrived.

We had therefore to march through the worst part of the rainy season with a number of men of whom not more than a tenth had ever before travelled any distance into the interior, and who, not being accustomed to carrying loads, gave trouble at almost every step by straggling and laziness.

Nor did the evil end here, for the majority of

the men were thieves, and pilfered unceasingly from their loads. Indeed, the effects of this ill-advised haste in starting pursued me throughout my journey across the continent.

Bombay was commissioned to find us thirty good men and true, to be our soldiers, servants, and donkey drivers. He promised all diligence and obedience, and whilst within ken of the English consulate exerted himself apparently to the best of his power. I afterwards learnt that he picked up his men anywhere in the bazaar, and a motley crew they proved.

Besides these thirty askari we engaged a few men as porters, and bought twelve or thirteen donkeys at an average price of eighteen dollars a head.

We then embarked with our stores, men, and beasts in two hired dhows, and left Zanzibar early on Sunday morning, February 2nd, 1873, and passing through the ships of the squadron with the union-jack and white ensign flying, made our way with a fair wind to Bagamoyo, arriving there the same afternoon.

Bagamoyo, the principal point of departure for caravans bound to Unyanyembé and the countries beyond, is a town on the mainland directly opposite Zanzibar. It is hidden from the sea by sand-hills, but marked by the tall cocoa-nut palms which always indicate the habitations of man on this coast.

February, 1873.   It consists of one long straggling street with a few stone houses, the rest being mere huts of wattle and dab, having huge sloping roofs thatched with the plaited fronds of the cocoa-nut palm; and it boasts of two or three mosques, frequented only on high days and holidays. A varied assemblage of Indian merchants, Arabs, Wasuahili and Wamerima, slaves and Wanyamwési pagazi compose its population.

Taking with us only a few necessaries, we went on shore to look for lodgings, and were met on landing by a messenger from the French mission, shortly followed by Père Horner and one of the lay brothers, who came to offer their assistance.

After a great deal of chaffering and bargaining we hired for ourselves the upper rooms of a stone house, the owner, Abdûllah Dina (a Koja), taking twenty-five dollars instead of the forty-five he had at first asked. For our men and stores we secured a house which belonged to Jemadar Issa, the commandant of the Balooch garrison of H.H. Syud Burghash.

Early the next morning we superintended landing cargo, going backwards and forwards the whole time between head-quarters, barracks, and beach. Yet, notwithstanding all our care, a bag of salt, a case of paraffin, one of preserved meats, and, of still greater importance, our large cooking-lamp, were missing when the debarkation was completed.

At first we were disposed to blame a Hindi

whom we had engaged at Zanzibar to look after the transport of our stores, but I believe carelessness and not dishonesty was his failing in this instance.

February, 1873.

Jemadar Issa readily gave us permission to fly the colours and post sentries at head-quarters and barracks, and returned our call in the forenoon, offering us all the courtesies and assistance in his power.

We told him of our losses, and he promised redress. But as this consisted only in the offer of putting the unfortunate Hindi in irons and sending him over to the Sultan for further punishment we declined this friendly proposal and made up our minds to bear our losses philosophically.

At the conclusion of our morning's work we paid a visit to the French mission, to which we had been invited, meeting on our way two donkeys with European saddles and bridles kindly sent for our use. After luncheon we went over the well-cultivated grounds and plantations, where bread-fruit trees and vegetables, including asparagus and French beans, grew in abundance, and then visited the buildings, nearly the whole of which were greatly damaged in the hurricane of 1872.

About three hundred children were being trained here to different trades and useful callings, and a school for girls was placed under the control of the sisters belonging to the mission. In the boys' dormitories the arrangements were very simple,

February, 1873. the beds consisting merely of a couple of planks on iron supports with a few yards of merikani to serve as mattress and bedclothes; and in each room was a small screened space for the brother in charge.

A new chapel was being erected outside the former building, portions of which were removed as the other progressed, and though this was rather slow work owing to the scarcity of labour and the laziness of the natives, yet by this arrangement the religious services were never interrupted.

The foundation of a new stone (pucka) building had also been laid, and when completed was to be used as a dwelling-house and school.

The Fathers seem to be labouring hard and doing a good work both by precept and example, and amidst their many difficulties are cheerful and confident, and I have no doubt their efforts will tend much towards the civilisation of this part of Africa.

Nothing could exceed the kindness and attention shown to us by these estimable men during our stay at Bagamoyo. They frequently sent us vegetables and bundles of palmiste for salad, and on one occasion a quarter of wild-boar, which in the inefficient state of our cooking appliances was not a trifle tantalising, as we could devise no means of dressing it ourselves, and our followers—Mohammedan in nothing but their prejudices—declined to touch it.

A BALOOCH COMMANDER-IN-CHIEF.

Our Koja landlord Abdûllah Dina was so jealous of the female portion of his domestic circle that he padlocked the door leading to the stairs outside the house, and put up a most inconvenient ladder instead. His object was to keep us from passing through the small portion of the yard into which our stairs led, although it was already divided from the other part by a railing filled up with reeds, and quite sufficient to prevent our infidel eyes from spying out the secrets of his harem.

February, 1873.

A few days after our arrival, Jemadar Sabr, commanding all the Sultan's troops on this portion of the coast, called on us with a following like a Highland chieftain. They were all redolent of dirt and grease and covered with bucklers, pistols, swords, spears, and matchlocks, as though they had ransacked the stores of some transpontine theatre.

The leader of this imposing retinue was not above begging for a dustoori of a few dollars; nor was Jemadar Issa one whit behind him in this respect, besides always asking for a little brandy as medicine.

Jemadar Issa promised to accompany us the next morning to Kaoli to return the call of Jemadar Sabr; but as he did not put in an appearance at the appointed hour we went down to his house, and found him in his usual dirty shirt.

He immediately proceeded to array himself by putting on a gorgeous turban and a scarf, into which he thrust his dagger, an elaborately gilt

February, 1873. French breech-loading revolver for which he had no cartridges, and a single-barrelled flint-lock pistol. He then hung his sword and shield over his shoulder, gave his sandals to his henchman, and was ready to start.

The retainer was dressed in an old Kaniki loin-cloth and fez cap, and carried an ancient firearm that could not be induced to go off when the salute was fired on our entrance to Kaoli.

We took as an escort, in order to appear in due state, four of our askari, in their uniform and armed with rifles, commanded by Bilâl, whom we had rated second to Bombay. And after some persuasion they actually marched two and two, carrying their rifles at the trail or an approach to the slope, until the paths grew so narrow that it was necessary to walk in single file.

After passing through the main street of Bagamoyo and some straggling huts we reached the sea beach, and here the Jemadar informed us that we must take the more inland path as the tide was high. Two of the Jemadar's train now joined us, one being a good-looking young fellow with the colour showing through his skin, although as nearly black as a man could be. His shield, sword, and dagger were very handsome.

We now struck further inland, and found the path more winding than the labyrinth of Crete; but it led us through a fertile country. For some time our road lay along a large tract planted with yams, manioc, &c., and the Jemadar pointed to fields of rice and told us that oranges, mangos, and other fruits grew in the adjacent woods. The cultivated ground was surrounded by a thorn hedge with which no "bullfinch" in England could be compared, for it was from twelve to fifteen feet high and about ten thick. Through this we went by an arched opening and came to an uncultivated part of the country where the grass grew in large thick tufts, often so high that it flapped in our faces and hindered our progress.

At last, after a two hours' walk, we again reached the beach close to Kaoli, when the Jemadar and his friends began firing into the air to apprise the people of our arrival. The old matchlock and flint pistol did their work well, making reports like young cannon; but one of the Jemadar's personal attendants could not manage to make his fossil weapon produce any sound whatever. And the other, who was armed with a worn-out French fowling-piece, was little better, as there was at least a second between the explosion of the cap and that of the charge, which rather detracted from the effect. Together they might possibly have been heard, but separately their efforts were drowned by the rippling of the sea upon the beach.

On our arrival we were most warmly welcomed by Soorghi, as well as by Jemadar Sabr and his retinue.

We first visited Soorghi, the chief of the customs

February, on the mainland—to whom we had letters of
1873. introduction from Lakhmidass, who farms all the
Sultan's revenue—and made enquiries about pagazi.
He advised us to send to Saadani to beat up for
them, promising letters and soldiers to assist in
this work.

After a time, during which Jemadar Sabr had been absent, we received a message from him inviting us to his residence, where we found a repast already prepared. It consisted of three spatch-cocks, three sorts of Arab pastry in nine different dishes, and two plates of vermicelli swamped in sugar, and of course the inevitable sherbet was served to us on entry.

I tried the wing of a fowl, and knives and forks being unprovided had to use my fingers; then tea was brought, not bad in flavour but sweetened to cloying, and lastly coffee, happily guiltless of sugar, but nevertheless it failed to rid our mouths of the overplus of saccharine matter and a good draught of fresh water was most palatable.

On our leaving the room Jemadar Sabr invited our escort to enter and finish the remainder of the feast, and whilst they were thus engaged we sat in state under the verandah with the Jemadar and his notables. Our interpreter was meanwhile doing his best to assist our askari, and consequently the conversation was very limited.

The eating being at last concluded, we formed order of march for Bagamoyo and bade good-bye to our friends of Kaoli; our host and some of his sons, however, accompanied us a short distance on our way.

February, 1873.

We were rejoiced to find the tide ebbing, so that we were able to return to Bagamoyo by the shore on the hard sand just uncovered by the water. Directly we got back we arranged for starting Bilâl for Saadani the next morning. He was accompanied on this expedition by an intelligent native named Saadi, to act as interpreter and recruiting sergeant, by two of Jemadar Issa's soldiers, and three of our own men, to whom we served out arms and ammunition.

In the evening, by way of diversion, there was a fire in the town, and some eight huts were burnt to the ground. We went to the barracks where our ammunition was stored to make preparations in case of the fire spreading that way, and then visited the scene of action. The natives we found looking on in hopeless apathy, excepting a few who were arguing and vociferating at a great rate. Fortunately there was no wind, and the fire soon burnt itself out.

The greater portion of a day was frequently occupied in paying pagazi, and a most tedious and wearying work it proved, owing to the peculiarities of the men and the difficulty they seemed to experience in making up their minds and saying what they wanted.

A man's name being called out, he answers

"Ay-wallah," but makes no attempt at moving. When at last it pleases him to come to the front and he is asked how he wishes to receive his advance, he will probably stand, even for ten minutes, considering before giving an answer. Then he says, "So many dollars, and so many doti; so many of the doti must be merikani and so many kaniki." When paid, he often wants to change a gold dollar for pice, and all the filthy copper coins have to be counted; then, perhaps, he wishes to have one doti merikani changed for one of kaniki, or *vice versâ*, or begs for another doti; and thus a vast amount of time is wasted.

In the evening we occasionally took some men to the beach for target-practice, first making them fire a round of blank and then three rounds of ball at an empty case at one hundred yards, and although there were no hits the firing was fairly good.

We found it necessary to muster our forces every morning, the honour of bearing colours on these occasions being conferred upon Ferradi and Umbari, two of Speke's followers.

The uniform we established for our askari consisted of a red patrol jacket, red fez, white shirt and cummer-bund. Bombay and the leading men were distinguished by wearing non-commissioned officers' stripes.

The 8th of February was a great festival of the Arabs, and all our Moslem askari honoured us with a special salaam, and asked for something as a "tip," upon which we presented them with a shilling each to have an extra feed, it being explained to us by Bombay that this was the "Mohammedan Christmas." We also received visits from Jemadars Issa and Sabr, the former having actually put on a clean new shirt.

February, 1873.

We were now anxious to return to Zanzibar to take up our remaining stores, due by the *Punjáb*, and to make final preparations for starting for the interior, but the difficulties in obtaining a dhow seemed insuperable.

There was, however, plenty to do in collecting and hiring pagazi and making saddles for our donkeys. The stirrups and bits were a puzzle, but we contrived to solve it with the assistance of a native smith, and though his work was of the roughest description we hoped that it would answer our purpose.

DHOWS.

CHAPTER II.

PARTING VISIT TO ZANZIBAR.—COMPLETING EQUIPMENT.—FRENCH CHARLIE'S STORE.—FAREWELL DINNERS.—OUR FIRST CAMPAIGN.—A FRACAS.—UPHOLDING OUR DIGNITY.—THE FATHER PLEADS FOR HIS SON.—SHAMBA GONÈRA.—VISIT FROM DR. KIRK.—OUR FIRST TOUCH OF FEVER.—A NEW VOLUNTEER.—START FOR KIKOKA.—THE MARCH.—ALLIGATOR SHOOTING.—DESERTERS.

February, 1873.

IT was not until the 11th of February that we succeeded in getting a dhow to take us across to Zanzibar, for which we sailed early that morning, accompanied by Père Horner of the French mission, who was *en route* for France for a short and sorely needed holiday.

The wind fell light when we, in company with some other dhows, were half-way across, and two of the *Daphne's* boats looking out for slavers came among us and visited our dhow, and shortly afterwards boarded another, which I believe proved a prize. Having now drifted far to the south it was decided to anchor, but just before sunset a fresh breeze sprang up, and thus favoured we reached the town of Zanzibar.

Here we found the *Punjáb*, and Captain Hansard kindly insisted on our taking up our quarters on board during his stay, an arrangement which was far more comfortable than living in the English gaol.

February, 1873.

All the stores that we had ordered in England were on board, as also an extra supply of ammunition, two Abyssinian tents supplied by the Indian Government, and a portable india-rubber boat by Mathews, of Cockspur Street, for which we were indebted to the thoughtful kindness of Major Euan C. Smith, C.S.I., Secretary to Sir Bartle Frere, who telegraphed for them whilst we were at Cairo ; and thoroughly good and useful they proved. Murphy having been granted leave by the Indian Government also came by the *Punjâb*.

At Zanzibar we took the opportunity of completing our outfit as far as possible at the stores kept by Tarya Topan, French Charlie, Rosan, and the various Portuguese Joes, gathering together those little odds and ends so necessary in rough travel. For a caravan should be as thoroughly independent as a ship, or even more so, since after having started from the coast no opportunities occur of purchasing such small items as needles, thread, buttons, &c. &c., on which much comfort in a great measure depends.

Tarya Topan was one of the most influential of the Indian traders, and was also more inclined to assist us than any other.

French Charlie was an oddity who required to be known to be appreciated, and from being cook at the English consulate had now arrived at an important position in society at Zanzibar. All H.M. ships arriving there he supplied with fresh beef and bread, and he was proprietor of the only approach to an hotel in the island. He had a miscellaneous collection of stores of all sorts and descriptions, and being utterly unable to read or write had a most imperfect knowledge of what he possessed, and was content to ask a would-be purchaser to overhaul his stores, and if he succeeded in finding what he required to give a fair price for it.

Without learning English he had partially forgotten French, an amusing mixture of the two being the result. It is needless to say his affairs are rather in disorder; but nevertheless he thrives and is prosperous, one reason for this probably being his great generosity, for I believe few could find it in them to cheat him.

Rosan was an American who kept a miscellaneous store; and the Portuguese Joes are Goanese doing business as tailors, hair-cutters, grog-sellers, and in fact turning their hand to anything and everything.

Dr. Kirk obtained for us letters of recommendation from the Sultan and, what was perhaps still more important, from the Indian merchant who farms the customs, to whom nearly every trader in the interior owes money, so that his injunctions could not lightly be disregarded.

We were entertained at farewell dinners at the consulate and on board the flagship *Glasgow*, and again took our departure for Bagamoyo in a dhow well laden with our belongings. On arrival we had the satisfaction of being effusively and noisily welcomed by our men, who had, wonderful to relate, kept out of mischief during our absence.

February, 1873.

Without delay we settled down to work, and

VIEW IN BAGAMOYO.

re-entered with unflagging zeal into the task of engaging pagazi, the rapid approach of the rainy season or Masika, which would render travelling more difficult, making every day's delay an important matter. I numbered the rifles which had been supplied to the expedition by the War Office and served them out to the men, who were exceedingly

March, 1873.

proud of being armed with European guns; and I may add that during the whole expedition they kept their arms under very trying circumstances in a condition that would be a credit to any soldier.

Finding that pagazi came forward very slowly, and that those actually engaged could never be collected together, I resolved to form a camp a short distance out in the country to prove that we intended to start immediately, and that therefore nothing would be gained by men holding back with the hope that higher rates of pay might be offered. By this means I also hoped to introduce some form of discipline into the heterogeneous mass of which our party was composed. With this object Dillon and I went out prospecting, and fixed on a lovely spot some four miles from the town near a plantation called Shamba Gonèra.

Just before making this move rather an unpleasant *fracas* occurred one morning when inspecting arms and seeing the donkeys watered. It originated in a dispute between a slave-girl and one of our boys who had charge of the riding donkeys as to which should first draw water at the well. An Arab rushed at the boy and commenced thrashing him, upon which one of the askari flew at the Arab and hit him over the head with a big stick, knocking him down and nearly stunning him; but as I could not approve of such summary justice I had the askari arrested.

No sooner had the Arab recovered from the effects

of the blow than he made off, vowing vengeance, and in less than five minutes was back foaming at the mouth, brandishing his sword, and swearing that he would "kill a dog of a Nazarene and then die happy!" He was followed by a crowd of yelling and infuriated friends, who were, however, wise enough to prevent him from carrying out his murderous intention. I ordered our men to return their arms and remain perfectly passive, as there seemed every prospect of a serious row; and it would have been impossible to prevent one had a rifle been fired.

Dillon, Murphy and myself were altogether unarmed, but had to walk up and down between our men and the crowd and appear perfectly cool, though once or twice the madman—for by this time he had worked himself into a state of fury which could not be distinguished from madness— broke loose and, before his friends could seize him again, came close enough to make it unpleasant. Once he approached me so nearly that I was calculating the chances of being able to catch his wrist to prevent his cutting me down.

After a time Jemadar Issa appeared with the Balooches forming the garrison and scattered the crowd, and I informed him that having made a prisoner of the man who struck the blow I expected him to secure the Arab, with which request he promised compliance, and we returned to our lodgings.

[March, 1873.

Shortly afterwards in came our landlord in much alarm telling us that the Arab and his friends had broken into his shop, turned everything topsy-turvy, and threatened to kill him if he refused to show the way to our rooms, but that the Balooches had dispersed them. I again sent for Jemadar Issa, acquainting him that the British flag had been insulted by the attack on the house over which it was flying, and unless he arrested the culprit at once I should refer the matter to the admiral at Zanzibar. At the same time I despatched messengers to Jemadar Sabr requesting his immediate presence to restore order.

A lull now took place, and, a passing thunderstorm having afforded us a large supply of water, we thought it a capital opportunity for washing our dogs. And whilst engaged in this interesting operation, in a light costume consisting only of pyjamas and soapsuds, the turban of Jemadar Sabr appeared at the top of the ladder, and we had to bolt incontinently and dress sufficiently to receive him with due respect.

At first he professed his inability to do anything; but we upheld our rights as Englishmen and still insisted that the man who had threatened and insulted us should be secured, or we would report the case to Zanzibar, adding that he well knew that if we adopted such a course neither his nor Jemadar Issa's place would be worth five minutes' purchase.

Both the Jemadars still attempted to run with the hare and hunt with the hounds; but seeing that we were determined not to withdraw from the position we had assumed promised compliance with our demands, and in the evening reported that the man was in prison.

March, 1873.

Two days' palaver about the matter then followed. We wished the man to acknowledge his offence or to be sent to Zanzibar to be dealt with by the Sultan; whilst the two Jemadars and the principal inhabitants desired that no further action might be taken in the affair.

On the third day the father of the offender, a fine, dignified, grey-bearded old Arab, called on us and made me feel almost ashamed of myself by kneeling down and kissing my hands. His son was very ill he said, and promised that himself and some of the principal inhabitants would be responsible for his actions. This old man's humiliation was more than I could bear and I readily agreed to the immediate release of his son, but added that in future we should all carry pistols, and told him to caution his son that if he again attempted to draw his sword near any of us we should immediately shoot him down.

Thus this disagreeable business was concluded, and, I believe, did us no injury but rather good, as it proved that, although we would not allow ourselves to be insulted with impunity, we were not at all vindictive.

March, 1873.

Very shortly afterwards we moved to Shamba Gonèra and pitched our tents under a clump of large mango trees on an open grassy slope, at the bottom of which was a stream running to the Kingani. The donkeys, numbering twenty-four, were picketed at night in two lines and in the daytime were tethered in such places as afforded good grass and

CAMP AT SHAMBA GONÈRA.

shade, the riding donkeys having in addition a feed of corn.

Much opposition to our obtaining porters being still offered at Bagamoyo, and the people, taking advantage of our desire to start, becoming more extortionate, I wrote to Dr. Kirk asking if he would pay us a visit in order to show that we were still under the ægis of the British Government. Although very busy he came almost immediately in the *Daphne*, and used his influence, which is greater than that of any one else at Zanzibar, to assist us.

March, 1873.

Accompanied by Captain Bateman of the *Daphne*, and some of the officers of that ship, Dr. Kirk visited our camp and told us that he was delighted with all he saw, at which remark from so experienced a traveller we were much gratified.

The result was that affairs went more smoothly for a time, but in a few days returned into the old groove. There was no doubt that Abdûllah Dina, whom we employed as a sort of agent, and Jemadar Issa, notwithstanding profuse asseverations that they were doing their utmost to help us, were really thwarting us in every way. They argued that the longer we were detained the more money they would make out of us.

The establishment of the camp at Shamba Gonèra proved of no service as far as keeping the men together was concerned, for the moment they received their rations they disappeared again into the town. I thought at one time of sending Dillon and Murphy with the men we had engaged to Rehenneko or Mbumi, on the other side of the Makata swamp, there to await my arrival with such additional pagazi as I could collect; but I found this impracticable, as Murphy, having exposed himself too much to the sun and dew, was unable to travel.

March, 1873.

I then compromised matters by sending under the charge of Dillon all the men we could muster and most of the donkeys to Kikoka, the outpost station of H.H. Syud Burghash, on the other side of the Kingani.

Soon after his departure both Murphy and myself had a sharp attack of fever, but whilst I was fortunate in shaking it off in three days it seemed inclined to keep a hold upon Murphy, and I therefore asked Dillon to return and give him the benefit of medical treatment.

The same day a letter arrived from Dr. Kirk stating that Sir Bartle Frere and staff were coming to Bagamoyo in the *Daphne*, and requesting me to inform the French mission of the same. I at once rode over to deliver this message, and also mentioned Murphy's illness, when Père Germain insisted on proceeding to our camp and taking him on a litter to the mission, that he might be nursed in the infirmary.

The *Daphne* arrived the next day, and Sir Bartle on landing was welcomed by all the Hindis in the place, a set of cringing sycophants who had done all that lay in their power to hinder us during the whole time we had been at Bagamoyo, but now came to make their salaams to the big man and assure him of their loyalty and non-participation in the slave-trade. Sir Bartle remained the entire day at Bagamoyo, but his staff went to the Kingani to try their hands at the hippopotami with which the river swarmed.

March, 1873.

Another volunteer came to us in the *Daphne*, Robert Moffat—a grandson of Dr. Moffat and nephew of Dr. Livingstone—who, hearing of the expedition, had sold a sugar plantation at Natal which formed his sole inheritance, and hastened to Zanzibar prepared to devote all his energies and every penny he possessed to the cause of African exploration.

It may perhaps be well to mention that Zanzibar is not alone the town or even the island commonly so called, but is the correct term for the whole of the Sultan's dominions, meaning "the coast of the blacks." Unguja is the native name for the town of Zanzibar.

I took advantage of Moffat's having joined to proceed at once with Dillon to Rehenneko, leaving Moffat and Murphy to bring up the rear division of the caravan, as this course would allow the latter time to recover and give the former a chance of completing his kit. And having—with the assistance of Moffat, who proved willing and hardworking—mustered all the men I possibly could, we loaded them and the donkeys and started for Kikoka.

From having unwisely worn slippers while walking in the long grass near our camp, my feet had been cut and poisoned, and were now covered with small sores which prevented my putting on

March, 1873.

boots, or moving about with any degree of comfort, so I mounted a donkey and led the way.

At the outset we marched over grassy country, and all went merry as a marriage bell until we reached Stanley's famous bridge across a muddy creek.

This my donkey, "Jenny Lind," refused to face, and on my getting off to lead her broke away and bolted back to Shamba Gonèra, leaving me to wade across this place with bare feet and to struggle along through black and sticky mud for the remainder of the journey to the Kingani. This caused the sore places on my feet to become so much inflamed that I could not even wear slippers on arriving at the river. Here we and our stores were ferried over without delay, but it was too late to get the donkeys across that night.

Neither our tent nor cook had arrived, so we had no alternative but to sleep out on the river bank and make our supper of roasted Indian corn, which we obtained from the garden of a Balooch who was supposed to guard the ferry. Luckily the night was fine, and we slept comfortably alongside a large fire.

We were astir by break of day, and before the ferryman was ready to tow the donkeys across amused ourselves by potting at the numerous hippopotami. A huge crocodile floating downstream towards the ferry varied our sport, and I succeeded in lodging a bullet and a shell in the middle of his back. He gave a convulsive plunge, throwing his whole length at least six feet into the air, and then sank to be no more seen.

March, 1873.

The donkeys being landed on the northern bank without accident, and the tent and cook having turned up, we started for Kikoka, arriving there at eleven o'clock.

Moffat, who had accompanied me thus far, I now sent back to Bagamoyo with my parting orders to Murphy, and then with Dillon endeavoured to collect our men for the road. This was not an easy matter, for notwithstanding our distance from Bagamoyo its Circean charms proved so strong that there were always thirty or forty absentees at the morning muster.

I offered the guard at the ferry a reward if they would not allow any of my men to cross without a pass from me; but this proving ineffectual, I sent Bombay with a party of askari back to Bagamoyo to hunt up the absentees and bring them out loaded with food.

At the end of four days—which I afterwards heard he had spent loafing about Abdûllah Dina's —he returned without bringing in any of the deserters.

Whilst Bombay was away a Comoro man called Issa, who had acted as interpreter on board the *Glasgow* and held very good certificates, volunteered to join the expedition, and as I required a native leader for Murphy's portion of the caravan

March, 1873.
I engaged him. His duties were eventually to be those of storekeeper and interpreter of the main body, being the only man who could read and write; and on account of his having travelled in Manyuéma and other countries rarely visited by caravans I trusted that his experience would stand me in good stead.

During our stay at Kikoka two caravans of Wanyamwési bringing down their own ivory passed us, but I could not tempt any of their number to join us as porters for the up journey, as they wanted to have their spree at Bagamoyo before returning to their own homes.

LOADED DONKEY AND PAGAZI.

CHAPTER III.

LEAVING KIKOKA.—FORM OF CAMP.—MODE OF HUT BUILDING.—FORAGING FOR PROVISIONS.—A "SHORT CUT."—BOMBAY AS A GUIDE.—A LUCKLESS CRUISE.—A NEEDLESS SCARE.—LEVY OF MHONGO.— MSUWAH.— FORTIFIED VILLAGES.—AN ARTFUL DODGER.—AN ARAB CARAVAN.— OFFERINGS TO SPIRITS.—BAOBAB TREES.—KISÉMO.—THE LUGERENGERI.—THE KUNGWA HILLS.—SIMBAWÉNI.—ITS QUEEN.—RUMOURED TERRORS OF THE MAKATA SWAMP.—LAZY PORTERS.—HONOUR AMONGST DESERTERS.

TIRED of the innumerable delays we decided to start from Kikoka on the 28th of March with whatever men we might have in camp, leaving such loads as we were unable to get carried in charge of the Balooch guard, to be afterwards sent for by Murphy.

March, 1873.

I turned the hands up at 5.30 A.M., and found that seven more pagazi had deserted during the night; this raised the total number of absentees to twenty-five, and so many more were skulking about the village and in the grass and jungle that it was ten o'clock before we made a move.

It was altogether impossible to make the askari load the donkeys properly; in fact, to tell the truth, we were obliged to do the work ourselves whilst our men looked on in idleness. If left to themselves they tried to tie the crupper round the donkey's neck and placed the pad so that it

March, 1873. afforded no protection whatever to the animal's back.

For two hours and a half we marched across a lovely country of rolling grass-land interspersed with belts of timber, and every here and there small knolls crowned with clumps of trees and shrubs. Away on our right lay the chain of small hills where Rosako and its neighbouring robber villages were situated, along the route which Stanley followed on his journey for the relief of Dr. Livingstone.

We camped on the top of a small knoll, the huts of the men being so arranged as to form a fence, while in the centre the tents were pitched and a large hut erected for stores and guard-room. Before sunset the donkeys were picketed inside the boma, and the entrance closed as a defence both against wild beasts and robbers.

The men divided themselves into small kambis or messes, numbering from three to seven each, for the purposes of cooking and building their huts.

Each kambi selects one man for duty as cook whilst the remainder busy themselves in building, and by this subdivision of labour a camp is formed in a wonderfully short space of time wherever grass and suitable wood are plentiful.

One man cuts the ridge pole and undertakes the general superintendence, whilst others prepare forked uprights and small sticks for rafters, provide bark to bind the structure together, and grass for thatch and bedding.

Every bit of grass is carefully rooted out from the inside to prevent the stubs injuring the mats. A thick layer of cut grass is also spread on the ground to form a sort of mattress, and on this the mats are laid.

March, 1873.

Some of the more luxurious build small kitandas, or bed-places, to raise them above the damp ground.

Within a couple of hours after arrival all is completed, and as soon as the men have been fed they dispose themselves to sleep until the time for their sunset meal, after which they smoke and yarn till eight or nine o'clock, when most of them turn in for the night.

Occasionally, however, the silence is broken by some fellow who, thinking he has something important to tell a chum at the other side of the camp, makes no scruple of howling out at the top of his voice and continuing to shout until he obtains an answer. Probably he will then have forgotten what he wished to say, and thus have disturbed the whole camp for nothing.

After two more days of marching through similar country the guides advised a halt to procure supplies, and I accordingly set out in the afternoon with Bombay and a party of men for a village said to be near, leaving Dillon to look after the camp.

I had taken off my travelling kit, and in order to appear in due form before the eyes of the natives had dressed in white shirt and

March, 1873.

trousers and put a green veil round my topee, Dillon remarking that I looked like a stage peasant got up as a bridegroom. Certainly I was not suitably equipped for a rainy afternoon, and so I found an hour later when it rained in such torrents

BOMBAY AND TWO CHUMS.

that in a few moments I was thoroughly drenched. The footpaths were ankle-deep in water, and a nullah which was perfectly dry when we passed it during our morning's march had now become a considerable stream.

FORAGING FOR PROVISIONS.

As the village was reported to be nearer than the camp I held on my way, and after a seven miles' walk arrived at a small group of round huts which formed the residence of the chief of the district. He happened to be away, and his son, apparently a great dandy in his own estimation, would not sell anything during his father's absence.

March, 1873.

After much bargaining and bothering I managed to obtain a goat and a few eggs from another source, but no food for the askari and pagazi was forthcoming.

We therefore went foraging about, and crossing an affluent of the Kingani which was up to our armpits discovered a few miserable huts, but from the inhabitants my men could get nothing more than a root or two of cassava.

It was now getting late and we turned our footsteps campwards, allowing Bombay to lead as he declared there was a short cut. So away we went ploughing our way through long wet grass, and as the darkness closed around without a single star to guide us we lost our road completely.

I was confident that Bombay was wrong, but he and all the men persisted that he was right. I trusted them, not then having practical experience of the inability of an African to strike out a new road, although they will remember every turn and step of those they have once travelled over.

About nine o'clock we found ourselves in a swampy wood, and hearing no answer to the guns

March, 1873.

I had ordered to be fired to apprise the people in camp of our whereabouts I thought it best to select some dry spot where we could kindle a fire, cook the goat, and make ourselves as comfortable as possible under the circumstances.

I squatted down close to the fire with my back against a tree and tried to eat some of the goat, but was too completely done up to get even a morsel down my throat. The men, however, made short work of it.

As soon as the first gleams of light heralded the approach of day I arose from my "wretched lair" and set off to look for the camp, and shortly met some people who had been despatched by Dillon to come in search of us. In another hour I reached my tent, though barely able to crawl into it, the night's exposure having brought on a violent attack of fever. I was only fit to turn into bed and get Dillon to doctor me.

To add to my annoyance I found that had we taken the direction I wished the evening before, we should have got into camp all right.

I was a very different-looking object on my arrival from what I had been on my departure on this luckless cruise. Shirt and trousers wet, torn, and mudstained; the colour of the veil washed out, and hat, face, and shoulders all rejoicing in a pea-green tint.

Three more days were we delayed at this camp, and then the men sent to the south of the Kingani returned with only a sufficient quantity of cassava for immediate use.

During our stay Moffat came out on foot with letters from Dr. Kirk and other friends at Zanzibar together with the mail that had arrived since we left Kikoka. He also brought the news that Murphy had almost recovered, and had broken up the camp at Shamba Gonèra and made his headquarters in Bagamoyo.

Moffat being rather knocked up by this walk, we gave him a donkey for the return journey to Bagamoyo, and started off again ourselves, marching for three days without interruption.

The country consisted principally of prairies with clumps of trees and occasional small ponds or water-holes in which beautiful large blue and white waterlilies grew, and here and there magnificent white lilies showed amongst the grass.

On this march I was suffering very much from fever; and was delirious when in camp. Yet I managed to pull myself together whilst on the road and was able to ride my donkey, though the moment the excitement of the march had passed I was hardly able to stand.

Upon Dillon during this time devolved the work of driving the caravan along, and owing to his unremitting attention all went smoothly.

On the third day we heard that a village was close in front and sent messengers to acquaint the chief of our approach. Astounding rumours were

April, 1873. brought back to the effect that the chief would not allow us to pass; but as every man who made any report differed from his fellows we decided that all were false.

We remained camped however for one day to await a definite answer, as there had lately been great difficulties between the chief and filibustering parties from Whindé, a village on the coast which owes a divided allegiance to H.H. Syud Burghash.

The hoped-for answer not having been received on the 7th of April, we started early in the morning and at noon arrived at the outskirts of the district of Msuwah. There was much cultivation all around us—pumpkins, Indian corn, sweet potatoes, &c.—but the only signs of any habitations were tiny spirals of blue smoke curling up from the midst of clumps of the densest jungle.

Our people were driven nearly wild with fright on this march, owing to a few who were rather in advance of the main body rushing back with fear depicted on every feature, declaring they had seen some *armed* men (as though every one in Africa did not go armed), and that we had better return to Bagamoyo at once, as it would be madness to proceed any further. After a time we somewhat allayed their agitation, and persuaded one or two of the bravest—or rather least cowardly—to talk to these much-dreaded armed men, one of whom, with spear, bow, arrows and all, returned with them and agreed to guide us to the chief's village.

We camped early that afternoon, and I was still so ill from fever and fatigue that I turned in at once.   April, 1873.

The following day the chief paid us a visit and gave permission to move close to his village, but informed us that owing to a treaty he had concluded with the people of Whindé we should be expected to pay mhongo before leaving.

Under this treaty entered into between the chief of Msuwah and the people of Whindé, the former was to pay the latter a certain number of slaves, and in compensation he was allowed to tax all caravans passing through his district provided that they started from any point on the coast excepting Whindé.

This agreement was arrived at after war had been carried on between both parties for some years without either side being able to gain a decided advantage, and we were doomed to be the first sufferers.

This incident shows how little real influence the Sultan of Zanzibar has over his subjects on the mainland, and how little he can do personally, even with the best intentions, to put down the slave-trade in his continental dominions.

Dillon returned the visit of the chief, who was very civil and arranged our mhongo at thirty doti.

The village of Msuwah consisted of six or eight large well-built huts, kept clean and in good order;

April, 1873.
but another in the middle of a dense patch of jungle we were not allowed to see.

These villages are built in the midst of jungle for the purpose of providing protection against attack, being only approachable by very narrow, tortuous paths, capable of being completely blocked and rendered perfectly impregnable against native warfare. Owing to these strong positions the people are able to harry their neighbours with a certainty of safety from reprisals, and make slaves, for whom they are always sure of finding a ready market in the towns on the seaboard.

Here we heard that the country to the front was "hungry," and we should therefore be obliged to buy food for the road before starting. And our civil and smiling friend the chief assuring us that it would be dangerous for our men to go in search of food, offered to send his own people to procure it—provided we paid in advance.

When he had received the cloth he made numerous excuses for not fulfilling his promises, and after five days' halt we had to start with only two days' supplies.

Some neighbouring chiefs hearing of our proximity took advantage of this delay to personally demand mhongo. To one, named Mtonga, I was foolish enough to pay thirty doti of merikani and kaniki and seven coloured cloths upon Bombay persuading me that his village lay on our road and there would be trouble if we did not satisfy these

CAMP AT MSUWAH. From a sketch by Dr. Dillon.

claims. But I afterwards found that the scoundrel had been cheating us, as his village was situated to the northward of us and if anything to our rear. Another, called Kasuwa, demanded two whole bales, but as I happily discovered that we had already passed him he got nothing. _{April, 1873.}

On the fourth day of our halt we were visited by the leaders of a large Arab caravan which had left the coast some time before us but had been detained by troubles along Stanley's route. They mustered over seven hundred men, of whom about a half were armed with muskets.

The halt was not altogether wasted, as it enabled us to improve our donkeys' saddles and gave me a chance of shaking off the fever; but during our stay we had the misfortune to lose one of our pagazi who died suddenly without any previous illness, and some half-a-dozen others deserted.

On the 14th of April we made another move after a great deal of trouble with the men, who if allowed to halt a day or two always made more fuss about starting than if they had been kept on the road altogether.

We passed through the Arab camp, in which there were seven tents belonging to the proprietors of different divisions, each being enclosed in a compound made of cloth screens or grass fences which served to keep the profane eyes of outsiders from penetrating the mysteries of the harem. They were in great tribulation, owing to many of their

April, 1873.

hired pagazi having bolted; and I found I had reason to congratulate myself on only having lost half-a-dozen whilst at Msuwah, as it is a favourite place for coast people to desert, and the jungle and villages afford so many lurking and hiding places that it is almost impossible to find them again.

The Arabs professed to be very anxious to join us, and I should not have objected but for rumours of scarcity of food and anticipations of difficulty in rationing so large a party.

I determined to press forward as quickly as possible towards the Makata swamp, every day's delay now increasing the chances of its being in bad condition for crossing. And we covered a good ten miles, halting only for half an hour—passing over a level tableland about four hundred or five hundred feet higher than Msuwah—and descried right before us a glorious cloud-capped range of mountainous hills.

The country through which we had come was well cultivated and dotted with numerous hamlets peeping out of woods and bosquets. Where the ground was not cultivated or covered with jungle the grass was excellent.

I was much astonished at the total absence of cattle, as we noticed no tsetsé and the country seemed admirably adapted for grazing, being well-watered and provided with trees to afford shade during the heat of the day.

Every plot under cultivation had in it a miniature hut, under which offerings were placed to propitiate the evil spirits lest they should injure the growing crops.

April, 1873.

Several graves of chiefs bestrewn with broken earthenware were pointed out to me. They also had huts erected over them with a small tree, usually of the cactus species, serving the purpose of a centre post.

On this march we first met with baobab-trees, which may be termed the elephants or hippopotami of the vegetable kingdom, their smallest twigs being two or three inches in circumference and their forms of the most grotesque ugliness. This is, however, toned down by their beautiful white flowers and the tender green of their foliage.

At Kisémo the chief brought a goat to our camp and asked for fifty doti as mhongo; but as he was "a small thief" this request was not complied with. We gave him four doti as the price of the goat and four more as a present, and he professed himself perfectly satisfied although it was so great a reduction from his attempt at extortion.

Our road at starting led up a steep ascent and across a tableland gradually sloping towards the west with occasional slight undulations, until we came to the steep and almost cliff-like descent into the valley of the Lugerengeri. Frequent outcrops of sandstone and quartz were noticeable and crystalline pebbles were plentiful, and the soil, which was in some places of a reddish hue, was at other points a pure white silver sand, both being covered with a considerable layer of vegetable mould.

Many beautiful flowers gladdened our eyes on the march, amongst which were tiger-lilies, convolvuli, primulas of a rich deep yellow, and another having somewhat the appearance of a foxglove opened back. In the valley of the Lugerengeri I saw some thorn-bushes of osier-like growth bearing large purple bell-shaped flowers. From the coast, thus far, we had frequently met with white primulas, a large yellow daisy, and small red and blue flowers very similar to forget-me-nots.

The Lugerengeri here lies at the bottom of a valley with a broad and very nearly level sole which it floods when swollen by exceptional storms, carrying destruction far and wide.

The year before we passed, one of these inundations—caused by the rains accompanying the hurricane which did so much damage at Zanzibar—swept away about twenty villages with great loss of life, though no reliable account of the numbers who perished could be obtained. The inhabitants, like veritable fatalists, had reoccupied many of the old sites, only a few being sufficiently wise to guard against the recurrence of a similar disaster by building on small eminences.

We camped near a village built by some of the wiser ones and were well received by the chief, who placed a couple of neighbouring huts at our disposal for our stores.

Before us, on the opposite side of the Lugerengeri, were the hills we had sighted two days previously.

April, 1873.

Bombay on arrival said, "Master, Lugerengeri live close by, jump him to-morrow;" but when to-morrow came there arose the same old cry of "Master, country very hungry in front," and we were compelled to spend a day looking for provisions, being rewarded by obtaining sufficient for three or four days.

About noon a division of the Arab caravan passed us and camped on the opposite bank of the Lugerengeri, the remainder of the Arabs being bound for the country of the Warori and Wabena.

By five o'clock the next morning we were on the move, and Hamees ibn Salim, the owner of the Arab caravan, hearing us astir, sent his drummer to play us past his camp. Crossing by the ford just as the day was beginning to dawn we found the Arabs not yet packed up, but Hamees turned out to salute us as we passed. When we forded the Lugerengeri it was only about thirty yards wide and knee-deep, but it must be impassable whenever a freshet comes down. The channel exceeds two hundred and fifty yards in width, with banks on each side twenty-five feet high; and many old plantations in the vicinity were covered with sand brought down in the floods of 1872. The bed consisted of white sand with quartz and granite pebbles, and large boulders of granite much water-worn were strewn about in considerable numbers.

April, 1873.

After traversing seven miles of thickly wooded country without any inhabitants, Hamees' caravan overtook us. I had been walking in front and was obliged to sit down and rest, being still weak from fever, on seeing which Hamees kindly offered me his donkey, and upon my refusing sat down to keep me company until my own arrived.

After this we had some rough marching over very steep hills, through patches of tiger-grass, and across ravines forty and fifty feet deep with almost precipitous sides, at each of which we were obliged to unload the donkeys and carry the baggage up and down by the help of the drivers.

Notwithstanding the extra work of superintending this, besides dragging one's weary legs along, the scenery was so delightful that we scarcely thought of fatigue.

All the hills were exceedingly rocky—being composed mostly of granite but in some instances of nearly pure quartz—but they were thickly clothed with trees wherever the inequalities of the surface allowed sufficient soil to accumulate. The greater number of the trees being acacias in full bloom, their red, white, and yellow blossoms, and those of other flowering trees, stood out in masses of gorgeous colour.

Late in the afternoon we arrived at the camping-place, a rocky pass having at the bottom pools of

THE KUNGWA HILLS.

water in granite basins. Out of these two streams issued, one running west and the other east, but both ultimately falling into the Kingani.

April, 1873.

This was the direct road through the range of hills that had been in sight since leaving Kisémo, and I now ascertained they were named Kungwa, though by Burton and Speke they are grouped with others as the Duthumi hills.

The tail of the caravan, owing to the long and tiring march, was all over the country and many of the stragglers were not up till after sunset.

Next morning saw us off betimes, our path, with a watercourse beside it, leading us through a regular pass. Along this route we had trouble in forcing our way through sword-grass and bamboo —the first we had seen—which was covered with a creeper very like the English sweet-pea, bearing many twin and a few double flowers.

Five miles of this work brought us into a valley enclosed by the Kungwa hills and full of conical knolls, many of which were crowned by villages. The Arabs camped in one called Kongassa, while we halted at another named Kungwa from the mountains, the highest peak of which overhung us.

The sides of the knolls were planted with Indian and Kaffir corn and sweet potatoes, whilst the damp bottoms served to produce rice, and in the village ebony or blackwood trees were growing.

A large unfinished house—the building of which

April, 1873. had been commenced by an Arab with a view of settling here, but now falling into decay—afforded good shelter for our stores and many of our men. Those who were unable to get quarters in it shared the huts of the natives, in order to escape the rain, which fell almost continuously and prevented us from starting till late the following day.

Our next resting-place was a deserted village five miles distant. Here we had to remain a day to obtain supplies; for, as usual, the men were lazy and wanted an excuse for delay, and this place, which had been the "hungry country" three days before, was now represented as a land of Goshen, whilst all in front was said to be a barren waste.

Dillon and I enlisted the services of two of the aborigines as guides whilst we went out shooting. Although we saw tracks of pig and antelope the beasts themselves kept out of sight, and after having been out an hour our worthy guides started off in pursuit of a honey-bird which they heard calling, and in their excitement created such a row as to entirely upset any chances of sport.

The soil in the bottoms was black and heavy, and had become converted by the rains into sticky and slippery mud; but the knolls, being sand, remained comparatively dry during the heaviest rain.

The Arabs who halted at Kongassa again appeared and camped close to us, and we went up the valley in company.

The hills closed in on either side, and the path was so blocked with bamboo cane-grass as to render it a matter of great difficulty to fight one's way along. The thick growth also shut out the view of the hills, which, when we were privileged with an occasional peep, was delightful; so to the physical labour of driving our way through the tough grass was added the tantalisation of knowing that we were surrounded by charming scenery without being able to enjoy it.

April, 1873.

Our camp on this day (April 20th) was by the small village of Kiroka, which the Arabs, having the start of us, had appropriated, and we were obliged to form our boma outside. Hamees' tent was already pitched when I arrived, and pitying my hot and thirsty condition he kindly took me inside to have a glass of sherbet. Owing to its sweetness this unfortunately only increased my thirst; still I fully appreciated the good intention.

From Kiroka the valley continued to close in, and at the western end we left by a pass situated at some height.

By the side of our path was a torrent bed more than twenty feet deep with nearly perpendicular sides, and into this fell a baggage donkey carrying about 140 lbs. of ammunition—a quantity of which consisted of percussion shell—but luckily without causing injury either to himself or his load, although he pitched straight on his head. A little

April, 1873.

hair rubbed off his forehead was the only visible result of his tumble.

The latter part of the pass was very slippery sandstone and quartz, and at its highest point the hills clothed to their summits with trees rose some three hundred feet above us. A steep descent of greasy red clay brought us into the broad valley of the Lugerengeri bounded on the south by the Kigambwé mountains, from which many torrents come down to the river, and on the north by a range of detached conical hills.

The valley of Lugerengeri is very fertile with pleasing alternations of open wood, jungle, grass and cultivation; but the torrents from the Kigambwé hills are very serious drawbacks to the safety of the inhabitants. The Mohalé must be over a mile wide in spates, and even when we crossed several streams knee-deep were flowing between thickets of bamboo which seamed the bed. We rested for the night in the village of Mohalé, and in the morning passed the famous town of Simbawéni "the stronghold of the lion," once the habitation of Kisabengo, a notorious freebooter and the terror of all surrounding tribes.

But its glories have now faded, and we marched past with colours flying and altogether disregarding the demands of its present ruler. She is a daughter of Kisabengo and possesses the will but lacks the power of rendering herself as obnoxious as was her robber sire.

Crossing the Mwéré torrent we proceeded to the Lugerengeri, over which we passed by a rough bridge composed of fallen trees, and camped by its banks. It occupied more than two hours getting loads and donkeys across, as the river was twenty yards wide and four to six feet deep with steep banks rising fourteen feet above the water.

April, 1873.

Hamees unwisely pitched his camp by the side of the Mwéré, and in consequence had to pay seventeen doti mhongo to Simbawéni, a tax which we escaped. Our men were also anxious to remain on the Simbawéni side and did not work willingly. But we got across without accident, except to one pagazi who preferred trying to wade the river to trusting himself to the slippery bridge and was swept away by the current. He was rescued with no further damage than wetting his load, though such an escape was scarcely to be expected.

An Arab caravan for the coast passing us here we availed ourselves of the opportunity of despatching a mail for Zanzibar.

Buying provisions for crossing the Makata swamp occupied the next day. There was no trouble in obtaining the supplies we required, as the natives crowded into camp with beans, pumpkins, vegetable marrows, honey, eggs, and corn for sale. Concerning the difficulties of this passage there were rumours almost sufficient to deter the stoutest from attempting it if allowance had not been made for the tendency of the negro to exaggeration. Hamees came over to see us in the afternoon, which was miserably wet, and Dillon endeavoured to amuse and astonish him with some card tricks; but great was his surprise on finding that Hamees could outdo him.

A branch of a tree falling upon my three-pole tent made a rent six feet long; and if I had not taken the precaution of having an inner lining fitted at Kikoka I should have been compelled to seek fresh quarters with Dillon in his Abyssinian tent.

An enormous amount of bother fell to our lot in the morning, for the men had gorged themselves to such an extent that they were very much disinclined to march and would fain have remained a few days more in this veritable land of plenty. We had to drive them out of camp one by one, and no sooner were our backs turned than they would dodge in again or hide with their loads amongst the bushes and long grass.

By dint of perseverance we at length got them away, and marching close under the end of the Kihondo mountain range—which rises sheer out of the plain to a height of seven or eight hundred feet—arrived at Simbo, the last camp before entering upon the toils and labours of the Makata swamp.

I may mention that Simbo is more a generic than a particular term and, unless a more definite name can be borrowed from some neighbouring village, is frequently applied to places where water is found in holes or by digging—that being the meaning of the word.

The range of Kihondo inosculates with Kigambwé, and in the angle formed by their junction are the sources of the Lugerengeri river.

On mustering in camp at Simbo we found one

RETURN OF THE DESERTER.

of the pagazi, Ulédi by name, had disappeared with his load. I instantly despatched five askari in search of him, and in the evening they returned in triumph, having recovered him at Simbawéni, where he had gone thinking to find a hearty welcome owing to our having refused to pay mhongo. The queen, Miss Kisabengo, however, handed him and his baggage over to the man in

60　　　　　　　　ACROSS AFRICA.　　　　　[Chap. III.

April, 1873. charge of the search party upon his paying seven doti as a fee.

I ordered him to be flogged as an example, and the men agreed that the punishment was well deserved, for on this part of the road, although it was not thought any disgrace to desert, yet it was considered a point of honour that a man should never run away with his load.

FLOWERS.

CHAPTER IV.

THE MAKATA SWAMP.—MUD TRAPS.—THE MAKATA RIVER.—A NATIVE BRIDGE.—TRANSPORTING DONKEYS.—REHENNEKO.—LAID UP.—A STRIKE AMONG THE MEN.—ROUTINE IN CAMP.—VISITORS.—A SWAGGERING HALF-CASTE.—NEWS FROM MURPHY.—HIS ARRIVAL.—DEATH OF MOFFAT.—ORGANIZING THE FRESH ARRIVALS.—THE STRENGTH OF THE EXPEDITION.—WOMEN AND SLAVES.—LOSSES BY DEATH AND DESERTION.—ARMAMENT.—OUR DOGS AND DONKEYS.—READY.

ON the 26th of April we started from Simbo for the dreaded Makata swamp, a large level plain lying between the Useghara mountains and those near Simbawéni, offering no particular difficulties of passage in the dry season, but becoming converted by the rains into a vast expanse of mud with two or three troublesome morasses on the western side.

April, 1873.

Two hours' marching through pleasant wooded country with red sandy soil gave us our first introduction to the Makata, which then appeared in its worst form.

The footprints of elephants, giraffes, and buffaloes had formed numerous holes in the clayey mud, some being at least knee-deep and full of water, and many of our donkeys were trapped in them. But they managed to bring their loads into camp in safety, although one had nearly been strangled

April, 1873.

by its driver, who made a running noose round its neck and attempted to drag it out of a hole by main force.

Five hours in heavy rain were occupied in getting over five miles of this road, and during that time we had often to lend a hand in loading and unloading the poor donkeys, besides preventing the men from straggling, since they all wished to halt in the middle of the mud.

This would have been a fatal mistake, there being no bushes with which to build huts or to provide fuel for the camp-fires, and a night's exposure to the rain and cold with no dry sleeping-place must have crippled most of them. So I continued on the march until 3 P.M., when we arrived at the site of an old camp, a comparatively dry spot where we found fuel and materials for hut-building.

It rained hard all the night but began to clear shortly after daybreak, and at eight o'clock we commenced our march over a level plain sparsely wooded and with a few fan-palms, and the mud not nearly so troublesome as on the previous day.

One hour's distance from camp we crossed a swift little stream, fed by small drains in the soil, which falls into the Makata river, and then came upon another too deep to ford.

To my vexation, on ordering the indiarubber boat to be made ready to ferry the loads across, I found that a part of the caravan had taken a different road in order to ford the stream where it was shallower, and unfortunately the man carrying the boat had gone with those who did not require his services.

April, 1873.

We sent after him, but in the meantime decided to cross by swimming, Dillon and myself going backwards and forwards to tow over those who were unable to swim. And after most of the men were safely landed on the opposite bank the boat appeared upon the scene, and we used it to transport the bales.

Finding one of my boxes amongst the baggage I took the opportunity of changing my wet clothes, but could not persuade Dillon to follow my example, and he remained in the water until he became thoroughly chilled.

I observed wrack of grass and twigs in the branches of small trees on the banks of these streams, about ten feet above water, showing how high the floods over the country must be at times.

Another half-hour brought us to the Makata river, a swift swirling stream about forty yards wide by eight or nine feet in depth. At this point was a rough bridge composed of trunks and branches of trees lashed together with creepers and supported by large branches, and in one or two places near the banks by a rough form of trestle.

According to African ideas this construction, which was then almost under water, answered

April, 1873.

very well for bipeds, but the unfortunate donkeys were obliged to be hauled across at a clear place further up the stream, in a manner they did not at all relish.

Each one was brought up in turn and bundled into the river from a high bank whilst a dozen men on the opposite side ran away with a rope made fast round the neck of the beast, which never

CAMP.

appeared after the first plunge until his feet struck ground at the opposite bank.

We camped a few hundred yards from the river and, the afternoon being fine, occupied ourselves in drying such of our stores as had been damaged by the wet. But during the night the rain came down again in torrents, our camping-ground became a swamp, and the river rose until the bridge over which we had passed was quite under water.

April, 1873.

We congratulated ourselves on our good-fortune in not being delayed another day before crossing, otherwise we might have been compelled to wait a week for the waters to subside, the current being far too swift to admit of our using the boat.

A portion of the plain rather raised above the general level now afforded us dry and good marching, and a striking feature on the route was presented by the number of fan-palms (*Borassus flabelliformis*), the swelling in the middle of their tall trunks having a very peculiar appearance to eyes unaccustomed to such an apparent deformity.

The numerous runs of game with which the country was intersected were also noticeable. One was so worn that, having separated from the main body of the caravan just before reaching camp, I followed it instead of the proper path for about half a mile without discovering my mistake.

We halted close to a village called Mkombenga, and Dillon became very ill with fever, his first attack, which was doubtless brought on by remaining so long in the water on our crossing the Makata river; and my right foot and ankle were so swollen and painful that I was perfectly unable to move.

Neither of us were better for a day's rest, but we thought it advisable to endeavour to reach Rehenneko, the descriptions we had heard of it leading us to believe that it was very healthy.

April, 1873.

It was distant one long march, but we decided on proceeding by easy stages. I was suffering such pain that I could neither walk nor ride but was carried in a hammock, whilst Dillon managed to get along on his staid old donkey, named "Philosopher" on account of the equanimity with which he endured the vicissitudes of travel. We rested at a small hamlet belonging to a chief named Kombéhina; but the next morning Dillon was too ill to mount his donkey. Having only one hammock, we decided that Dillon should remain here and nurse himself while I pushed on to Rehenneko which was reported as being near at hand, sending the hammock back for Dillon as soon as I arrived there. Several large villages were passed on the way and the country was very thickly cultivated, excepting in places where it was too marshy or flooded, such as we met with on two occasions. Each of these flooded tracts was three-quarters of a mile across with water varying from one to three feet in depth.

When I arrived at Rehenneko I located myself comfortably under the verandah of the chief's hut and immediately sent the hammock for Dillon.

Rehenneko proved to be a large and populous village and I was soon surrounded by a wondering crowd, the people being all well dressed after the fashion of the slaves at Zanzibar. They wore also a very peculiar necklace, consisting of a disc of coiled brass wire projecting horizontally from the neck and sometimes as much as two feet in diameter, having an effect which forcibly reminded me of a painting of John the Baptist's head in a charger.

These curious and uncomfortable ornaments I only saw in Rehenneko, but I heard that they were worn throughout the surrounding district.

The village was situated at the entrance to a rocky gorge leading into the mountains of Useghara, and I at once saw it would not prove a suitable place for a permanent camp on account of its low-lying position. I therefore selected the summit of a small hill for the site, and was carried there and had my tent pitched.

Only half-a-dozen men hutted themselves that night owing to their very great fear of wild beasts. Indeed, they were so timid that when I wanted water to drink after sunset I could not persuade any man to fetch some from a stream some four hundred yards off.

Dillon arrived the next day very ill, and I had the camp properly laid out for a long halt if necessary.

The men's huts formed a large outer circle and in the centre a plot was fenced in for our tents, the guard-room, and store-house; the space between the men's huts and our own compound was used for picketing the donkeys at night. During the day they were allowed to roam about and graze under the charge of a couple of men detailed for this

May, 1873.

duty. In addition to fever Dillon had an attack of dysentery and was confined to his bed until the 20th of May, having arrived on the 2nd; and I continued very lame, the swelling of my foot proving to have been caused by a large abscess which formed on my instep.

To add to our troubles a strike occurred amongst the men directly after our arrival, as they wanted extravagant amounts of cloth in lieu of rations. I was obliged to be firm even at the risk of losing many by desertion, for had I yielded to their request the whole stock of cloth of which we were possessed would very soon have been exhausted. I could purchase eighteen days' rations for one man for two yards; yet each man wanted two yards for every five days, and the smallest concession on my part would only have induced them to increase their demands.

My usual daily routine during Dillon's illness was to hobble round the camp after morning cocoa and visit the donkeys before seeing them turned out to graze, dressing with carbolised oil any that had sores. Then I mustered the men, inspected arms, and heard any complaints; after which the camp was cleared up, rations served out, and parties sent to the surrounding villages to buy the following day's provisions. Breakfast came next, and then writing, saddle-making, and different small employments occupied the time until evening, when a meal—dinner and supper combined—was served. I then took sights and smoked a pipe by the camp fire until it was time for bed.

May, 1873.

Occasionally the day was diversified by the arrival of a visitor; Ferhan, chief of a large village and slave of Syud Suliman—who was minister both to Syud Said and Syud Majid and is now one of the counsellors of Syud Burghash—having thus come to pay his respects and make us a present of a goat and some fowls. And another day the son of an Oman Arab settled at Mbumi, Syde ibn Omar, brought a present from his father and excuses for his not appearing in person on account of illness.

These two visits were very pleasant; but a third proved rather the contrary when a bumptious, overbearing half-caste came swaggering into camp to demand that we should give up to him one of our pagazi on the plea of a debt contracted two or three years before.

I investigated the case, and the pagazi declaring that he owed nothing to the Arab I refused to let him be taken away; upon which our friend bounced out of the camp without deigning to respond to my "kwa-heri," or good-bye.

Whilst remaining here I succeeded in getting all the donkeys' saddles into good working order, and designed a pad of a most useful pattern which would have enabled us to work with donkeys the whole journey across Africa had it been made of

May, 1873.

more lasting materials than those at our disposal. The saddles were fitted with two girths, breast straps, breechings and cruppers, and at the top there were toggels and loops so that the loads could be put on or taken off almost instantaneously when they had to be passed across any of the numerous obstructions on the road.

Seven donkeys carried panniers for ammunition and gun-gear, which would have answered admirably had they been stronger; but we put more weight into them than they were intended to bear, and that, together with constant banging against the trees, so shortened their natural span of life that none of them reached further than Ujiji.

Beginning to grow anxious respecting Murphy, I sent back several small parties to try and obtain news of him, and at length, on the 20th of May, I received a letter from him dated at Mohalé, on the 16th. He there stated that both he and Moffat had suffered from several attacks of fever and Moffat was very ill indeed.

Some days elapsing without hearing anything further I again endeavoured to communicate with him, and then received a report from an up caravan that he was about to cross the Makata.

On the 26th a caravan hove in sight, headed by a white man riding a donkey; but only that one white man could be seen amongst the crowd of dusky figures by which he was surrounded.

"Where is the other?" was the simultaneous

ejaculation of Dillon and myself, and "Who is the missing one?"

As the party approached nearer we became still more anxious, and at last, unable longer to bear the suspense, I limped down the hill to meet it.

I then recognised Murphy, and to my question, "Where is Moffat!" the answer was "Dead."

"How! When! Where!" was quickly asked, and then the sad tale was told of his having fallen a victim to the climate at a camp about a couple of hours' march from Simbo.

His remains rest beneath a tall palm-tree at the commencement of the Makata plain. His name is added to that glorious roll of those who have sacrificed their lives in the cause of African discovery. Mackenzie, Tinné, Mungo Park, Van der Decken, Thornton, are a few of that noble company in which, too—though we did not know it at that time—the name of his uncle, Livingstone, holds a most distinguished place.

Poor boy! He came to Bagamoyo so full of hope and aspirations for the future, and had told me that the day he received permission to join the expedition was the happiest of his life.

Murphy's entire party did not come up until the following day, when they arrived in charge of Issa. Immediately they were settled in camp I numbered and served out the loads, making a list of the contents of each so that it might be possible to find at once anything that was required.

May, 1873.

One great difficulty was providing carriers for Murphy who was still ill from fever, owing in a great measure to his having neglected the use of quinine.

Being no light weight he required three relays of four men each, thus making a serious drag on our means of carriage, and the six donkeys he had brought up were so knocked about that they were unfit for work. It taxed all the ingenuity of myself and Issa to put matters straight.

The total strength of the expedition at this time consisted of Dillon, Murphy, and myself, Issa—our storekeeper—thirty-five askari, including Bombay who was supposed to command them, one hundred and ninety-two pagazi, six servants, cooks and gunbearers, and three boys. We had also twenty-two donkeys and three dogs, and several of the men had with them women and slaves, so that numerically we were an imposing force.

Our total losses up to this time among our men had been one askari and one pagazi by death, and thirty-eight pagazi by desertion; one donkey had died at Shamba Gonèra, and another, having been lamed by a kick from one of his companions, was left by Murphy at Bagamoyo.

As regards our arms, Dillon and I each possessed, besides revolvers, a double-barrelled No. 12 rifle and a fowling-piece of the same bore, all by Lang, and right good weapons they proved; Murphy had a double-barrelled No. 10 fowling-piece and a

No. 12 of Lang's, which poor Moffat bought at Zanzibar.

Our men were provided with six navy and thirty-two artillery sniders; and Issa, Bombay, and Bilâl carried revolvers. Many of our pagazi also had flint-lock, Tower, or French trade muskets, and every man not otherwise armed, a spear, or bow and arrows.

RIDING DONKEYS.

The donkeys had all been elaborately named at Bagamoyo, but the only two that retained them were Dillon's and my riding donkeys, the Philosopher and Jenny Lind.

The three dogs, which were a great delight to us, were Leo, a large rough nondescript bought at Zanzibar, my special friend and a great wonder amongst all the natives on account of his size and appearance; Mabel or May, Dillon's dog, a bull

May, 1873.

terrier given him by Mr. Schultze, the German Consul at Zanzibar; and Rixie, a very pretty brindled fox terrier brought by Murphy from Aden.

On the 29th of May everything was ready and we hoped to make a fair start on the following morning. Murphy was only partially recovered from fever and I was still lame, but Dillon was perfectly well, and we were all full of hope for the future.

AFRICAN FIREPLACE.

CHAPTER V.

OUR PORTER'S VANITY.—A ROCKY GORGE.— CAMPING ON A SLOPE.—
AN IMPUDENT BEGGAR.—MIRAMBO.—MONSTER TREES.—WIFE-BEATING.—
ITS REMEDY.—A BLUNDER AND ITS CONSEQUENCES.—FORTUNE SEEKERS.—
SEVERAL CARAVANS JOIN US.—AN ELEPHANT-HUNTER.—A DISTRESSING SIGHT.
—A TEREKESA.—A DRY COUNTRY.—DEATH FROM EXHAUSTION.—WATER
ONCE AGAIN.—STRANGE DOCTRINE OF A "TRUE BELIEVER."—TEMBÉ HUTS.
—THE WADIRIGO.—A WARLIKE RACE.—THEIR ARMS.—HARVESTING.—BITTER
WATERS.—THE MARENGA MKALI.—SHARP-EYED WAGOGO.

ON the morning of the 30th of May, several hands were absent and five had deserted. Amongst the latter was the man whom I had refused to surrender to the bumptious Arab who demanded him for debt.

May, 1873.

It was annoying beyond measure to find that after feeding men in idleness for a month, they bolted the moment they were required for work and had received their rations for the road.

And another trouble was, that notwithstanding my having taken the pains to see each man told off to his own particular load, yet they made a rush and struggled for the favourite ones. This was not so much from any desire to shirk a heavy load as to carry one which entitled the bearer to a more dignified position in the caravan, the order being—tents first and foremost, then wire, cloth, and beads, the miscellaneous gear such

May, 1873. as boxes and cooking utensils, bringing up the rear. By dint of perseverance we adjusted all our difficulties and started at ten o'clock.

Our road wound through a rocky gorge and up the steep side of the mountain, rendered more difficult by numerous torrent beds channelled in the solid granite, and which were worn quite smooth and polished and made slippery by the draining down of water. Before some of our donkeys would cross the worst of these it was necessary to blindfold them.

None of the men appeared fit for work, being out of training from a long stay in camp; so after a short march we encamped on a slope almost as steep as the roof of a house, that being the most level spot we could find.

Consequently we were obliged to chock up our "rolling stock" to prevent their starting for the Makata plain, some eight hundred feet below.

Several men complaining of illness and weakness we rearranged loads. This employed us until late in the evening, when the askari whom I had sent in search of deserters returned without having obtained any news of them.

Leaving here the next morning without difficulty we made a long and fatiguing march over very mountainous country to a camp on the left bank of the Mukondokwa—the principal affluent of the Makata—meeting on our way a large Arab caravan taking ivory to the coast.

The leader, a very miserable-looking wretch, unhesitatingly asked us for a bale of cloth, but when that modest request was politely refused lowered his demands and begged for a single doti.

June, 1873.

From him we heard that Mirambo, a chief to the west of Unyanyembé, who had been fighting the Arabs for some three or four years, was still unconquered; for although all the Arabs at Taborah aided by numerous native allies had taken the field against him they had been unable to drive him from the vicinity of their settlements. Travelling round about Taborah was therefore considered dangerous. The road was a succession of very steep ascents and descents, worn in many places into steps composed of quartz and granite either in slippery sheets or loose blocks that rendered walking very difficult indeed, and it was almost a marvel that the pagazi and donkeys with their loads avoided coming to grief.

Our camp was on an uncomfortable slope even steeper than that of the previous night, and everything seemed inclined to follow the universal law of gravity.

Just below flowed the Mukondokwa, a broad and shallow but swift stream, and the hills covered to their summits with acacias looked, as Burton justly observes, much like umbrellas in a crowd; and in the dips and valleys where water was plentiful the mparamusi reared its lofty head.

The mparamusi is one of the noblest specimens

June, 1873.

of arboreal beauty in the world, having a towering shaft sometimes fifteen feet in diameter and a hundred and forty feet high with bark of a tender yellowish green, crowned by a spreading head of dark foliage. Unfortunately, these magnificent trees are often sacrificed to serve no more important purpose than the making of a single door, the wood being soft and easily fashioned; and since it rots rapidly unless well seasoned, the work of destruction is constantly proceeding.

As the last men left camp for our next march a leopard having a monkey in its clutches fell from an overhanging tree within fifteen yards of where our tents had been pitched.

For two hours we followed the left bank of the Mukondokwa and then crossed the river below a sharp bend in its course, whence a level path through plantations of enormous matama, with stalks over twenty feet high, brought us to camp close to the village of Muinyi Useghara.

The stream at the point where we forded it was fifty yards wide and mid-thigh deep, running two knots an hour, the ford being marked by the finest mparamusi I ever saw. It had two stems springing from the same root and running at least one hundred and seventy feet in height before spreading into a magnificent head.

Near this was the former village of Kadetamaré. It had been much damaged by the late floods and hurricane and was now inhabited by some of his slaves under the orders of a headman in charge of the provision grounds. June, 1873.

Kadetamaré, profiting by experience, had built a new village for himself on the summit of a small knoll.

Soon after our arrival at Muinyi Useghara's we witnessed a curious custom, said to be universal in Oriental Africa.

A woman rushed into camp and tied a knot in Issa's turban, thereby placing herself under his protection in order to be revenged upon her husband who had beaten her for not cooking some fish properly.

The husband came and claimed her, but before she was restored to him he was compelled to pay a ransom of a bullock and three goats, and to promise in the presence of his chief that he would never again illtreat her.

A slave can also obtain a change of masters by breaking a bow or spear belonging to the man whom he selects as his new owner or by tying a knot in any portion of his clothing, and the original owner cannot redeem him except by paying his full value, and he is invariably obliged to promise not to use him harshly.

From this place we despatched a party of forty men to Mbumi, for food to take us to Mpwapwa; but some of them returned a day later with a woeful story of disaster and death.

When sifted to the bottom, the affair proved

June, 1873. much less than they represented, though bad enough in all conscience.

It appeared that the party arrived safely at Mbumi and completed the purchase of the corn we required, when a false alarm was raised that some of the wilder tribes living in the hills were coming to attack the villagers. There was naturally very much excitement, in the midst of which one of our men's rifles was discharged by accident and shot a native through the body, killing him on the spot.

The people then turned upon our party, and those who did not escape by running were seized and put in chowkie, and the corn that had been collected was lost.

Syde ibn Omar, the Arab whose son visited us at Rehenneko, lived near Mbumi and wrote to acquaint us of the occurrence, and afterwards came in person and was of the greatest possible assistance in arranging the affair. Still this unlucky business delayed us and cost three loads of cloth. But we were fortunate in getting off so easily, for many caravans have lost very heavily in conflicts with natives of the Useghara mountains arising from far more trivial circumstances than the death of a man.

By a caravan passing down from Unyanyembé, we sent letters and also Moffat's Bible, watch, and an old rifle that had belonged to his grandfather, Dr. Moffat, to be forwarded from Zanzibar to his mother at Durban.

Three up caravans also arrived and attached themselves to us in order to benefit by the protection of numbers in passing through Ugogo.

June, 1873.

One was composed of Wanyamwési taking home the proceeds of the ivory they had sold at the coast. But on passing Rehenneko two or three days after we left, they were attacked and dispersed by the chief and people of that place; and, according to their account—which I believe was greatly exaggerated—they had lost fifty or sixty loads and eight or ten men.

Another was a party of about twenty, belonging to a blacksmith who indulged in the hope of making a fortune at Unyanyembé by repairing muskets during the war with Mirambo.

The last and largest was a heterogeneous assemblage joined together for mutual protection. It consisted of small parties under the charge of Arabs' slaves and poor freemen who could only muster two or three loads and slaves to carry them; but, full of hope, were bound for lands of fabulous riches where ivory was reported to be used for fencing pig-styes and making door-posts.

When we marched on the 11th of June we were altogether over five hundred strong.

The track was rough and broken, and in some places overhanging the river there were holes so nearly hidden by scrub that very wary walking was requisite, a false step being sufficient to send

June, 1873.

one tumbling through scrub and thorns into the Mukondokwa.

Fording this stream again and then following up its valley, we crossed it for the third and last time close to a small village called Madété, where we camped.

Here we met an elephant-hunter from Mombasa, awaiting the return of men he had despatched to the coast with ivory. He was armed with bow and arrows, the latter so strongly poisoned that one deep, or two slight, wounds proved sufficient to kill an elephant.

The arrow-heads were neatly covered with banana leaves to prevent accidents, and a stock of the poison was carried in a gourd.

A short distance below the place where we last crossed the Mukondokwa, the Ugombo joins it, and following the valley of that river, on both sides of which the mountains are very bold and precipitous—some peaks, apparently formed of solid masses of syenite, being excellent landmarks—we arrived the next day at Lake Ugombo.

This sheet of water varies from three miles long by one wide to one mile long by half a mile wide, according to the season, being mainly dependent on the rains for its supply.

It affords a home for a number of hippopotami and its surface is usually dotted with various kinds of water-fowl, while on the neighbouring hills guinea-fowl were abundant.

Although I had been assured that all our donkeys were properly tethered in camp, I heard during the night the screams of one evidently in great pain or fear at some distance from us. It was impossible to proceed to its assistance, owing to the darkness, and when day dawned the poor animal was found to have been so dreadfully torn and mangled, most probably by a hyæna, that we were obliged to shoot it.

A distressing sight was witnessed on the day of our departure, when a mixed multitude of men, women and children, driving cattle and goats, and hurrying along with a few of their household belongings, passed by our camp.

They proved to be the homeless population of some villages near Mpwapwa which had been plundered by the Wadirigo, a predatory highland tribe of whom more anon.

From Ugombo to Mpwapwa, two long marches distant, the country was reported to be waterless, and for the first time we underwent a *terekesa* or afternoon march, one of the most trying experiences of African travel.

A terekesa is so arranged that by starting in the afternoon from a place where water is found and marching until some time after dark, leaving again as early as possible on the following morning for the watering-place in front, a caravan is only about twenty hours without water instead of over thirty as would be the case if the start were in the morning. And as the men cook their food before moving from the first camp and after arrival at the second, no water need be carried for that purpose.

The tents and loads were in this instance seized upon and packed by the carriers at 11 A.M., leaving us exposed to the sun's rays without a particle of shelter till we started at one o'clock.

From that hour until after sunset we toiled along a parched and dusty country, with outcrops of granite and quartz all bleached and weathered by the scorching sun and pouring rains of the torrid zone. The vegetation was sparse and dry consisting of a few baobab-trees and kolqualls and some thin wiry grass, much of which had been burnt down by sparks from the pipes of passing caravans.

Our halting-place was at Matamondo, where the river-bed was perfectly dry and not so much as a drop of water was to be seen.

Issa, however, had heard at Ugombo that some was to be found near this place, and after a long and tiresome search in the dark a pool was discovered about two miles distant.

To this the men immediately went to quench their thirst; but the state of the road rendered it impossible to send the unfortunate donkeys there at night.

In order to escape the heat of the sun as far as possible we started again at 5 A.M., and after dragging along through dusty scrub, up and down steep hills and in and out of rocky nullahs, we approached the foot of the hills on the slopes of which Mpwapwa lies about two in the afternoon.

June, 1873.

The sight of fresh green trees and fields of maize, matama and sweet potatoes, and streams of beautiful crystal water running in threads through a broad sandy course, then gladdened our eyes.

Those only who have traversed a barren scorching road such as we had gone over can imagine how great was the delight and refreshment to our weary eyes and aching limbs when this scene first burst upon our view.

Directly I reached the water I sent some of the least fatigued with a supply for those who had lagged behind, faint with heat and thirst; but, notwithstanding this precaution, one pagazi and a donkey never lived to taste of the fountains of Mpwapwa.

Proceeding up this watercourse, bounded on both sides by very large trees, we found water becoming more plentiful and pitched our three tents under an enormous acacia, one half of which afforded us ample shelter.

We were soon favoured by a visit from an Arab who was working his way down to the coast in company with a caravan under charge of a slave of a large merchant of Unyanyembé, having failed to make his fortune in the interior. He seemed half-witted and certainly was the coolest fellow I ever met; for he did not hesitate to take

June, 1873.

the pipe out of my mouth, and after a whiff or two to pass it on to a circle of greasy, dirty natives who were squatting round us staring as only a negro can stare.

After a while our eccentric friend retired, and soon afterwards a tremendous noise occurred in the camp of the Wanyamwési.

On going to ascertain the cause of the excitement, I found the Arab, followed by some slaves from his caravan, driving the Wanyamwési out of their camp on the plea that heathens had no right to possess any goods, and therefore the remnant of stores they had saved from the rapacious clutches of the chief of Rehennoko ought by right to belong to a true believer.

He was now attempting to carry this doctrine to its logical conclusion, but I sent the lunatic back to his master, and seeing quiet restored the Wanyamwési returned to their occupations which had been so suddenly and unexpectedly interrupted.

The chief, a dirty, greasy old fellow with a moist and liquorish eye and a nose which denoted his devotion to pombé, came afterwards with the leader of the Arab caravan to thank me for having prevented a serious disturbance.

In order to recruit after the fatigues of the trying march from Lake Ugombo, and to prepare for crossing the Marenga Mkali, another waterless track of more than thirty miles, we remained here two days.

CONTRIVANCE FOR CARRYING WATER.

And having now experienced the disagreeable consequences of the lack of water, I resolved to take a supply by filling four indiarubber air-pillows, each holding three gallons. It required some little ingenuity to fill them; but by taking out the screw-plugs of the nozzles by which they

June, 1872.

TEMBÉ.

were inflated, and using the tube of a pocket-filter as a siphon, the difficulty was overcome.

At Mpwapwa the *tembé* was first met with, and continued thence throughout Ugogo the sole habitation of the natives.

The tembé is formed simply of two walls running parallel, subdivided by partitions and having a roof nearly flat, sloping only slightly

June,
1873.

to the front. They are usually built to form a square, inside which the cattle are penned at night. It is about the most comfortless form of habitation that the brain of man ever devised, and as the huts are shared by the fowls and goats they are filthy in the extreme and swarm with insect life.

The people are armed with bows and arrows and knobsticks for throwing or using as a club, and also have long, narrow, oval-shaped shields of bulls' hide.

Their ornaments are brass-wire earrings and necklaces; and, having been so much in communication with people of the coast, they dress like the Arabs' slaves.

A great contrast to the Mpwapwa people were some of the Wadirigo who came over to look at us. They stalked about among the timid villagers, openly telling them that whenever they thought fit they would plunder them.

The Wadirigo are a tall, manly race, despising all such refinements of civilisation as clothing, the men and many of the women being stark-naked with the exception, perhaps, of a single string of beads round the neck or wrist.

They carry enormous shields of hide, five feet high by three wide, stiffened by a piece of wood bowed to form a handle down the centre, and having a small withe round the edge to keep it in shape. On the right-hand side of the centre-piece are two beckets. In these are kept a heavy spear for close quarters and a bundle of six or eight slender, beautifully finished assagais—ornamented with brass wire and balanced by a small knob of the same metal at the butt—which they throw upwards of fifty yards with force and precision.

June, 1873.

Such is their reputation for courage and skill in the use of their weapons that none of the tribes on whom they habitually make their raids ever dare to resist them.

After resting three days on we went again, marching first to a village called Kisokweh, and meeting on our way many women of Mpwapwa bringing in the harvest in large baskets carried on their heads.

Several had babies slung in a goatskin on their backs, and wore an apron made of innumerable thongs of hide having a charm dangling from each to preserve the infant from the evil eye and other forms of witchcraft.

Kisokweh was occupied by the Wadirigo who were well-enough disposed towards us, and as is usually the case with people of their description, it was "light come, light go," so that we were able to purchase from them a couple of bullocks, half-a-dozen goats, and some ghee, for a very small amount of beads and brass wire.

A short march from this brought us to Chunyo ("bitter"), so called from its undesirable reputation of having bitter water which poisons beasts should they drink it. As we found it fairly good on tasting we allowed ours to drink, arguing that if good enough for man it could not harm a donkey, and the result proved we were right.

The water in the pillows we reserved for the Marenga Mkali, for which we started on the 20th of June.

The walking was good, over a level sandy plain with numerous small granite hills in different directions; and although there was not much vegetation for the first part of the road, but only a little thin grass and some thorn scrub, this seemed to afford sufficient sustenance for large herds of antelope and zebra.

One herd Dillon and I stalked for some distance, but could not get within effective range owing to the paucity of cover.

On this occasion we marched almost without intermission from 9 A.M. to 9 P.M., when we camped in a grove of stunted acacias. The men scarcely appreciated this long stretch, and were desirous of halting with a down caravan which we passed at sunset; but knowing that the next morning would be the most trying part of the march we pressed forward wishing to shorten it as much as possible.

The scene in camp was very striking, for no tents being pitched or huts built we all bivouacked in the open.

Overhead was the sky of a deep velvety blackness studded with innumerable silver and golden stars, while the dusky figures moving about amongst the fires formed a weird and effective foreground, the smoke hanging like frosted silver amongst the treetops.

Ugogo was reached the next day after a very tiresome march of five hours across a country intersected by many nullahs, which in the rainy season are temporary streams.

When we arrived within the limits of cultivation our men, unable any longer to withstand the pangs of thirst, commenced gathering watermelons of a very inferior and bitter sort; but some sharp-eyed Wagogo detected them and demanded about twenty times the value of what had been picked. And upon camping at noon our beasts were not allowed to be watered until we had obtained leave by payment.

EARTHEN POT. UGOGO.

CHAPTER VI.

ENTRY INTO UGOGO.—CHARACTER OF THE WAGOGO.—DEFEAT OF AN ARAB EXPEDITION.—UGOGO.—WATER SUPPLY.—A WAKE.—WANYAMWÉSI AND THEIR INGRATITUDE.—THE WAGOGO.—EXTRAORDINARY EARRINGS.—FANTASTIC COIFFURES.—PERSONAL ADORNMENT.—A STRUGGLE FOR PRECEDENCE.—CURIOUSLY FORMED TREES AND EXCRESCENCES.—ASTONISHING THE NATIVES.—ADOPTED FATHERS.—A THIEVING TRIBE.—BOMBAY IN A FOG.—A CHILLY MORNING.—MANUFACTURE OF SALT.—SMALL-POX.

June, 1873.

WE had now fairly entered Ugogo, and having heard many wonderful stories of the extortions practised by the Wagogo, anticipated some difficulty in passing through their country.

They were reputed to be great thieves, and so overbearing that any insult they inflicted was to be borne without resistance. But should a Wagogo be struck or receive some imaginary injury a fine was exacted, and if not immediately paid, the Wagogo being a brave and warlike race would attack and plunder the caravan.

Such was the character we received of them, and though we found them disposed to be rude and extortionate, they were in truth the veriest cowards and poltroons it is possible to conceive. Arabs, Wanyamwési and others with whom they are principally brought in contact, approach Ugogo in fear and trembling, apprehensive of being fleeced of half their stores in passing through; for they are completely dependent on the Wagogo for their supplies of food and water from day to day. And they, like true cowards, bully and oppress those who are at their mercy, knowing they can offer no resistance.

June, 1873.

The tribute which is levied is not, however, altogether unjust, and would indeed be perfectly fair if conducted on any fixed principles; for if the Wagogo did not live in the country and keep the watering-places in repair, it would be impassable in the dry season which is always preferred for travelling.

Some years ago an Arab, braver but not wiser than his fellows as subsequent events proved, determined to fight his way through Ugogo without paying tribute, and with this view collected about nine hundred people and openly declared his intentions.

The Wagogo never even waited for his approach, but filled up the pools, burnt their houses and such stores as they could not carry, and retreated into the jungle with their wives, children, cattle, and all their movables. The Arab and his men though quite prepared to contend with human foes were beaten by hunger and thirst; and while some returned to Unyanyembé whence they had started, many more died of starvation, and only eight or ten reached Mpwapwa in safety.

June, 1873.

It is said that six or seven hundred men perished in this attempt.

Ugogo is about one hundred miles square, but is divided into numerous independent chieftainships in each of which mhongo has to be paid and delay experienced.

The country is arid and parched during the dry season, but in the rains which last from November to May is well watered, and large crops of matama which ripens in June are easily raised. It is upon the stalks of this that the cattle are principally fed in the drought, and they appear in good condition notwithstanding its seeming lack of nutriment.

Every tribe possesses a herd of cattle which is attended to by all the grown-up males in rotation, the chiefs even taking their turn at this duty.

Numerous watercourses are met with, and in their beds water may frequently be obtained by digging. There are also a few small natural ponds; but where both these resources fail, the inhabitants dig pits to contain sufficient rain to last them until the season again arrives. After a time the water in these holes becomes indescribably nauseous, and is very often rendered brackish by the large amount of salt in the soil.

On the 22nd of June we moved to Mvumi, the village of the chief of the first division of Ugogo, and were thoroughly initiated into the vexations of paying mhongo and the manner in which negotiations respecting the amount are conducted.

At the moment of our arrival the chief and his people were celebrating the obsequies of one of his sisters who had departed this life a week previously, and consequently every one was drunk.   *June, 1873.*

This circumstance detained us three days, during which a gang of Wanyamwési engaged by Murphy at Bagamoyo bolted *en masse*. He had entrusted their payment to Abdûllah Dina, and that worthy gave them such villainous cloth that they considered themselves cheated when they saw the "superior material" which our other people had received. Not contented with deserting only, they stole a load of cloth from one of the small parties accompanying us, which we felt bound to replace, being responsible for the acts of our servants.

They joined the Wanyamwési whom we had protected at Mpwapwa, and who thus commenced to show their ingratitude by aiding their countrymen to desert and rob us.

As the chief had given orders that none of the inhabitants should enter the camp, on account of trouble having arisen on several occasions between them and passers-by, with loss of life on both sides, we were obliged to send about the country to procure food during our halt here.

The Wagogo are easily distinguished from other tribes by the custom of piercing their ears and enlarging the lobes to a monstrous extent, wearing in them pieces of wood, earrings of brass wire,

June, 1873.

gourd snuff-boxes, and a variety of miscellaneous articles; in fact the ear to a Mgogo answers much the same purpose as a pocket to people indulging in wearing apparel. The lobes are often so enormous as to descend to the shoulders, and in old age frequently become broken or torn. In this case the indispensable earrings are either suspended by a string across the top of the head, or a fresh hole is made in one of the hanging ends, which ultimately becomes as large as the former one.

Their arms are double-edged knives, spears, bows and arrows and knobsticks. A few also carry hide shields similar in shape to those of Mpwapwa, but with the hair scraped off and patterns painted on them in red, yellow, black, and white.

Small copper and brass bracelets, worked at Zanzibar, are much worn as well as *kitindi* of iron and brass wire, which are also placed round the upper arm and above and below the knee. And a peculiar ornament carved in horn, shaped like a double chevron with spikes projecting from the upper angles covered with wire and tipped with small knobs of brass, is worn on the upper part of the left arm.

But it is in the adornment (?) of their heads that the Wagogo principally exercise their inventive powers; and nothing is too absurd or hideous to please them.

Some twist their wool into innumerable small

strings artificially lengthened by working in fibres of the baobab-tree, and either make them project wildly in all directions or allow them to fall more naturally, cutting them level with the eye-

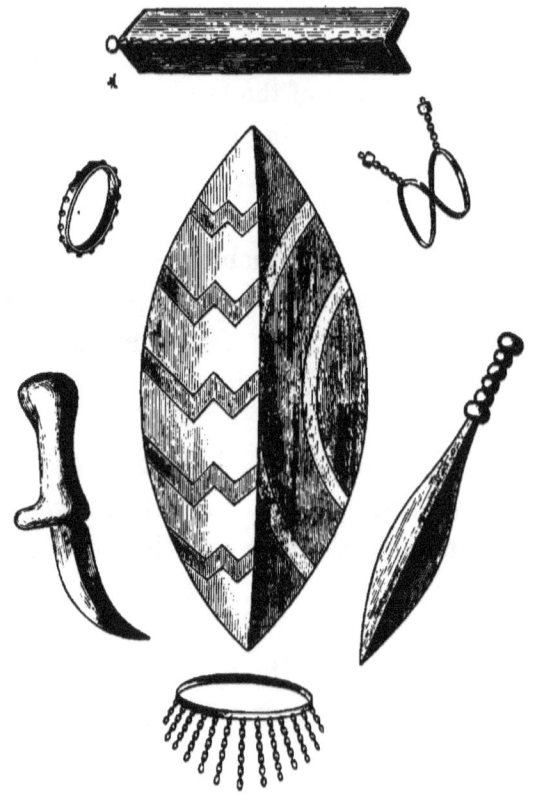

ARMS AND ORNAMENTS.

brows but letting them lie in a mass on the back of the neck. On the ends of these strings there are often little brass balls and different coloured beads.

Others cover their heads with copper pice brightly polished, or shave the greater part of the crown, training from the unshorn portions a varying number of stiff tails frequently wound round with copper or brass wire, whilst their brows are bound with a strip of white cowhide.

From the traders they obtain white cloth which they dye a dirty yellow with clay, and they smear themselves with red earth, sometimes in patches and spots but at others uniformly over the whole body.

Adding to this the circumstance that the Wagogo are usually dripping with rancid ghee or castor-oil, and never wash, some slight idea of their objectionable appearance and smell may be formed.

Having concluded the payment of mhongo at Mvumi, we left on the 25th of June, arriving the same afternoon at a pretty little ziwa or pond, surrounded by fine trees and with short, turf-like sward stretching back from the water's edge, forming a complete oasis in the midst of the sterile country through which we had journeyed. It was about four hundred yards long and two hundred wide, and was the chosen haunt of numerous water-fowl.

Dillon and Murphy took the boat and managed to bag a few birds somewhat like teal; but I was unable to move about owing to my boot having chafed the place on which I had an abscess when at Rehenneko and rendered me again quite lame.

Our march had been almost devoid of incident,

excepting that the caravan was brought to a standstill on one occasion by some of the cloth carriers attempting to take precedence of the more aristocratic wire carriers.

June, 1873.

And a second time, some Wagogo refused to allow us to pass their tembé without mhongo; but having already paid at Mvumi, to which district these people belonged, this was a barefaced imposition. I told the Wagogo they might take payment in lead from our rifles, although our timid men wanted to persuade me to allow myself to be cheated. And seeing three white men with rifles who evidently did not intend to submit to any extortion, they thought it most prudent to draw in their horns and let the caravan pass without further opposition.

The country was only partially cultivated, and some places were so sterile as to produce nothing but stunted acacias and a thorn which I called the "angular" tree. Every bend was at a sharp angle and there was not a curve in any portion of its branches.

Under the acacias were strewn numerous natural caltrops, formed by a sort of excrescence on the trees from which protruded four sharp, stiff thorns, each three inches long. When dry these fall to the ground and offer a serious impediment to barefooted men.

In one portion of our road there were many narrow rifts, seemingly occasioned by a recent earthquake, but I failed to make any one understand my enquiries as to their cause.

On reaching the tembé of the chief of this district, which was called Mapalatta, we were again compelled to pay mhongo, but owing to the headman being drunk this matter could not be arranged on the day of our arrival. The chief was very civil and gave us permission to take any matama stalks we might require for building huts and feeding the donkeys, during the time we were detained waiting for the headman to become sober.

Many visitors came to inspect our wonderful belongings—watches, guns, pistols, compasses, &c.— and one old man who was the chief's uncle and adopted father, after staring for a long time in mute admiration said, "Oh these white men! they make all these wonderful things, and know how to use them! Surely men who know so much ought never to die; they must be clever enough to make a medicine to keep them always young and strong, so that they need never die."

I believe the old gentleman had some idea that we were a few thousand years old and had evolved guns, watches, and all out of our inner consciousness.

He was very communicative, telling us that six circlets of skin on his left wrist were of elephant's hide and denoted the number he had killed. This induced me to enquire whether the yellow ones on his right wrist were trophies of lions he had killed;

but he replied, "Oh, no! goat's skin, worn as a fetish." *June, 1873.*

Honey was plentiful here, but as a party of Wadirigo were reported to be lurking about in the jungle no one could be persuaded to go out to collect any for us.

On the day following mhongo was settled satisfactorily to the chief, in particular, and relatively to us, for he was greatly pleased with what we gave him and we rejoiced at having paid less than we expected. A timely present to his adopted father on the day of our arrival had probably something to do with the moderation of his demands.

Perhaps a word may be necessary in explanation of the term "adopted father." It arises from the custom observed on the death of a chief, when the son is supposed to look upon his father's eldest surviving brother as his new or adopted father; but only in private, and not in public, matters.

When preparing for the road on the 29th of June, the remaining goats of those purchased from our friendly thieves, the Wadirigo, were missing; so Issa and a few askari were left to look after them while we proceeded with the caravan to Mpanga Sanga.

This was a clearing in the jungle three miles in diameter, with half-a-dozen tembés and the residence of yet another independent chief.

On the road a little cultivation was passed with some tembés dependent upon it and our camp was pitched near the chief's hut on the edge of a partially dried-up lake.

In the absence of Issa the payment of mhongo was entrusted to Bombay; but the old man got in a fearful fog about it, and it ended in a dispute between the chief and myself. I considered his demands unreasonable and directed Bombay not to unfasten any bales in the open camp but in my tent, to prevent the prying eyes of the natives from seeing my good cloth. Because I knew they would most assuredly report to the chief what I possessed, and he would base his demands on this information instead of on the number of bales.

Bombay, however, became confused and frightened and opened several loads in the presence of a number of Wagogo. They instantly told their chief they had seen a couple of expensive Indian cloths, intended by me for presents to Arabs or important chiefs; but which, of course, were now demanded.

I naturally upbraided Bombay for having acted in this manner and desired him to inform the chief that he could not have the cloths. He then became still more foolish, and whilst away on this errand left a bale of common cloth exposed. This dangerous proceeding, in a place where every man's fingers are fish-hooks, resulted in two whole pieces of merikani being stolen; and in the end I was obliged to part with one of the Indian cloths besides losing the merikani.

When Issa arrived he brought one only of the six stolen goats, although the chief at Mapalatta had given him every assistance in looking for them. The others had been carried off by a party of Wadirigo—supposed to be attached to those of whom we had bought them—so that our encouragement of dishonesty brought its own reward.

It was not, perhaps, a very correct thing accord-

ZIWA, NEAR MPANGA SANGA.

ing to a high code of morality to become a receiver of stolen goods; but I thought we might as well accept the offer, especially as the original owners, the fugitives whom we met near Lake Ugombo, could not have benefited in the slightest degree by our abstaining from purchasing from the Wadirigo.

Leaving Mpanga Sanga on the 1st of July,

July, 1873. we marched for some hours through jungle with open spaces and ziwas, at the last of which we made a mid-day halt. It was of considerable size with a goodly number of water-fowl about, so we launched the boat and succeeded in bagging four or five ducks.

This was a favourite camping-place, and various passing caravans had ornamented it with trophies of horns and skulls of buffaloes and antelopes which had been shot when coming to drink.

In the afternoon we marched on with scarcely any intermission through a rough country covered with jungle and forest, until, owing to the lateness of the hour and the men being tired, it was hopeless to attempt to reach the next watering-place that evening. But the next morning we started before sunrise and for the first time in Africa felt cold, the air being very chilly.

Arriving at a camping-place near a partially dried-up ziwa, we found a down caravan on the point of leaving, and in answer to our enquiries ascertained that Mirambo was still to the fore.

They had heard that Livingstone was all right; but their knowledge of his whereabouts was so vague that we placed no trust in their reports.

At this camp which was on the outskirts of Kanyenyé, the largest and most ancient of all the districts in Ugogo, we were visited by a grandson of Magomba the head chief, who brought us a liberal present of milk and honey. He said they had long heard of us, and his grandfather had ordered him to advise us to follow the direct road to his tembé. Otherwise a son of the old chief would endeavour to persuade us to pass by his place with the view of extorting presents, which he had no authority for doing. And truly enough, emissaries arrived from this son in the afternoon

July, 1873.

VIEW IN UGOGO.

trying to induce us to pay him a visit. We politely declined.

Kanyenyé is a broad depression in the centre of Ugogo, principally remarkable for the manufacture of salt, large quantities of which are exported to their neighbours.

It is scraped from the surface of the earth where

July, 1873.

patches of salt efflorescence are found, mixed with water and boiled down, and made into cones like sugar loaves about eighteen inches high.

From this we moved to Great Kanyenyé, crossing a plain studded with baobab-trees and at a ziwa we noticed a fine herd of cattle being watered. The country was almost wholly under cultivation, and numerous tembés were passed on this march. At the entrance to one we noticed many people suffering from small-pox; the first instance, since leaving the coast, we had seen of this fell disease which at times sweeps like a devouring fire throughout large portions of Africa.

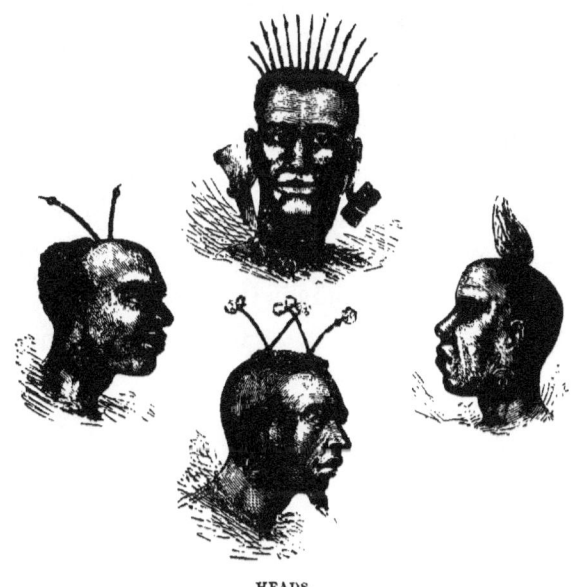

HEADS.

CHAPTER VII.

KANYENYÉ.—A VERITABLE METHUSELAH.—HARSH-TONGUED PEOPLE.—A DRUNKEN OFFICIAL.—LAZINESS OF OUR PAGAZI.—A FANCY FOR GOGGLES.—A LITTLE VISITOR.— SAMBO SHOT. — A THICK HEAD. — RETRIBUTIVE JUSTICE. — FINES FOR SHEDDING BLOOD. — HYÆNAS.—A RAIN-SPIRIT.—PIGEON-SHOOTING.—WITCHCRAFT.—THE PENALTY OF FAILURE.—WIZARDS ROASTED ALIVE.—USEKHÉ.—OBSEQUIES OF A CHIEF.—THE WAHUMBA.—COST OF PROVISIONS.—ADMIRING SPECTATORS.—IMMENSE TUSKS.—A DISTRESSED BRITISH SUBJECT.—EXPENDITURE IN MHONGO.

July, 1873.

OUR camp at Kanyenyé was one of a group of some half-dozen built by various passing caravans, and on arriving there was a tremendous rush by our pagazi to secure the best huts. It was a regular case of "each for himself, and the devil take the hindmost."

Meanwhile, we were left to shift for ourselves without assistance and had much trouble in getting a place cleared for our tents, for the pagazi considered their work was over directly they were in camp and had deposited their loads.

Afterwards, when travelling with Arabs, I found that we had treated our men with too much consideration, and they in consequence tried to impose on us and were constantly grumbling and growling. Our loads were ten pounds lighter than the average of those carried for the Arab traders. And since

July, 1873.

they do not employ askari, their pagazi, besides carrying loads, pitch tents and build screens and huts required for the women and cooking; so that they are frequently two or three hours in camp before having a chance of looking after themselves. With us, the work of our porters was finished when they reached camp, for the askari pitched our tents, and the task of placing beds and boxes inside was left to our servants and gunbearers.

Bombay, whom we trusted to keep order amongst the askari was jealous of Issa and allowed the men to abuse him as they liked, and they were often so impertinent and insubordinate that Bombay himself was afraid to give an order. For instance, when directed to have a certain thing done, such as gathering wood for our camp-fire, and after a time being asked why it had not been brought in, he would reply, "Oh, no man want go!" On enquiring who had refused and desiring that the offenders should be brought to me for punishment, his next answer would be, "Tell all man, all man say no go." Of course, as no individual had been singled out for the duty, they considered that what was every man's business was no man's business, and it usually resulted in my having to give the order myself.

Magomba, who was chief of Kanyenyé when Burton passed in 1857, was still in power, being reported by his subjects to be over three hundred years of age and to be cutting his fourth set of teeth, the third set having, according to our informant, worked out about seven years before our visit.

From that time he had subsisted on pombé, being unable to eat meat, the only other food which one occupying his rank and position could deign to touch.

I have no doubt that this ancient chieftain was considerably over a century, for his grandchildren were grey and grizzled.

Another instance of the extraordinary longevity of the African races was noticed by Dr. Livingstone at Ma Kazembé's. He found there in 1871 or 1872 a man named Pembereh, who had children upwards of thirty years of age when Dr. Lacerda e Almeida visited that place in 1796. And this Pembereh was still living, according to the Arabs, in 1874, and must then have been at least a hundred and thirty years old.

No restrictions were placed upon the intercourse between the natives and ourselves, and throughout the day the camp was crowded with them, staring, yelling and gesticulating. They were a cowardly but merry set of thieves, laughing and joking among themselves at every new and strange sight.

Their voices were particularly unpleasant and jarring, their tones resembling snapping and snarling, even in ordinary conversation, and when excited the noise reminded one of a hundred pariah dogs fighting over their food.

July, 1873.

Magomba's chancellor of the exchequer, chief of the customs, or whatever the title of the official deputed to arrange mhongo may be, was busily engaged repairing his tembé and we were told to wait until he had completed his architectural labours. When these were ended, he celebrated the event by a debauch on pombé, and remained in a drunken state for three days.

After he had recovered sufficiently to resume his official duties, he made the extravagant demand of one hundred doti; but luckily his notice was attracted by a pair of worthless blue goggles which so took his fancy that he insisted on having them.

Of course we declared they were of priceless value, and our apparent anxiety to keep them so whetted his desire that he consented to settle the mhongo at twenty doti if the goggles were included, a bargain which we gladly accepted.

It was simply a caprice on his part, for had we offered to dispose of the goggles we should have been laughed to scorn. I should not advise any future travellers to lay in a stock of these articles with a view to trading in them, as the investment would most likely prove as profitless as Moses' gross of green spectacles.

But it is generally so with uncivilised men when something new catches their eye; they must have it, *coûte qui coûte*. Yet a few days later, just like children tired of a new toy, they are ready to throw or give it away.

Some caravans from Unyanyembé arrived during our stay here. From the owner of one I heard that Livingstone had returned to that place after having started with the men sent up by Stanley, finding that he had not a sufficient number of carriers for all his stores, but had again left about five months since. I could discover no foundation for this story, and I fancy my informant had only passed through Unyamyembé on his way down from Karagwé, and had not obtained very reliable news.

July, 1873.

A great-grandson of Magomba paid us a visit the day after our arrival. He was the heir-presumptive, and was better dressed and cleaner than the commonalty, and the nails of his left hand had been allowed to grow to an enormous length as a sign of high rank, proving as it did that he was never required to do any manual labour.

It also provided him with the means of tearing the meat which formed his usual diet, though poorer people could only occasionally indulge in a small piece as a "kitchen" to their ugali or porridge.

In consequence of this Nebuchadnezzar-like growth of nail he was unable to use his left hand for any ordinary purpose, and it was much smaller than his right. As soon as he withdrew I had a little visitor, about seven years old—a small Arab boy whose mother was taking him to the coast to be educated, his father having been killed in one of the fights with Mirambo. The boy was a perfect little

July, 1873.

gentleman and behaved admirably, and was much delighted with the pictures in some old illustrated papers and a book on natural history which I showed him.

I heard afterwards that he was very grieved at the thought that such good people as the English must go to perdition for drawing pictures of men.

As he was leaving my tent I heard the report of firearms in the camp, and running out, found that Sambo had been accidentally shot in the head by my servant, Mohammed Malim, with one of my Derringer pistols which he had been cleaning in his hut and had reloaded.

It appeared that on returning with them to my tent he was caught hold of by Sambo, who was rather a "character" and always skylarking, and a struggle ensued in which one of the pistols went off and the bullet struck Sambo just outside the eye. His skull proved so thick that the ball did no damage but only travelled along between the scalp and the bone, and could be felt standing out in a lump at the back of his head. It was soon cut out, and a little patching with diachylon plaister mended his pate most satisfactorily.

I put my servant under arrest pending the investigation of the case, but some insolent ruffians came to me demanding that he should be put in chains or otherwise they would shoot him.

This gross piece of impertinence annoyed me very

much, so I gratified their desire for seeing some one in chains by clapping them in themselves.

July, 1873.

This affair delayed us another day as I had to enquire thoroughly into the whole matter; and so much lying and false testimony was, I suppose and hope, never before heard in so short a time. The chief, or rather his advisers, also demanded four doti as a fine for blood having been shed on his soil, and although I felt much inclined to refuse, I unwillingly paid, fearing complications and delays.

Hyænas came prowling and howling around our camp nightly, and being anxious for a shot at one we used the carcase of a donkey which had died of a low fever as bait. This attracted a large spotted brute with a jaw strong enough to break the bone of a horse's hind leg, and he was shot by Dillon.

The yells of the hyænas excited our dogs to such an extent that we were obliged to fasten them up at night to prevent their bolting out of camp and getting killed.

I took a few lunars here and found that they and my dead reckoning agreed well; and though a little different from Speke's longitude, his latitudes coincided exactly with mine.

Having pardoned the offenders whom I had put in chains, and received promises of better conduct in future, we left here on the 9th of July, and after two hours across level country arrived at a steep and rocky ascent which gave us an hour's hard climbing.

July, 1873.

The summit was tableland, well-wooded and grassy, with numerous pools, some partially dried up, and in all directions there were fresh tracks of elephants and other large game.

When evening came, having fitted paper night-sights to our rifles, we sallied out to one of the pools, and ensconcing ourselves behind some bushes spent about three hours vainly hoping that game worthy of our lead might come to drink; but we saw only a few skulking hyænas at which we would not fire for fear of frightening a possible elephant.

ROCKY HILLS IN USEKHÉ.

Our next march was to Usekhé, the village of another independent chief and, consequently, the place for another demand for mhongo.

But I need not recapitulate the vexatious delays which occurred at the villages of each of these petty tyrants, through the drunkenness of themselves and their advisers.

On this march jungle gradually gave way to large granite boulders scattered amongst the trees, and afterwards there appeared a range of hills composed of masses of granite of most fantastic

VII.] AN IMPROBABLE STORY. 115

shapes and forms, piled together in grotesque con- July, 1873.
fusion. Passing through a gap in this range we
came upon an open and partially cultivated plain,
bestrewn with piles of rock and some enormous
solitary blocks of very striking appearance.

A short distance from camp there arose abruptly
a grand mass of rocks having on the top a small

CAMP, USEKHÉ.

pool with smooth steep sides, and according to
report an elephant which had endeavoured to
drink there had fallen in and been drowned.
But the drawback to this story was the absolute
impossibility of any elephant reaching the pool,
for the rocks were so slippery and difficult to climb
that to visit the scene of the reported tragedy I was

July, 1873. obliged to take off my boots and clamber up in my stockings.

Returning thence to camp we visited a place where the people were accustomed to perform incantations for obtaining rain in drought. And a charred post and heap of ashes marked the spot where some wretched wizard had paid with his life for failure to procure the much wished-for rains.

Witchcraft is one of the curses and banes of the whole country, every illness being attributed to sorcery or evil spirits, and of course the wizard is resorted to in the hope of obtaining deliverance from the malign influence supposed to be exerted.

By means of playing alternately on the hopes and fears of their credulous dupes the workers of magic for a time realise a comfortable livelihood, but at last a day of retribution arrives. The magician is suspected, or denounced by a rival, of having caused the illness of some great person, and unless he can save himself by flight or turn the tide of popular opinion against his accuser he is seized and lashed to a stout post round which a circle of fire is kindled. The unfortunate wretch is then slowly roasted until he confesses, when the fire is heaped upon him and his life and agony quickly terminated.

Often while suffering these tortures the magicians seem possessed by a sort of mania to uphold their reputation and boast of crimes they pretend to have caused, saying, " I have killed such a one," "I have prevented rain falling," "I caused the Wahumba to carry off so-and-so's cattle." In many cases also they have faith to a great extent in their own powers, and certainly are thoroughly believed in and feared by their dupes.

July, 1873.

White magic, such as divination, curing fevers, boils, &c., by means of charms and incantations, finds many professors and is considered harmless. A large proportion of those working white magic are women, but nearly all professors of the black art are men.

The son often succeeds to his father's profession; but where a magician has been suspected of practising against the welfare of a chief, his whole family is sometimes destroyed with him to prevent any of them harbouring ideas of revenge against the chief or his successor.

Whilst at Usekhé we amused ourselves with shooting pigeons which came in flocks just before sunset to drink at a watering-place near our camp; and at these shooting matches, which provided a little variety for our evening meal, the losers had as a penalty to fill a number of cartridges. We also found in the crevices of the rocks some coneys which were very good eating, being to the taste much like rabbits. Owing to a peculiar formation of their feet these coneys can cling to the face of the rocks like flies to a wall.

Usekhé was at one time the richest and most

July, 1873.

prosperous section of Ugogo. But many of the Arab caravan previously mentioned as attempting to pass without paying mhongo, died near here, and no rain fell for two years afterwards. This circumstance was attributed by the superstitious Wagogo to a curse, and numbers of the inhabitants therefore emigrated, and those who remained were forced to kill the greater part of their cattle in consequence of the failure of their crops.

The wave of population is now returning and they are fairly prosperous; but their flocks and herds have not increased to their former proportions.

During my rambles about here I again chafed my unlucky foot and had to give up walking for a few days, and Murphy complained of a slight attack of fever. Dillon said, however, that he never felt better, and that he could go on with a wild life for an unlimited number of years.

Mhongo being settled we moved again, passing through a strip of jungle to the large settlement of Khoko ruled over by Miguu Mifupi (or Short-shanks), who bears the worst reputation of all the potentates of Ugogo. But he is growing old and unable to personally enforce his demands, and mhongo was easily arranged.

Khoko was the most populous place we had yet seen, and was principally formed of an aggregation of tembés with passages between them. But at one end there were many houses inhabited by

Wamerima merchants from Bagamoyo who had made this their head-quarters, and the huge thatched roofs of these dwellings lent to the settlement an air of semi-civilisation.

July, 1873.

Three enormous sycamore trees (a species of fig) growing just outside the town formed a prominent mark for miles around. Under the spreading

ENORMOUS SYCAMORES.

branches of one of this group our own party and a down caravan camped, as it afforded ample shelter for over five hundred people.

One of the Wamerima brought a large musical box into my tent, asking me to become the purchaser of it and assuring me it would prove a most valuable investment. When, however, it had

July, 1873.

been set going and had played a few bars of a waltz to the time of a funeral march, the music suddenly terminated in a grand crash which proved a permanent finale, the spindle of the fly-wheel having broken.

Here we learnt some particulars of the manner in which the obsequies of a chief are performed. In the first instance he is washed, and one is almost inclined to wonder that so unwonted a proceeding does not restore him to life. The body is then placed in an upright position in a hollow tree, and the people come daily to mourn and pour pombé and ashes on the corpse, indulging themselves meanwhile in a sort of wake.

This ceremony is continued until the body is thoroughly decomposed, when it is placed on a platform and exposed to the effects of sun, rain, and dew, until nothing remains but the bones. And these are then buried.

In former days a number of slaves were sacrificed on such occasions, but I was assured that this practice had ceased for many years.

The bodies of commoners are simply thrown into the nearest jungle to be devoured by beasts of the field and fowls of the air.

Large numbers of Wahumba who have partially forsaken the wandering habits of their tribe are settled in the neighbourhood, and act as herdsmen to the Wagogo who occupy themselves more particularly with agriculture. They are a branch of the great Masai nation and inhabit the country just to the north of Ugogo, where they possess large herds but do not cultivate the ground or maintain permanent habitations.

Their diet consists entirely of milk mixed with blood and meat, which they devour almost raw.

They move from place to place in search of pasture, sheltering themselves at night under a framework of small branches covered with one or two dressed hides.

Their arms are short heavy spears unfit for throwing, and double-edged swords similar to those worn by the Roman Legionary, and they also carry a huge shield like that of the Wadirigo.

As might be expected from the nature of their arms, they are more courageous than their neighbours, and being great robbers are much feared. None but themselves and other members of the Masai family have, they assert, any right to possess cattle, and they therefore consider themselves perfectly justified in "lifting" any they meet with.

The last station in Ugogo is Mdaburu, distant one march from Khoko, the limits of the two clearings being only a couple of miles apart.

The fields were divided from each other and the road by rough fences, and the ground seemed much more carefully cultivated than usual.

Mdaburu is intersected by a wide and deep nullah bearing the same name. Even in the

July, 1873.

driest weather it contains large pools of good water, while in the rainy season it becomes an impetuous river rushing down to the Lufiji, of which it is one of the principal affluents. I questioned one of the natives who seemed more intelligent than his fellows, and ascertained that he had been to the junction of the Mdaburu with the Ruaha, as the upper portion of the Lufiji is called, and that the Ruaha was also merely a chain of pools in the dry season but a great river during the rains.

On the march a pagazi deserted with his load, which was a very serious matter since our stores of cloth were melting away owing to the high price of provisions and the large tribute we had so constantly been compelled to pay. I ordered Bilâl, with half-a-dozen askari, back to Khoko to look for the deserter, and also sent to the chief of Mdaburu telling him of the occurrence and requesting him to give directions for the return of the man and his load; but all our endeavours to trace him proved futile, and the scoundrel got clear away.

Times had evidently changed since Burton passed through Ugogo, for while he was able to buy sixty-four rations for a doti we could never get more than twenty, and rarely more than ten! Eggs were unattainable luxuries, and milk and honey were exorbitantly dear.

Reckoning the doti at its Zanzibar value only, eggs, butter, and milk were more expensive than in England, and it was consequently necessary to exercise the most rigid economy in our living.

July, 1873.

In the afternoon a headman and his retinue called upon us and squatted in my tent for a couple of hours, which was the reverse of pleasant, all of them being anointed with rancid ghee.

The headman informed me that, having been to Zanzibar, he had already seen something of white men and their ways; but now they had entered his own country he wanted to see everything they possessed, and we were obliged to satisfy his curiosity. Anything he had previously seen he scarcely noticed, but examined minutely each novelty.

He recognised some pictures of animals which we showed him, but invariably looked at the back of the paper to see what was there, and remarked that he did not consider them finished since they did not give the likeness of the other side of the animal.

Still he was evidently pleased with the entertainment, and decided to detain us for three or four days for the benefit of the people who had never yet seen a white man and were anxious to have a look at us.

Charming as the idea might have been to the native mind, we scarcely appreciated being looked upon as a sort of Wombwell's menagerie travelling for the amusement of the natives.

Admission, too, was not only free, but we were

July, 1873.

actually obliged to pay for permission to come into the country to be stared at.

On the day of our arrival a caravan belonging to Said ibn Salim al Lamki, the Arab governor at Unyanyembé, came in from that place bound for the coast, with a large quantity of ivory intended for the purchase of powder for carrying on the fighting against Mirambo, who was still unconquered. But the Arabs were determined, as soon as further supplies of ammunition and reinforcements arrived, to strike such a blow as should finish him completely.

Some of the tusks were so immense that they required two men to carry them; and an idea of their weight may be formed when it is remembered that a Mnyamwési porter will bear 120 lbs. of ivory as a load.

Although content with single hire, the carriers of these enormous weights require double and treble rations, and whenever they feel so inclined compel the leaders of caravans to halt.

Amongst the hangers-on of this caravan was Abdul Kader, Stanley's Hindoo tailor, who was going to the coast in the endeavour to return to his native land.

According to his account he had been constantly ill since leaving Mr. Stanley and was now only just sufficiently recovered to be able to march. He had subsisted during his sickness on the charity of the leading Arabs at Unyanyembé, and as he was a British subject representing himself to be destitute and unable to work I gave him four doti of cloth to assist him on his journey.

July, 1873.

The Wagogo informed us that the Wanyamwési who withdrew from us at Mvumi, and aided and abetted deserters from our camp after having been under our protection, had been declaring that we had robbed them, and were trying to raise the country against us; thus proving, on a second occasion, that they had no idea of gratitude.

One of their headmen, however, had the impertinence afterwards to come to our house at Unyanyembé and ask for a present on the plea of old acquaintanceship.

The Wagogo did not at first entertain a very high opinion of our firearms, telling us that we trusted in guns which would be useless after the first discharge, when men with spears could fall upon us and annihilate us. But upon initiating them into the mysteries of breech-loaders and fixed bayonets they altered their tone and came to the conclusion that our fighting power was very considerable, and that it would be dangerous to attack us except in large numbers.

Having settled mhongo and written some letters which we entrusted to the charge of the leader of Said ibn Salim's caravan, we left Mdaburu on the 18th of July, for the Mgunda Mkali, or hot field, which lay between us and Unyanyembé.

In passing through Ugogo we had altogether

July, 1873. paid as tribute seventy-seven coloured cloths, more than two hundred doti of common cloth, a coil of wire, and three pounds of beads.

This at Zanzibar prices would amount to five hundred dollars, and in Ugogo represented nearly double that amount; but, happily, we were now leaving the mhongo-paying district.

ROCKS, USEKHÉ.

CHAPTER VIII.

THE MGUNDA MKALI.—A SERIOUS MISUNDERSTANDING.—RESTORATION OF PEACE.—REJOICING IN THE VILLAGE.—THE MABUNGURU NULLAH.—AN UNEXPECTED CHASE.—NATIVE FARMING.—AN INTELLIGENT AND INDUSTRIOUS PEOPLE.— JIWÉ LA SINGA.—COMPLIMENTARY BEGGARS.—MOONSTRUCK ASKARI.—HATRED OF SNAKES.—PITFALLS.—A DRY MARCH.—BURNT-UP COUNTRY.—A HUNTER'S PARADISE.—A WELL-FORTIFIED VILLAGE AND WELL-DRESSED CHIEF.—DISCOVERY OF A DEN OF THIEVES.—A HAUNTED WELL.—AN ATTACK BY RUGA-RUGA.

THE Mgunda Mkali on which we were now entering, was only just beginning to be cleared when Burton and Speke were in the country.

Few watering-places were then known, and provisions were obtainable in one locality alone between Mdaburu and Unyanyembé. Consequently travellers were obliged to cross by forced marches, and no caravan succeeded in passing it without losing a considerable number of porters on the road.

Now, however, things are much changed for the better; the Wakimbu, a tribe of Wanyamwési driven by wars from their former homes, having attacked the jungle. Water has been found in many places, large spaces have been cleared and brought into cultivation, and under the dominion of man, some of the most fertile and peaceful spots

July, 1873. in Africa are now scattered in the midst of what was formerly virgin forest affording shelter only to wild beasts.

After passing one or two clearings and a few pools covered with yellow waterlilies, we camped near two villages situated amidst jungle at a height of 3,938 feet above the sea—the country still rising rapidly.

The following day we arrived at Pururu, a village of Wakimbu situated in a very picturesque valley, where we intended to halt for a few hours to purchase food before making an afternoon march to the next camping-place. But we had scarcely settled down when a great disturbance arose amongst our men who seized and loaded their guns, exclaiming that there was a row with the natives.

Taking our rifles we went towards the village which we found prepared to resist attack, the gates closed and guns and spears protruding through the stockade by which it was surrounded.

A single accidental shot would now have been sufficient to originate a fight which might have had disastrous consequences, for the natives were all well under cover, and had any of our men been killed or wounded it would have resulted in the remainder bolting.

At this critical moment we decided to drive our men back to the halting-place, and then directed Issa to enquire of the chief the cause of the hostile attitude assumed by the village, our men being in such a state of mingled fright and excitement that no reliable explanation could be obtained from them.

The chief's statement was that our second kirangosi, who had come from Bagamoyo with Murphy, had taken ivory from this village on the understanding that he would exchange it for powder at Zanzibar; but being a Mnyamwési he had failed to procure any ammunition for the village, orders having been issued that no Mnyamwési should be allowed to take powder from the coast whilst the war continued between the Arabs and Mirambo.

To make amends he had offered the chief some cloth; but its value was not considered equal to that of the ivory with which he had been entrusted.

In order to arrive at an understanding, the chief and some of the headmen wanted to talk the matter over quietly with him. To this he objected and his chums commenced hustling the chief, saying, "Don't you treat our kirangosi like that," and then the row began.

On our promising to investigate the case and see justice done, peace was instantly restored.

We then accepted the invitation of the chief to enter the village, which was clean and tidy. The huts were flat-roofed and built in the form of long parallelograms, the whole being surrounded by a heavy stockade with only two entrances. Over each of these was a sort of crow's-nest, where the defenders of the gate took up their position and were furnished with a supply of large stones to

July, 1873.

be used on the attacking party coming to close quarters.

After sitting and talking for some time we were offered pombé if we would remain a little longer; but we preferred going to our tents, which had been pitched since it was too late to contemplate going further. Shortly after we returned to our quarters this hospitable chief and half-a-dozen men appeared with huge pots of pombé, which they handed to us after tasting the liquor themselves to prove that it was not poisoned.

I discovered that the kirangosi who had caused the trouble and delay possessed sufficient cloth to satisfy the demands of the village, and I therefore ordered him to pay as he acknowledged the debt, though he had attempted to plead poverty to avoid paying the amount in full.

Upon this decision the villagers gave themselves up to rejoicing, and were drumming, singing, dancing, and drinking until four o'clock in the morning.

We made a move at seven o'clock, and marched through wooded country with numerous large outcrops of granite, both in sheets and boulders, and small rocky hills on the sides of the larger slopes, and arrived at a pretty little pond in convenient time to halt for breakfast and a rest during the noonday heat.

Butterflies—which I always found in a dry country a sure sign that water was near—were

VIII.]   THE MABUNGURU NULLAH.   131

very numerous by this pond, and I noticed at least ten different varieties.

July, 1873.

Marching again through similar country, we reached the Mabunguru nullah, the westernmost affluent of the Ruaha, about sunset. Even at this period of the dry season it was almost a river, stretches of its channel a mile or two in length

HALTING-PLACE NEAR A POND.

being full of water and separated from each other only by sand-banks and bars of rock from fifty to a hundred yards wide.

These creeks were now thirty yards across, and there were signs of the water in flood spreading two hundred yards on either side. I do not suppose it to be a permanent stream during the rainy season,

K 2

July, 1873.

but more probably it goes off in freshets, the whole country being very rocky and therefore able to absorb but little water.

On the road we interchanged greetings with an Arab caravan, and ascertained that an account of Dr. Livingstone having returned to Unyanyembé was untrue; but doubtless the man who told us had been misinformed and did not intentionally deceive us.

Numberless tracks of large game were passed, as also bones of animals, one skull being that of a rhinoceros, frequently met with in these districts.

Our next day's march, also a double one, was through much cultivated land, and, according to report the country had once been much more thickly populated; but two or three years previously a party of wild Wanyamwési had looted it and destroyed many villages.

The men seemed delighted at getting towards the end of the first portion of our journey, and during the latter part of this day the kirangosis kept up a sort of recitative, the whole caravan joining in chorus with pleasing effect.

Dillon and I started ahead of the caravan in search of sport; but people from villages a short distance in front had been about and everything was scared, though fresh marks of antelope and buffalo were abundant.

We pitched our camp on the banks of a little

ziwa embosomed in grass and covered with red, white and yellow waterlilies.

July, 1873.

Cattle being cheap we purchased a bullock for our men, but the brute broke away and galloped off at a furious rate when being driven into camp, and we had to give chase and shoot him down.

Jiwé la Singa (the rock of soft grass) was the point to be aimed at on our next journey. The road was across a clearing, extending as far as the eye could reach, and which boasted of many herds of cattle, populous, stockaded villages and much cultivation.

The fields were divided by ditches and banks, and in one place we saw some rude attempts at irrigation. To cultivate these fields must require a considerable amount of perseverance and industry, the ground being neatly hoed into large ridges; and each year when preparing for a new crop these are turned completely over so that the ridge of one year becomes the trench of the next.

The villages I visited were remarkably clean, and the huts wonderfully well-built considering the means and materials at disposal. Indeed, except in the matter of "book-learning," these people cannot be considered as occupying a low place in the scale of civilisation.

We were now crossing the watershed between the basin of the Rufiji and those of the Nile and Kongo.

Having been unnecessarily delayed owing to our stupid kirangosi leading us round two sides of a

July, 1873.

triangle, we did not reach Jiwé la Singa until two in the afternoon, whereas many of our people who followed the direct route arrived in camp at noon. It is a prosperous place, and some Wamerima from Bagamoyo have settled there as traders.

They welcomed us with expressions of the highest esteem, even asserting that they regarded us much in the same light as their own ruler, Syud Burghash. Therefore they suggested that we could not well refuse them some paper, powder, needles, thread, and such small articles, thinking no doubt they had paid handsomely for them by their compliments. One who had been to Katanga told me that the Portuguese had established there a regular trade in ivory, copper and salt.

Here we were detained two days by the necessity of laying in provisions that we hoped might last us to Unyanyembé, and the appearance of a new moon during this halt caused us some trouble.

To celebrate the event according to Mohammedan custom, our askari commenced firing their rifles, and would not desist when desired to do so. One man to whom I had individually spoken discharged his rifle in despite of my orders, upon which I had him disarmed and promised punishment on the morrow. Another then suggested that I had better punish them all, as it was their custom and they intended to follow it, and him I also disarmed.

This custom of firing on the occasion of a new

moon was not only a waste of ammunition but was also very dangerous, as the men never looked in what direction their rifles were pointing but sent the bullets whizzing about the camp. I therefore determined to put a check upon the practice.

July, 1873.

When about to proceed, on July 26th, I found that some pagazi as well as the askari who had been disarmed for disobedience of orders when "moonstruck" had deserted; but one of these pagazi was exceptionally honourable, for though personally breaking his engagement he had been thoughtful enough to hire another man to carry his load as far as Unyanyembé.

Crossing two small ranges of rocky hills and then through forest and jungle with many palmyras, we halted for breakfast; and resuming our march continued on the move until sunset, when we were obliged to camp without reaching water.

On the way several antelopes and a lemur were seen, and Bombay and Issa reported having passed a herd of twelve elephants.

Suddenly there was great excitement amongst the men, and a cry was raised that a venomous snake was in camp. They immediately rushed upon it with their sticks and when I arrived it was so mangled and crushed that it was impossible to discover the species whether venomous or not. The men declared that its bite was deadly, for the notion usual amongst uneducated people that every snake is poisonous prevailed here.

July, 1873.

Kipireh, the point we had hoped to reach the night before so as to enjoy the advantage of its fresh spring water, was arrived at two hours after leaving camp; and here a dispute arose between ourselves and our men.

The day being still young and the inhabitants assuring us that water was to be found a short way in front, we thought it best to push forward, although our kirangosi declared that we could not arrive at any watering-place till the next day. Suspecting the kirangosi of laziness, and the natives appearing unfriendly, we forced our men forward; but after marching another mile were obliged to allow them to halt.

This I thought a favourable opportunity for calling all the askari before me and giving them a lecture as to their duties, in the vain hope of making them behave better for the future.

The halt being long, I went with my dog Leo as a companion to look around, and noticed some well-constructed fences and pitfalls for game. One of these pitfalls had been cleverly placed in a slight gap in a fence which I thought was merely a weak spot and made straight for it. Fortunately for me, Leo jumped on the covering just as I was about to step on it, and exposed the trap by falling through, thus saving me from a very nasty tumble. The pit was so deep that it was with difficulty I managed single-handed to pull the unfortunate dog out; but on succeeding I was delighted to find him unhurt.

After our rest we toiled on through alternating tracts of jungle and prairie, and to add to our troubles the grass had been burnt in many places, leaving miles of country blackened and charred, while the gritty ashes filled our mouths, ears, and throats, aggravating a thousandfold the suffering of thirst.

July, 1873.

Sunset came upon us and yet we had found no water, and not until nearly 8 P.M. did we discover a pool of liquid mud with which we were obliged to be content.

From this it was plain that the natives at Kipireh had wantonly deceived us, and we were compelled to admit that our kirangosi was right in advising a halt near that village.

Shortly after moving onward the next morning, some tolerably clear water lying in a cavity in a bed of granite gladdened our eyes. Directly we sighted it the men threw down their loads, and in a moment a mingled mass of men, dogs, and donkeys were all slaking their thirst at one and the same time.

A fair idea of our daily life and routine may be gathered from the introduction here of a few pages of my journal.

"*July* 28*th*.—Off at seven for Ki Sara-Sara, which we reached at 11.15. The country just the same— large rocks scattered about, soil sandy or a black loam lying on the granite; open woods with occasional small mbugas or plains. Lots of tracks, but

July, 1873. no game to be seen. Just after leaving camp we found a pool of water in a hole in a sheet of granite. It would have been a blessing had we known of it before, as the water we had been using was so thick that the 'pags' had been calling it pombé in derision. Nearly all the grass has been burnt in the woods, and all the kambi we have passed have shared the same fate, as the fires are left burning and any breeze scatters the sparks and away flashes the grass. One passes tracts of miles at a time as black as a coal; I can't say my hat, or my boots, as the first is white, and the second are brown. One donkey died to-day of a sort of low fever which seems to attack the coast donkeys. The Wanyamwési thriving wonderfully. Water supposed to be scarce at the camp, but we found some by digging about two feet close to the tents. I fancy water must lie all about here on the top of the granite, which is everywhere close to the surface, as the whole rainfall is either absorbed or evaporated, there being no drainage.

"Another pagazi ran last night; it is very considerate of them now, as it will save their pay at Unyanyembé. Some men came in from there to-day and say that there are numerous robbers about the road in front and we must look out or we shall lose some loads. They talk of a road to Ujiji of twenty-five marches; but fourteen of these are without food, so the bother would be to carry it; otherwise it would be grand to get there in five weeks from Unyanyembé. I think I shall try and get some more donkeys at Unyamyembé, as where there are grass and water they are all right.

July, 1873.

"*July* 29*th*.—Got away in the morning. On account of another pagazi having run, were delayed till past eight. About twelve we arrived at some puddles of water, which, in the rainy season, form part of a river, according to the natives; but as the whole country shows signs of being a swamp in the rains and there is no riverbed I expect they only form a long narrow pond. Game very plentiful, and one of the pagazi got a zebra after a very long stalk. Dillon and I went out; we saw several antelopes and a herd of mimba or gnu, at which we got a long shot, and I think both hit on our first barrels, as the shells burst and did not send up any dust; but they (the gnu) were off 'like a flash of greased lightning through a gooseberry bush.' There were tracks and droppings of all sorts of four-footed animals, and if one only had time to devote a few days to shooting this would be a perfect hunter's paradise.

" On our return to camp we found a caravan we had heard of at Ki Sara-Sara passing through. The mtongi was a handsome old Arab, with a beard perfectly white, but he was as lively on his pins as a kitten. He says all the Arabs have left Unyanyembé to go after Mirambo, who has now lost his last village, and is being hunted in the

July, 1873.

bush. The only Arab now in Taborah is a cripple, so we shall find the place quite deserted. Course N.W. seven miles.

"*July* 30*th*.—Got off a little after seven. I went off to one side in the bush with Issa and tried for game; but having to work down wind saw nothing but two antelopes, which were out of range, and some monkeys. I thought three and a half hours enough of this, and began to work in towards the road, and took my fowling-piece instead of the heavy rifle and had two or three shots at birds. Soon after I was met by some excited askari, who thought the firing must have been caused by meeting with Watuta (a wild tribe and much feared) or Ruga-Ruga (bands of brigands of any tribe). I got back to the road as soon as possible, and found all the caravan halted and in a great funk. I got them on again, and we arrived at the first village in Urguru at one o'clock, where we formed our camp. Soon after the tents were pitched a messenger came in from the chief of the district of Urguru, saying that the Arabs of Taborah had sent to ask him to look out for us, and wanted to know (this being the case) why we had stopped just short of his capital, which was only half an hour in front. I sent and said we were too tired and hot to strike camp again then, but that as I found we wanted provisions we would halt there (at his village) the next day to get some. The country seems very fertile, and water underlies the surface soil everywhere; at least digging three or four feet in the depressions always gave a supply.

"*July* 31*st.*—Marched at 7.30 A.M., and arrived at eight. The village was large and clean, and surrounded by a stockade or the outer walls of houses. The part where the chief lived was divided off from the rest of the village, as also was the gateway. The gates were heavy slabs of wood hewn out of the solid trunk, and people could only go up to the principal ones one at a time, a wing of palisading projecting on either side in the form of a long U with holes to use spears and arrows through, so that it would be dangerous for an enemy to attempt to force the gate. There were some other doorways in the outer walls of the houses, forming part of the *enceinte*, which closed in a sort of portcullis fashion. A number of heavy logs had holes in their upper ends, and the wall plate was rove through them; when the doorway is open these logs are triced up, inwards, out of the way; when closed, the outer sides of the lower ends butt against a strong fixed log, and are secured by a movable log inside.

"The chief was the best-dressed man I had seen amongst the natives. He wore a handsome double Indian déolé and a Muscat Sohari, masses of sambo on his legs, heavy bangle and wire, and ivory bracelets on his arms, and a necklace of elephant's hair neatly bound round with wire, from which hung an ornament, made out of the bottom of a shell

August, 1873.

brought from the coast, and ground down till quite white and smooth, called a Kiongwa. He was apparently lighter in colour than most of his subjects.

"The people kept a large number of pigeons and a few fowls and sheep. Provisions about the average price, *i.e.* ten kibabah to a shukkah. We had visitors in our tents all day, and at night found that they had left evidences of their presence behind them."

On the 1st of August we left our friends at Urguru and made a long march through a forest with great quantities of game, and reached Simbo. During this march Murphy saw a giraffe, but seemed so occupied with staring at it that he forgot to use his rifle until the animal was out of range.

Passing through an open grassy strip, Dillon and I went after some buffalo; but they winded the caravan and were off before we could get within range. We then came to more forest, and each took one side of the road, and saw many antelopes. I shot one, but was disappointed of my prize through being unable to extricate it from a tangled mass of thorns into which it had run to die.

Partridges and jungle-fowl were plentiful, and in one place I flushed a flock of guinea-fowl that quite darkened the sky, but unfortunately I was only provided with shell and ball cartridge.

During this solitary ramble, when in some jungle of thick growth, I suddenly came upon a heavy stockade partially covered over. It struck me at once that this might be a halting-place of the dreaded Ruga-Ruga, then hovering about in the neighbourhood, and against whom we had been warned. I therefore approached most cautiously, and, seeing no signs of its being tenanted, ventured to the entrance. On looking in I saw many pots and cooking utensils lying near the still smouldering fire which proved that it must have been occupied but a short time previously, as also skins, and well-picked bones of animals which had doubtless provided the morning meal.

My suspicions being thus confirmed I left as stealthily as I had approached; and I need hardly say that I did not continue my attempt at making a bag, fearing that the report of firearms might have attracted attention and ended in my being bagged myself.

I afterwards found that this was beyond doubt the den of some Ruga-Ruga, and had they been at home at the time of my visit nothing could have saved me from capture, as their intentions were decidedly hostile. Indeed the cause of absence from their domicile was their having gone to the front to lie in wait for the caravan.

I soon rejoined the caravan and we camped at Marwa, respecting which there are some curious superstitions. The camping-place is in the midst of a group of enormous rocks, and water can only be obtained by digging at the base of one of

August, 1873.

the largest of them. This is supposed to cover the site of a village upon which it fell, destroying every one of the inhabitants, and the ghosts of the dead villagers are believed to haunt the place.

Should the spring be disrespectfully spoken of as "Maji" merely—the ordinary word for water—instead of as "Marwa," which in different dialects signifies pombé, palm wine, and other kinds of drink; or should any one wearing boots pass the spot or fire a gun in the immediate vicinity, the ghosts at once stop the supply. Upon drawing water a small present of beads or cloth is customarily thrown in to propitiate the guardian spirits of the well; and as I declined to conform to this rule, Bombay, fearing some terrible disaster if the full ceremonies were not complied with, made the offering himself.

As a long march lay before us I roused the camp at 3 A.M., but could not get away before five o'clock owing to the pagazi hiding in the jungle to endeavour to escape carrying their loads in the darkness.

When fairly started, Dillon and I left the road in the hope of shooting something for the pot; but a few antelope out of range, and two lions six hundred yards away, quietly strolling home after their night's ramble, were all the game we saw. Unable to get any sport we rejoined the main body, and halted for breakfast at a small pond in which some water still remained, although it had been reported as dried up.

Some Wanyamwési—taking ivory and honey to Unyanyembé—who joined us the night before now went on by themselves, and much to our astonishment we shortly met them returning in haste and disorder. They reported that they had been attacked by Ruga-Ruga, losing two women slaves, their ivory and honey, and one of their men had been wounded. They also said the Ruga-Ruga were on the look-out for our party, and therefore it behoved us to be careful.

August, 1873.

Hearing this, we closed up the caravan, distributed the guns along the line at equal intervals and prepared to resist any attack that might be made on us. And on arriving in the afternoon at a ziwa of some size we decided to camp and build around us a strong boma, or fence, with one flank resting on the water so that our supply of that necessary article should not be cut off. Soon after sunset a few arrows were shot into camp, and this hostile act being responded to by us with a few shots at some dim and dusky objects outside, seemingly with good effect, we were not again disturbed; but we kept strict watch and ward all night.

By daylight we were away again and crossed a dry river-bed, the nominal boundary between Urguru and Unyanyembé, and immediately afterwards came upon clearings and villages surrounded with heavy stockades, outside which were ditches and banks planted with the milk-bush.

We camped at Ituru—being now at last in

August, 1873. Unyanyembé with the first stage of our journey across Africa nearly completed—and sent messengers to the Arab governor to inform him of our arrival, etiquette requiring this formal notice before entering an Arab settlement.

VILLAGE IN UNYANYEMBÉ.

CHAPTER IX.

UNYANYEMBÉ.—MORNING CALLS.—EXCESSIVE HOSPITALITY.—THE FIGHTING MIRAMBO.—THE ORIGIN OF THE STRUGGLE.—THE GARRISON OF UNYANYEMBÉ.—ATROCITIES.—KIDNAPPING OUR PAGAZI.—A LETTER FROM SIR S. BAKER.—COMMUNICATION WITH MTÉSA.—A DIFFICULTY IN HIS CONVERSION TO MOHAMMEDANISM.—GROSS OUTRAGE UPON A PAGAZI.—MUTINY AMONGST THE ASKARI.—THE UNPLEASANTNESS OF THE SITUATION.—OUR TROUBLES AND WORRIES.—FEVER AND BLINDNESS.—DESERTION OF PAGAZI.—CONSEQUENT EXPENSE.—KINDNESS OF THE ARABS.—AN AUCTION.—PUBLIC SALE OF SLAVES.—THE DEATH OF LIVINGSTONE.

IN answer to our formal announcement of arrival we received a letter the following morning from Said ibn Salim, the governor, inviting us to breakfast with him and stating that he had placed a house at our disposal during our stay at Unyanyembé. We at once proceeded to his residence at Kwikuruh and were welcomed most warmly, and found prepared for us a capital breakfast of curried fowl, wheat cakes, butter, milk, coffee, and tea. To this meal we did such ample justice that I fancy we must have rather astonished our host.

Our appetites being appeased, the governor, accompanied by many other Arabs who had gathered together to welcome us, conducted us to the house in Kwiharah, and when we had been shown over the premises left us to make ourselves comfort-

August, 1873.

August, 1873. ably at home. The house—which had previously been lent to Livingstone and Stanley—was a large and substantial building of mud bricks with a flat roof. The interior arrangements will be understood by reference to the accompanying plan.

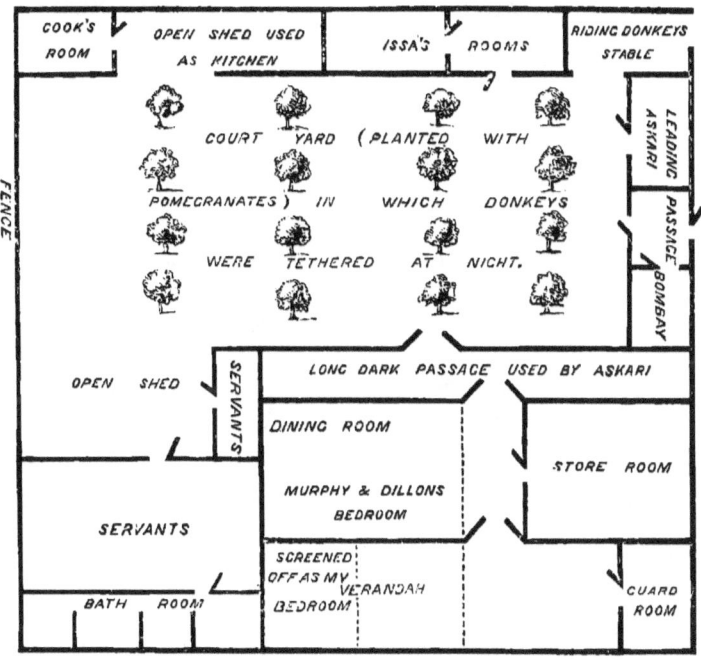

Our first business was to pay and discharge the pagazi whom we had engaged to accompany us thus far, after which only thirteen bales of cloth remained.

In the afternoon Said ibn Salim called to acquaint us that on the morrow we should pay visits to the principal Arabs, and that the most convenient arrangement would be for us to commence the day by breakfasting with him.

August, 1873.

He had formerly been detailed by Syud Majid to accompany Burton and Speke on their famous journey when they discovered the Tanganyika and Victoria Nyanza; and also was sent with Speke and Grant on their journey, but did not go further than this place on account of illness. He cherished an affectionate memory for his former masters and was very kind to us for their sakes; not only lending the house, but giving us a supply of milk morning and evening, and constantly sending presents of fowls, eggs, and goats.

A harder day's work than we anticipated was in store for us, and had we known what making calls upon all the Arabs involved we should not so readily have undertaken it, although the customs of a country must be observed.

We began with a sumptuous breakfast with Said ibn Salim, after which he conducted us, with much state and ceremony, to pay the promised round of visits to the local magnates. According to usage we were expected to eat and drink at every house we entered, but though doing our utmost to show appreciation of the kind intentions of our hosts, our capacities were but limited, and I am afraid we were scarcely equal to partaking of the proffered hospitality to the extent they would have wished.

August, 1873.

The Arabs at Unyanyembé live in great comfort, having large and well-built houses with gardens and fields in which they cultivate wheat, onions, cucumbers, and fruits introduced from the coast. They maintain constant communication with Zanzibar in peaceful times, and thus obtain supplies of coffee, tea, sugar, soap, candles, curry powder, and various luxuries.

But at this time they were much harassed by Mirambo, with whom they had waged war for years without seeing any prospect of a speedy and successful termination to the hostilities.

The whole truth of the cause of this war I did not ascertain whilst at Unyanyembé; but I learnt some particulars afterwards. It appeared that Mirambo was originally the chief of a small district of Unyamwési, and for a number of years evinced a strong friendship towards the Arabs and even yet maintained friendly relations with many of them. Several had houses situated close to his village, and he had frequently given fifty cattle at a time as a present to any one whom he esteemed.

But some unprincipled fellow took advantage of this good-nature to obtain a large quantity of ivory on credit, and when payment became due laughed at Mirambo for having trusted him. Mirambo then applied to the Arabs at Unyanyembé to assist him in bringing the matter to a just settlement, but as they turned a deaf ear to his complaints he determined to arrange affairs according to his own wishes.

Shortly afterwards a caravan commanded by a partner of the man who had cheated Mirambo arrived on the borders of his territory and he refused to allow it to pass unless the outstanding debt was paid. The Arab yielding to adverse circumstances consented to meet a portion but not the whole of the debt, but Mirambo being in no humour for half-measures took the law into his own hands, and the caravan was worsted in the struggle.

August, 1873.

Since that time an irregular, desultory warfare has been carried on, greatly to the detriment of trade and causing an immense amount of misery; for Mirambo is always on the move and brings destruction wherever the people decline to join him. On more than one occasion he has invaded the settlements of the Arabs in Unyanyembé and carried off their cattle from under their eyes, whilst they have simply barricaded themselves in their houses, being afraid to offer any resistance.

A thousand Balooches in the pay of Syud Burghash were quartered at Unyanyembé, and during our stay the force was strengthened by the arrival of two thousand coast people. Besides this little army the Arabs have native allies, and had they any union amongst themselves Mirambo might easily have been defeated and his power altogether broken long since. There were, however, many different cliques jealous of each other, and no settled plan of campaign was ever followed out.

On both sides the war was prosecuted with the

August, 1873. most revolting barbarity and cruelty. They had no idea of fair fighting, but considered that the greatest glory was won by burning villages inhabited by unoffending people, and surprising and murdering small parties and individuals by stratagem.

This barbarous system was fostered by the Arabs, who rewarded any man bringing in a trophy of a fallen foe by presenting him with a slave and a concubine.

Such a course naturally provoked retaliation on the part of Mirambo's men, and so the struggle became more and more embittered. For my own part I cannot but admire the pluck and determination shown by Mirambo.

Two days after our round of visiting and entertainment I was attacked by fever, Dillon and Murphy quickly following suit. Indeed during our stay here we passed the greater part of our time down with fever.

The pagazi engaged for the journey to Unyanyembé having taken their departure after payment, those whom we had hired by the month apparently thought this a favourable opportunity for going on strike and demanding two months' pay in advance. As long as possible I resisted, but ultimately agreed to advance one month's wages. They would have deserted *en masse* had I not yielded to some extent and some fifty or sixty deserted after obtaining this partial compliance with their demands.

Although the more respectable Arabs showed us great kindness and rendered much assistance, I am compelled to add that many of the smaller traders threw every possible obstacle in our way, tempting our men to desert and even carrying them off in some cases against their will.

August, 1873.

One case was especially galling, some of our pagazi whilst drunk being enticed away by a man on the point of starting for the coast, although he well knew they belonged to us. On hearing of this proceeding I sent to remonstrate, and in reply received a message to the effect that he should retain the pagazi unless I agreed to pay him three doti a man, which he averred he had advanced to them.

Not feeling inclined to submit to this extortion I represented the matter to the governor, who investigated the case, and ordered the men to be given up. Before the conclusion of the affair another attack of fever laid me low, and Dillon, not knowing the full particulars of the case, yielded to the man's demand.

When I recovered I found to my chagrin that not only had the cloth gone, but the men had also disappeared, having been marched out of Unyanyembé in chains.

Whilst remaining here a caravan belonging to Mtésa, chief of Uganda, arrived, bringing a letter from Sir Samuel Baker addressed to Dr. Livingstone. I thought it advisable to open the letter

August, 1873. to ascertain whether it contained any news of Livingstone. It was dated from Fort Fatiko, and in it Sir Samuel mentioned having had some trouble with Kabba Regga (Kamrasi), chief of Unyoro, by which he had lost many followers, but that Mtésa having sent men to assist him he had passed through the difficulty.

As these people said they should at once return to Mtésa's, I entrusted them with a letter for Sir Samuel, and also two for Mtésa—one in English, which was, of course, only a matter of form; the other in Arabic, the contents of which would, I knew, be explained by a Mohammedan missionary who had resided with him for some years.

I also forwarded two good cloths as a present, for at that time there appeared some possibility of receiving directions from Dr. Livingstone to proceed to the Victoria Nyanza.

We heard that the only obstacle in converting Mtésa to the Mohammedan religion was the difficulty experienced in finding any one sufficiently bold to perform the rite of circumcision, for it was feared that death would be meted out to one who caused him pain.

At the end of August Shaykh ibn Nassib and Abdallah ibn Nassib, two brothers in command of the Sultan's troops, came in from the scene of the latest fighting with Mirambo. They were fine specimens of Arab gentlemen and we speedily became great friends; and as their settlement was only a few hundred yards from our house, visits were constantly interchanged. They also proved of great service on one occasion when our askari mutinied and the expedition narrowly escaped being altogether broken up.

August, 1873.

The mutiny arose through one of the askari taking the law into his own hands on discovering that a doti of cloth had been stolen from him by a pagazi. Instead of reporting the man to me for punishment he proceeded to wreak vengeance on the thief, and with the assistance of three comrades triced up the culprit by the heels and left him hanging.

Issa, passing that way, fortunately saw the poor wretch and immediately came to me exclaiming that four of the askari were killing a man. On running to the rescue I found the miserable creature with his heels in the air and blood pouring from his nose, mouth, and ears, leaving no doubt that all would soon have been over with him.

I then ordered Bombay to put in chains the four ruffians who had committed this outrage; but he instantly returned with the startling intelligence that the askari refused to obey orders.

As I was still attending to the pagazi, who began to show symptoms of recovery, I told Bombay to give the askari notice that if they would not obey orders they should no longer be soldiers of Englishmen; but that they should be stripped of their red

August, 1873.

coats, made to lay down their arms, and be dismissed.

He then left me, but instead of making any attempt at enforcing the order to put the four men in chains he merely said, "Master, no want you; put down coats and guns and go." Of course the whole number, with the exception of our servants and a few who were sick, immediately went, and the four original offenders escaped.

In this difficulty I appealed to Shaykh and Abdallah ibn Nassib, who promised their assistance and sent to acquaint the governor of the occurrence and to obtain his permission to act. This resulted in the four men who commenced the trouble being captured and brought in the following morning in chains, while the others made their humble submission.

On the intercession of the Ibn Nassibs I reinstated the askari, but punished the ringleaders by keeping them a fortnight in chains. Bombay had acted most stupidly, and indeed during our stay at Unyanyembé was generally drunk and useless; but he now promised reformation, and as I hoped that he really intended to do well I did not punish him.

Several attempts were made at starting from Unyanyembé, but were unsuccessful owing to the pagazi I engaged so constantly deserting. They are always paid in advance on being engaged, according to custom, and at last it almost amounted to paying a man, feeding him for a few days, and then seeing his face no more.

The unpleasantness of our situation may be judged by the following extracts from letters sent home by Dillon and myself at this time. Writing on August 23rd, Dillon, who was usually blessed with buoyant spirits, commenced his letter,—

"Now for a dismal tale of woe! On or about (none of us know the date correctly) August 13th Cameron felt seedy. I never felt better, ditto Murphy. In the evening we felt seedy. I felt determined not to be sick. 'I *will* eat dinner; I'll *not* go to bed.' Murphy was between the blankets already. I did manage some dinner; but shakes enough to bring an ordinary house down came on, and I had to turn in. For the next four or five days our diet was water or milk. Not a soul to look after us. The servants knew not what to do. We got up when we liked, and walked out. We knew that we felt giddy; that our legs would scarcely support us. I used to pay a visit to Cameron, and he used to come in to me to make complaints. One day he said, 'The fellows have regularly blocked me in—I have no room to stir. The worst of it is one of the legs of the grand piano is always on my head, and people are strumming away all day. It's all drawing-room furniture that they have blocked me in with.' I was under the impression that my bed was on the top of a lot of ammunition panniers, and I told Murphy

September, I was sorry I could not get away sooner to *call on*
1873. *him;* but I had the King of Uganda stopping with
me, and I must be civil to him, as we should
shortly be in his country. Murphy pretty well
dozed his fever off, but I never went to sleep from
beginning to end. We all got well on the same
day, about, I suppose, the fifth (of the fever), and
laughed heartily at each other's confidences. The
Arabs sent every day to know how we were, or
called themselves, bringing sweet limes, pomegra-
nates, or custard apples. . . . .

"*September 8th.*—We have had a second dose of
the beastly (excuse the word) fever. On the morning
of the third day of our attack (about the seventh of
Cameron's) I saw Murphy get up and steer for the
open end of the room, staggering as he went, and
endeavouring to get clear of a lot of ammunition
which had been emptied from the panniers, but he
failed to keep in the right line; apparently seeing
that he must go on to the 'rocks ahead,' he stag-
gered slower and slower, taking very short steps,
till, coming in contact with the edge of a heap of
empty cartridges, he gradually subsided on the top
of them, with a groan, on his hands and knees.
The sight appeared to me to be so ludicrous—a
big, powerful fellow not being able to get out of a
room without a door or fourth wall—that I laughed
as loud as my prostrate condition would admit of.
This had the effect of bringing him to his senses,
and he struggled to his feet and balanced himself

out. The whole thing must have been seen to have been appreciated, and by one in a similar state of helplessness as the victim. You can't imagine how this fever prostrates one. A slight headache is felt, one feels that one must lie down, though one does not feel ill. The next morning one walks, or tries to walk, across the room; one finds one must allow one's body to go wherever one's foot chooses to place itself, and a very eccentric course the poor body has to take sometimes in consequence. Drink! drink! drink! cold water, milk, tea—anything. Bale it out of a bucket, or drink it out of the spout of the teapot."

September, 1873.

Writing myself on September 20th, with my troubles uppermost in my mind, I said,—

" I am very savage just at this moment, as I have been trying for two days to get enough men together to form a camp a short way out, in order to see all right for marching, and all the pagazi declare they are afraid. I think I am past the fever here now, as although I have had it six times the last attacks have been getting lighter; and the only thing bothering me now is my right eye, which is a good deal inflamed, but I think is getting better. I think it was caused by the constant glare and dust round the house.

"*September 30th.*—Here I am still, trying to make a preliminary start, but not one of my pagazi will come in; at least I can't get more than a dozen together out of one hundred and thirty I have

September, 1873. engaged, and I can't manage much with them. I am still greatly bothered with my eye, as, if I use the other much, it brings on pain.

"*October* 14*th.*—Just able to try and write again, but I have been quite blind, and very bad with fever since my last words. I have been more pulled down by the latter than any I have had before, and was feeling very much as if I should like to be with you all for a day or two. . . . . I am in great hopes of getting out of here soon now. Dillon is more alive, and growling at not getting away. . . . . I am writing this bit by bit, as my eyes allow me, so don't expect much coherence or sense in the epistle."

In a letter to Mr. Clements Markham, I wrote,—

"*September* 15*th.*—We have all been down with fever since we have been here, but are now pulling round again. It is a great nuisance, as the fever makes me lose my lunars; I tried directly I was able to *think* to get some, but was so shakey and dazed it was utterly impossible.

" Since I wrote the foregoing I have been down with fever, but am now, thank God, clear of it. We are waiting for a few pagazi, and putting our donkeys' saddle-bags to rights prior to starting for Ujiji, which I find can be reached in twenty-two marches or about thirty days. I am afraid Dillon must go back, as he is getting quite blind, in fact the last day or two he has been quite unable to read or write; one eye was affected first, and now the other is going: he ought decidedly, in my opinion, to go back, and I have strongly advised him so to do. September, 1873.

"*September* 20*th.*—It is something dreadful this waiting here. Here is the 20th September, and I am bothered still by the lack of pagazi. If I had been well, we should have been away weeks ago; but out of forty-five days, I have had one fever of eight days, one of seven, one of five, one of four, and now just getting well of a violent attack of headache, which lasted for five days (and of course do not feel particularly bright), so I have only had sixteen days. Dillon is much better, and has decided to go on; he is not all right yet, though. . . . .

"*September* 26*th and* 27*th.*—Still detained by lack of pagazi, but I hope to be off in about ten days or so. I have just had another attack of fever, and this is the first day I have been able to do anything. Dillon seems to have fever every other day nearly, but not very violently; but what I am most afraid of is his sight. He has quite lost the use of his left eye, and has occasional symptoms in his right. It is atony of the optic nerve. If he gets quite blind further on, I do not see my way to sending him back; in fact it would be impossible for the greater portion of our route, and he himself says getting back to a temperate climate would be the only thing to do him good. . . . .

"*September* 29*th.*—Yesterday, by dint of great labour, I got sixteen pagazi together at about 2 P.M.,

October, 1873. and to-day I hear they are all collected at Taborah, and afraid to go on, and I am here with my tent cleared out, and not a soul to move a thing. I shall go mad soon, if this state of affairs continues. I am thinking of going on by myself as light as I can, if I can get enough of the pagazi I have engaged, and making a drive somehow. . . . .

"I have sent over to Taborah to try and get the pagazi to come over and go on, but it is dreadful. Oh for a chance to get out of this fever-stricken place, and to feel one is doing something! I should feel as happy as a king, ay, and far happier too, if I only heard I could go on, even if I had to walk barefoot the whole way. If I go on by myself I should take nine askari, and arm six of the best pagazi with spare rifles, which, with my servant, would give me sixteen well-armed men, besides myself; and if I can only get them to stick together, I should feel perfectly confident. *Coûte qui coûte*, *I* must go somehow or another, as I don't feel justified in stopping here any longer.

"*October* 18*th*.—Since I wrote the last, I have been quite blind of both eyes, and very bad indeed with fever, so I have been helpless.

"These horrible fevers and my blindness have quite prevented my doing anything since I last wrote, and my eyes now are anything but perfect in work or feeling; however, they are now getting better rapidly, but of course the moon has passed, and I have got no lunars."

The above is sufficient to show how constantly we were ill, and of this the men took advantage to absent themselves. They also worried us into allowing them extra provisions, and cloth, which they well knew would have been refused but for our illness. I managed to hold out against their importunities; but while I was delirious they asked Dillon and Murphy to allow their rations to be doubled, and by dint of persisting obtained compliance.

October, 1873.

In consequence of the great losses we sustained by the desertion of pagazi I was obliged to buy cloth at a price four times as high as at Zanzibar, or we should have been regularly stranded.

The Arabs were perfectly right in charging this price, since no caravans from the coast had arrived for some time and stores had become very scarce. In fact, I cannot speak too highly of the behaviour of the upper classes of Arabs towards us during our stay at Unyanyembé.

When we were ill they called or sent daily to enquire for us, and limes, tamarinds, and other fruits, as also dishes of well-cooked curry far beyond the attainments of our own *cordon bleu*, were constantly sent to us, besides such presents as a bullock, a goat, a dozen fowls, or a basket of eggs. In our intervals of convalescence we used to return their calls, and were always most warmly welcomed.

Hearing that a great auction was to be held at Taborah, for the sale of the effects of some Arabs

October, 1873. who had been killed while fighting with the Warori—a savage tribe whose territory lies in the route to the southern end of the Tanganyika— I went to see their manner of conducting it.

In two large rooms were assembled nearly a hundred and fifty traders—Arabs, Wasuahili, and Wamerima—and three men acted as auctioneers.

The first part of the sale consisted of household utensils, kettles, coffee-pots, bedding, and a small quantity of trading stores; and the auctioneers carried each article round the assemblage, gesticulating violently and insisting that it was the best thing of its sort that had ever been brought to Unyanyembé, and asking each and every one what amount they would bid for it. After two or three rounds the article was knocked down to the highest bidder, whose name and the price given were entered in the inventory which had been previously prepared.

The second part was devoted to the sale of slaves. They were led round, made to show their teeth, to cough, run, and lift weights, and in some instances to exhibit their dexterity in handling a musket.

All these slaves were semi-domestic, and fetched high prices; one woman who was reputed a good cook going for two hundred dollars, and many of the men reached eighty dollars, whilst in no instance was the price under forty.

A sad and eventful day now arrived.

It was on the 20th of October, as I lay on my

Ukhonongo October 1873

Sir

We have heared in the month of August that you have started from Zanzibar for Venyenyembe, and again and again lately we have heared your arrivel. Your father died by disease beyond the country of Bisa, but we have carried the corpse with us. 10 of our soldiers are lost and some have died. Our hunger presses us to ask you some clothes to buy provision for our soldiers. and we should have an answer that when we shall enter there shall be firing guns or not, and if you permit us to fire guns, then send some powder. We have wrote these few words in the place of Sultan or king Mbowra.

The writer Jacob Wainright
Dr Livingstone Exp'd

bed prostrate, listless, and enfeebled from repeated October, 1873.
attacks of fever; my mind dazed and confused
with whirling thoughts and fancies of home and
those dear ones far away, that my servant, Mohammed Malim, came running into my tent with a
letter in his hand.

I snatched it from him, asking at the same

A GOOD COOK. PRICE TWO HUNDRED DOLLARS.

moment where it came from. His only reply was,
"Some man bring him."

Tearing it open, I found Jacob Wainwright's
letter—a facsimile of which is here given.

Being half-blind it was with some difficulty that
I deciphered the writing, and then failing to attach
any definite meaning to it I went to Dillon. His
brain was in much the same state of confusion from

October, 1873.

fever as mine, and we read it again together, each having the same vague idea—"Could it be our own father who was dead?"

It was not until the bearer of the letter—Chuma, Livingstone's faithful follower—was brought to us that we fully comprehended what we had been reading. The writer had naturally supposed that the doctor's son was the leader of the Relief Expedition. We immediately sent supplies for the pressing needs of the caravan and despatched a messenger to the coast announcing Dr. Livingstone's death.

MANNER OF FETTERING SLAVES.

CHAPTER X.

ARRIVAL AND RECEPTION OF LIVINGSTONE'S BODY.—SOME PARTICULARS OF HIS DEATH.—THE FUTURE OF THE EXPEDITION.—ITS PARTIAL ABANDONMENT.—MURPHY RESIGNS.—DILLON COMPELLED TO TURN BACK.—THE PERSONNEL OF MY EXPEDITION.—PARTING FROM DILLON.—I GO FORWARD ALONE.—TROUBLES OF TRANSPORT.—I THROW AWAY PRESERVED PROVISIONS.—A NATIVE PLEA FOR SLAVERY.—THE DEATH OF DR. DILLON.—A SAD BLOW.—KASÉKERAH.—OFFENDED DIGNITY OF ASKARI.—SHIRKING THEIR WORK.—DETERMINED DESERTERS.—A PLEASANT MARCH.—VILLAGE CLUBS.—A VISIT TO MURPHY.—THE MANNER OF TRANSPORTING LIVINGSTONE'S BODY.—CAPTURE OF A THIEF.—I REDUCE MY KIT.—A DIRTY AND DRUNKEN CHIEF.—MUSCAT DONKEYS.—THE ROAD BLOCKED.

ON the arrival of the body a few days later Said ibn Salim, Shaykh ibn Nassib, Abdallah ibn Nassib and the principal Arabs without exception, showed their respect to Livingstone's memory by attending the reception of the corpse, which we arranged with such honours as we were able. The askari were drawn up in front of the house in two lines between which the men bearing the body passed; and as the body entered, the colours, which, contrary to our usual custom, had not been hoisted that morning, were shown half-mast high.

October, 1873.

Susi, on whom the command had devolved on the death of Livingstone, brought a couple of boxes belonging to him, and his guns and instru-

October, 1873. ments. He also stated that a box containing books had been left at Ujiji, and that shortly before his death the doctor had particularly desired that they should be fetched and conveyed to the coast.

Dr. Livingstone's death, as far as I could ascertain from the description given by his men, occurred rather to the westward of the place marked in the map published in "Livingstone's Last Journals." He had been suffering from acute dysentery for some time, but his active mind did not permit him to remain still and rest. Had he done so for a week or two after the first attack, it was the opinion of Dr. Dillon upon reading the last few pages of his journal that he would most probably have recovered.

It is not for me here to speak of Livingstone, his life and death. The appreciation of a whole nation —nay, more, of the whole civilised world, will testify to succeeding generations that he was one of the world's heroes.

And that title was never won by greater patience, self-denial, and true courage, than that shown by David Livingstone.

It was now necessary to consider what course we had better pursue, since he, to whom we were to have looked for guidance, was taken from us.

Murphy resigned his position and announced his intention of returning to the coast, on the ground that the work of the expedition was completed and that nothing further remained for us to do.

October, 1873.

Dillon and I decided upon proceeding to Ujiji and securing that box to which Livingstone had referred with almost his last breath, and, after having safely despatched it to the coast, to push on towards Nyangwé to endeavour to follow up the doctor's explorations.

We now redoubled our exertions to get away, and equipped Susi and his companions for the march to Bagamoyo. But unhappily Dillon and I were not destined to go forward together, for a few days prior to the date fixed for our departure he was attacked with inflammation of the bowels, and, much against his wish, felt constrained to return to the coast as that seemed the only course which gave hope of recovery.

I also was unfortunate and had a serious fall when riding a new donkey received in exchange for some of those we brought from Zanzibar. I pitched exactly on the small of my back upon a pointed block of granite, and was so shaken and hurt that I was unable to walk even the few hundred yards to the house, and was confined to my bed for some days.

When Dillon decided on returning to the coast, Murphy handsomely volunteered to continue with me. But I did not accept his offer on account of the great difficulty in obtaining pagazi, and I was

October, 1873.

also convinced that the only chance of the expedition moving forward lay in reducing it to the smallest possible limits.

Issa and Bombay quarrelled to such an extent as to render it impossible to retain both in the caravan, and the former having heard that his brother —an interpreter on board one of her Majesty's cruisers—had been killed at Kilwa, he was desirous of returning for the sake of his mother who had now no son at Zanzibar.

I much regretted losing Issa, for he was very useful and kept correct accounts of all stores expended, besides being most methodical, and possessing considerable influence amongst the men.

Bombay was certainly faithful and firm in attachment; in fact he reminded me of the old Scottish servant who, when his master said they must part, replied, "Na, na; I'm no' gangin'. If ye dinna ken whan ye've a gude servant, I ken whan I've a gude place." Sometimes he would work well, and prove really serviceable; but he was usually afraid of the men, and drink was his bane.

The *personnel* of my expedition now consisted of Bombay, head man; Bilâl Wadi Asmani, second in command—Asmani who had been with Stanley and Livingstone as guide, and now filled that post with me—accompanied by his inseparable friend, Mabruki; Mohammed Malim, my servant, a good interpreter and tailor; Hamees, gun-

KWIHARAH. From a sketch by Dr. Dillon. [PAGE 171, Vol. I.

bearer, engaged at Unyanyembé; boy Jacko, freed by Said ibn Salim to accompany me; Sambo, cook—his claims to that office rating on the fact of his having been cook's mate in an English merchant ship; Kombo, cook's mate, and a body of askari and pagazi amounting in all to about one hundred men, desertions and engagements causing the total to vary daily.

November, 1873.

On the 9th of November Livingstone's caravan, accompanied by Dillon and Murphy, started for the coast, whilst my cry was "Westward Ho!"

I was the first to start, although I was obliged to leave a quantity of stores behind under charge of Bombay, owing to the non-appearance of pagazi. Consequently I had to halt at Mkwemkwé, only a short distance from Kwiharah.

The evening before we parted was a solemn time both for Dillon and myself. We talked of our homes and of meeting in England; but whether we really cherished that hope of meeting again I scarcely know. We must both have had grave misgivings. I know that many such disquieted my mind at that moment, for I felt my health had failed and before me all was uncertainty. Yet though the wrench and pain of parting was great, neither would express in words any doubts or fears as to the future.

At this time I was nearly blind from ophthalmia and almost unable to walk from the pain in my back, while fever which was still hanging about

November, 1873.

me had reduced me to a skeleton, my weight being only seven stone four on leaving Kwiharah.

I must own that the likelihood of Dillon's reaching home appeared to me greater than of my ever again seeing England. Still I was determined to go on, trusting in the good mercy of God to enable me to accomplish the labour I had undertaken; and Dillon spoke cheerfully of the hoped-for benefit from change of climate, of regaining health and it might be sight. Little did I foresee that our separation for ever in this world was then so near.

From Mkwemkwé the men still deserted at every opportunity, going either to Taborah or Kwiharah; so I again asked the assistance of Said ibn Salim and the Ibn Nassibs, who promised to drive the men back to me whenever it was possible. I also ordered Bombay out to Mkwemkwé as personal supervision was needed to keep him up to the mark, replacing him at Kwiharah by Bilâl.

On returning from this visit to Said ibn Salim I was surprised to find Murphy in my tent. He had come to procure some medicine for poor Dillon, who, in addition to his previous illness, was now attacked by dysentery. Murphy said, however, that they intended to start without delay, arrangements having been made to carry Dillon on a litter.

I begged I might be sent for immediately should he become any worse, so that I might go to him.

But the next day some of Livingstone's men came to me with the gratifying news that Dillon was better, and they intended to march the following morning.

November, 1873.

Having by dint of perseverance managed to get my stores from Kwiharah, I broke up camp at Mkwemkwé and went to Itumvi, a large village lying on the direct road to Ujiji; but having only sufficient carriers for half my stores I experienced much the same trouble and delay here as at Mkwemkwé.

On paper and by rations there were about twenty men in excess of loads, yet whenever we started on the march many were absent; and when Bilâl was sent to look after absentees, and was fortunate enough to recover half-a-dozen, twenty more were found to be missing when he returned.

By this wearying and worrying behaviour of the men I was detained at Itumvi till the 20th of November, when I reduced the number of loads by restowage and throwing away the preserved provisions for my own use, and naturally left behind considerably less than had been the case at Mkwemkwé.

I endeavoured to obtain some assistance from the chief of Itumvi, and tried to enlist his sympathies by assuring him that England was the black man's friend and wished to see all men free, and was doing her utmost to stop the slave-trade on the coast.

November, 1873.

"What, then, are the poor Arabs to do for slaves, if you stop the trade?" said he; and though admitting that slavery was a very bad thing and saying he never sold a slave, yet he owned that he sometimes bought one.

As we were starting from Itumvi, a messenger from Murphy brought the dreadful news of poor Dillon's death on the 18th of November, caused by the terrible effects of African fever. By some unhappy chance firearms had been left within reach, and in the delirium of fever and the misery of the complication of diseases under which he was suffering he had shot himself in the head.

And agonizing though it is to dwell on this subject, I think it only right to point out that none but those who have experienced this fever can realise the extraordinary fancies that take possession of the mind. At times I have imagined, although not entirely losing my consciousness, that I had a second head and that I could not live in this state. The weight has been so great and the impression so marked that I have felt tempted to take any means to rid myself of it but without experiencing the slightest desire to put an end to my existence.

The day on which I received this news was the saddest of my life. I had lost one of the best and truest of my old messmates and friends; one whose companionship during the many weary hours of travel and suffering had helped to cheer and lessen the difficulties and vexations by which we were so frequently beset.

November, 1873.

And the shock so stunned me in my enfeebled condition that for some few days I appear to have existed almost in a dream, remembering scarcely anything of the march to Konongo and leaving my journal a blank. Perhaps it may not readily be understood how it arose, after having parted with

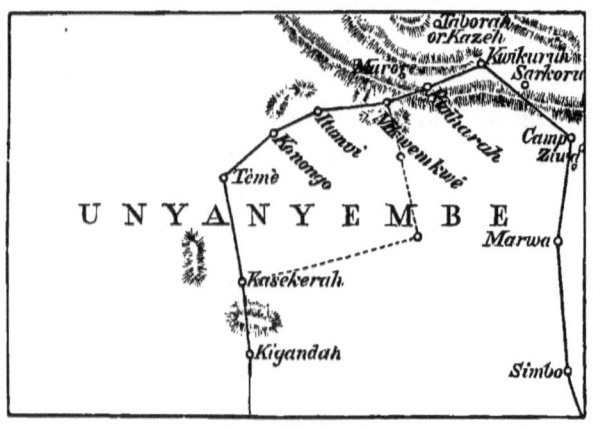

PLAN OF DR. DILLON'S ROUTE.

Dillon and Murphy for several days and while moving towards opposite coasts, that our parties should at this time still have been near each other. I have therefore given the accompanying sketch of the routes followed.

The absence of pagazi continued to cause delay and I had finally to abandon the idea of marching to Ujiji by the direct road, finding that

November, 1873.

not a soul would follow me if I persisted in the attempt. I accordingly decided to go round by Ugunda and try for a route between the recognised one and that taken by Stanley.

All the remaining preserved provisions excepting a tin of soup, one of fish, and two plum-puddings—which I kept for a possible Christmas—were now thrown away to further lighten the loads; for improvident as this almost seemed and reluctant as I was to leave behind that which might hereafter prove of such vital importance to us, it was evident that our only hope of reaching port in safety lay in lightening the ship as much as possible. There were also some large villages close by, so that starvation did not stare us in the face.

On the 27th of November I mustered a hundred pagazi for a hundred and ten loads and marched to Témé, a large village four miles distant, leaving Bombay to bring on the remaining loads with men hired for the day.

We passed two large villages, showing our colours and striking up with a drum which I had procured in the hope of inspiriting the men by a little noise. The whole population had, however, turned out and were busily employed in preparing the ground for the next crop, the rains having now commenced, so that this attempt at display fell a trifle flat.

Bombay kept me waiting at Témé the next day, in consequence of which a number of men bolted back to Kwiharah, and when Bombay did make his appearance we were in a worse plight than before. *November, 1873.*

I was astonished to find a Turk serving as a soldier under Abdallah ibn Nassib who was stationed here for the purpose of buying provisions for the Balooches at Kwiharah.

He was born at Constantinople, enlisted in the Turkish army, and was present at the opening of the Suez Canal. He deserted in Egypt, and, apparently without exactly knowing how he managed it, arrived at Zanzibar. Being in a destitute condition he then enlisted among the Balooches of Syud Burghash. He seemed very contented with his position, but still had a hankering after Constantinople and told me that he intended returning there some day.

More pagazi having offered themselves, I indulged in the faint hope that there was a possibility of a fair start in the morning; but more than twenty absconded during the night, and it was not without much delay that I succeeded in making a move again.

Three hours' march through a rolling country having villages and clearings interspersed in the jungle, brought us to Kasékerah, the scene of poor Dillon's death. From the natives I unsuccessfully endeavoured to ascertain where my old messmate was buried in order that I might visit his last resting-place and place some mark over the spot

December, 1873, where he lay. No one could tell me anything about it.

On meeting Murphy I found he had buried him in the jungle, having a fear (though a needless one) of the natives desecrating his grave. I learnt also that just before his death the poor fellow had destroyed those letters which I had given him for conveyance to the coast, so I immediately commenced writing another account of the history and prospects of the expedition.

Some of Murphy's men arrived with the information that he had halted two days' march in front, and, having had some cloth stolen from his tent, was sending to Said ibn Salim for a further supply to enable him to continue his journey to the coast.

Kasékerah was a large and neat village of flat-topped huts surrounded by an outer stockade, and within an inner one was an enormous circular hut, the residence of the chief, who was a daughter of Mkasiwah, chief of all Unyanyembé. There were deep verandahs in front of many huts, several of which were plastered with different coloured earths, forming patterns.

Again I had to wait for Bombay, and the day after his arrival it rained too heavily for us to proceed. But on the 2nd of December we started after the usual amount of bother, nine men having disappeared directly rations had been served out.

The askari too were inclined to give some trouble by setting forward as a grievance that carrying flags and a drum was not soldiers' work but the duty of pagazi. Bombay caused me much vexation by abetting the askari in their ridiculous pretensions; and not until after four hours' hard work could I start the caravan—minus the drum.

December, 1873.

Others made up their sleeping mats, clothes, and personal baggage to represent bales of cloth and put them amongst the loads; and from their being much lighter than cloth or beads, the pagazi singled them out and displayed much anxiety to carry them instead of their proper burdens.

A short walk through wooded country brought us to Kigandah, the last village in Unyanyembé; and between it and Ugunda—the next division of Unyamwési—lay a march of six hours through virgin forest.

To guard against further desertions I posted sentries at every entrance to the village; but this precaution proved unavailing and twenty-five men escaped, fragments of their scanty clothing on the top of the palisades being sufficient, at the dawn of day, to show the road they had taken.

To wait for the fugitives would have occasioned much delay and most probably the loss of many more. So putting the best face I could on the matter, I hired sufficient men to carry the deserters' loads to the first village in Ugunda, where it was stated pagazi were usually to be obtained. I also

December, 1873. despatched a messenger to the Arabs at Kwiharah and Taborah reporting the numbers that had deserted, most of whom were known being men belonging to the coast.

Marching through wooded country with beautiful open glades, the trees bursting into fresh leaf and the young grass clothing with a tender green the patches which had been burnt in the dry season, and everything looking fresh and spring-like, I felt better than at any time since leaving Kwiharah. And to my astonishment I found myself able to follow the shady path without suffering fatigue.

We rested at some pools of clear fresh water, and a baggage donkey appreciating the comfort of a bath, went into one and, lying down, commenced to roll. Pleasant as this might have been for the beast, it tended much to the detriment of a load composed of miscellaneous odds and ends, botanical paper, &c.

Resuming our march we reached, in a few hours, a large village in the centre of much cultivation. This was the residence of Mrima Ngombé, chief of Ugunda, and as such was called Kwikuruh, that name being invariably given to the village at which the chief of a district in Unyamwési dwells.

The men carrying my tent and cooking gear having lagged behind I took refuge from the sun's rays in the village public-house, where I became the centre of a wondering crowd.

There are two of these public-houses—or perhaps they may be more properly termed "clubs"—in nearly every village in Unyamwési, one for each sex. That appropriated to the women is not open to strangers; but at the one frequented by the men all travellers of distinction are welcomed by the chiefs and elders. As soon as a boy attains the age of seven or eight years he throws off the authority of his mother, and passes most of his time at the club, usually eating and often sleeping there.

They are generally larger and better built than the other huts, and a standing bed-place occupies a considerable portion of the interior.

The following day I visited Murphy, who was camped about a mile and a half to the eastward of me, and found him very comfortable and seeming much better than he had been since his arrival at Bagamoyo. He showed me much kindness on this occasion of meeting, giving me his waterproof coat and indiarubber sheet, which proved of great value to me afterwards.

Acting on Issa's advice, Livingstone's men had packed the corpse in bark and so lashed it up as to have the appearance of a bale of cloth, in order to smuggle it past the eyes of the prying Wagogo.

Had they suspected what the package really contained they would never have allowed the caravan with its burden to pass through their country.

A rumour now reached me that Asmani, whom

December, 1873. I had despatched in search of pagazi, was in the jungle unable to come in having been stripped naked by some Ruga-Ruga. I sent a piece of cloth to this unfortunate individual by some men, but instead of Asmani they brought back a deserter who confessed that it was he who was guilty of stealing the cloth which Murphy had lost.

He had been instigated to commit the theft by a half-caste Arab resident, who threw physic to the dogs to prevent their making a noise when the thief entered Murphy's tent.

For providing this magical medicine the Arab had received the greater part of the stolen goods, while the poor tool in trying to skulk back to Taborah, had been robbed of everything.

On enquiring into the case, and after patient investigation and hearing much cross-swearing, I considered that the weight of the evidence was against the Arab who had connived at the theft and received the goods. I therefore ordered him to make good Murphy's loss, under penalty of being sent in chains to Said ibn Salim for punishment.

After some little resistance and arguing he preferred paying to being delivered over to Said ibn Salim, who would probably either have shot him or forwarded him to the coast to be dealt with by the Sultan at Zanzibar.

He greatly feared being sent to Said ibn Salim; for the news had spread—although I was not aware of it till afterwards—that he and Abdallah ibn

Nassib had on several occasions very nearly resorted to force to prevent the more disreputable people at Taborah from enticing our men away from us. They would undoubtedly have adopted strong measures had they not been afraid of creating divisions whilst Mirambo was still unconquered.

December, 1873.

Mrima Ngombé, the chief of Ugunda, developed a strong friendship for me and constantly visited me, bringing pombé and insisting on my hobnobbing with him; but notwithstanding his efforts it was impossible to obtain any pagazi amongst his people as they would not leave home during the sowing season.

I therefore reduced my personal kit to a minimum, making all my clothes, boots, &c., into one load; yet even then there were not sufficient carriers, neither was there any chance of obtaining men on hire from day to day. So I left behind twelve loads of the cheapest beads and wrote to Said ibn Salim to forward them if an opportunity offered.

Having wished Murphy "Godspeed," I again made a start from Kwikuruh on December 8th, and after a long march reached Mapalatta.

When first the caravan arrived the people closed the doors of the village, for they had lately been harried by some slave-traders and had learnt to view all strangers with suspicion. But after a time they professed themselves satisfied with our peaceful intentions and allowed us to enter.

According to Asmani, who had rejoined us at

Mrima Ngombé's, no other villages would be met with for some days and consequently it was necessary to lay in a stock of provisions. Although according to previous experience this statement was probably incorrect, it was not advisable to risk a jungle march without food, and I ordered a day's halt to buy and clean the necessary corn.

The chief of the village was a disgustingly dirty old man suffering from delirium tremens—the only instance of this disorder which I saw in Africa, though drunkenness was by no means uncommon. The purchase of five days' food was, however, satisfactorily arranged with his wives, and we again proceeded on the 10th of December.

The country was perfectly charming, the trees delicately green and fresh, the open grassy glades enamelled with various wild flowers. Indeed it would have required no great stretch of imagination to fancy oneself in the wooded part of a well-kept English park, except that gazelles bounding away in the distance and the skulls of a lion and an elephant kept prominently in mind the fact that one was still in African jungle.

After marching eight miles a clearing was reached, and in the centre there stood a large new village named Hisinéné. Asmani, with his eternal grin, pointed it out with apparent delight, seeming to think that it would be a pleasant surprise. On the contrary I was disgusted, as it now appeared that the halt of the day before had been altogether unnecessary and each village was certain to tempt some of my men to remain behind. When leaving the place the next morning I was gratified to find that only one man had run during the night.

After every one had started I brought up the rear on Jasmin, the white Muscat donkey I obtained at Unyanyembé, which by this time had learnt to attach itself to me almost with the fidelity of a dog.

These Muscat donkeys are much valued, being highly bred and possessing good staying powers, but they require better care and feeding than the ordinary native animal. They stand about twelve to thirteen hands high, and their paces are equal to those of a horse and they are very pleasant to ride owing to their easy amble.

Suddenly the caravan came to a halt and a most unwelcome sight presented itself, the men having grounded their loads while Asmani and others were engaged in a violent altercation with some natives.

These proved to be an embassy from Taka, chief of Eastern Ugara, proceeding to Unyanyembé to hold a palaver respecting a misunderstanding which had arisen owing to the headman of a village having been shot by an Arab in a squabble.

Taka was now sending to Said ibn Salim and Abdallah ibn Nassib to arrange this matter, and meanwhile the road through Ugara was blocked.

Every effort to persuade this embassy to turn back and accompany me to Taka's village was

December, 1873. unavailing, and we were compelled to return to Hisinéné.

All the bright hopes of the morning were thus dashed to the ground, and a lengthened delay appeared inevitable.

DRUMS.

CHAPTER XI.

DRIVEN BACK TO HISINÉNÉ.—A MISERABLE CHRISTMAS.—SUPERSTITIONS REGARDING SNAKES.—CUSTOMS OF THE PEOPLE.—DANCING.—COOKING ARRANGEMENTS.—STORING CORN.—THEIR HUTS.—FOOD.—CURING.—PROVISIONS.—CLOTH-MAKING.—GRINDING CORN.—TRIBAL MARKS.—HAIR-DRESSING.—WARNED AGAINST MIRAMBO.—A SPY SHOT.—ON THE ROAD AGAIN.—A HOSPITABLE OLD LADY.—MISSING THE WAY.—SACK-MAKING.—AN ELOPEMENT.—DISORDERED STATE OF THE COUNTRY.—THE SOUTH NGOMBÉ.—A DAY'S SHOOTING.—A HUNTER'S STORY.

HISINÉNÉ being again reached I consulted Bombay and Asmani as to the best course to pursue in this unexpected difficulty. *December, 1873.*

To attempt to avoid Ugara would have lengthened the journey by three weeks or a month, while the country through which we should have been obliged to pass was reported to afford no supplies of provisions.

The ambassadors had assured me that the moment an arrangement had been arrived at the road would be opened, and they would conduct me to Taka's village, knowing that he would welcome me warmly. I therefore decided to send Asmani with them to Unyanyembé, to urge upon the Arabs the desirability of settling the matter as quickly as possible.

The chief of Hisinéné was allied with the Arabs

December, 1873. in the campaign against Mirambo, and a few days after our arrival the fighting men were mustered and despatched to the scene of action.

Hearing nothing from or of Asmani for ten days, I grew anxious and sent Mohammed Malim with half-a-dozen men and my two riding donkeys, to travel as fast as possible and ascertain what the news really was.

Now followed much dreary waiting and anxiety, which together with the unhealthiness of the place knocked me up, and I was attacked by fever and a sharp touch of dysentery. My back too was so exceedingly painful that I had no rest night or day for more.than a week.

Some good sport was to be had here, and when I rallied a little I frequently took my gun into a rice swamp about fifty yards outside the village and bagged some snipe. The men also constantly went shooting, bringing in on one occasion a zebra and on another a couple of gazelle. The zebra is the best meat in Africa and is eaten by all the Arabs and their people, though not one of them would touch horse or donkey to save their lives.

Christmas Day passed very miserably. A heavy rainstorm commenced the day and flooded the whole village; the ditch and bank round my tent were washed away, and I had over six inches of water inside it. Everything was wet, damp, and muggy.

A MISERABLE CHRISTMAS.

Then my dinner, for which I had kept a tin of soup and one of fish, besides one of the plum-puddings, was a failure. A village dog stole the fish, Sambo upset the soup, and the pudding was not boiled, and I had to content myself with a scraggy fowl and a bit of matama damper.

December, 1873.

A very curious superstition on the part of the

ZEBRA.

natives was noticeable here. One of my men came to me shouting that there was a large snake in a hut. I of course took my gun intending to shoot it; but when I arrived the natives would not allow the reptile—a boa about ten feet long—to be injured, but contented themselves with quietly turning it out of the village with long sticks. I asked the reason of this gentle treatment, and was told that it was a "pepo"—a spirit or ghost—and if injured some disaster would befall the village or its inhabitants.

[margin: December, 1873.]

During my long stay I had also many opportunities of observing the customs of the people.

Every morning as soon as it was light they came out of their huts and sat round fires smoking their matutinal 'baccy. This finished, all, excepting old women and young children, the chief and two or three elders, sallied forth to work in the plantations. Those whose fields were close to the village returned at noon to eat ugali or porridge, while others who worked further away cooked and ate their mid-day meal at the scene of their labours. Shortly before sunset they returned, and in the evening there was dancing, smoking, and singing, and drinking too when corn for making pombé is plentiful.

Drums are brought out and beaten vigorously by the hands, while men go circling round and round for hours at a time yelling and shouting.

The women never mingle with the men on these occasions, but sometimes engage in a dance by themselves, when the gestures and actions are often even more immoral and indecent than those of the men, though they are bad enough in all conscience.

Neither men nor women have any objection to be gazed on by the opposite sex whilst going through these antics, but as in most other tribes they never mix or dance together.

The huts in which they live are usually built of stout posts planted in the ground and the interstices filled with clay. The roof is flat with a slight slope to the front, and the rafters are covered either with sheets of bark or with bushes and grass, over which is spread a thick coating of earth.

Sweet potatoes cut in slices, pumpkins and gourds, are often laid on the roofs to dry for the winter provisions.

In the interior of these huts there are generally two and sometimes three divisions.

The first contains small bed-places covered with hides, and here also is the universal African fireplace consisting of the three cones of clay, which, in a few instances are hollow and form an oven. The only cooking utensils are earthen pots, nearly everything being prepared for eating by boiling.

In the next division kids and lambs are kept, and the innermost one is used as a granary, where corn is stored in "lindo" or bark band-boxes with the lids carefully luted on with clay.

These lindo are often of enormous size, some being sufficiently large to contain a dozen sacks. Smaller lindo are frequently used as trunks for travelling.

Light is admitted only through the door, which also provides the sole means for the escape of smoke, and as a consequence the rafters and walls

December, are black and shiny, and the cobwebs with which
1873. they are festooned are loaded with soot.

Amongst the rafters walking-sticks, bows, spears, knobsticks, and arrows, are stored, to become seasoned by the smoke.

As may be expected these dwellings are infested with vermin, the worst being enormous ticks, the bite of which is so annoying that the Arabs believe them to be venomous and often to cause fevers.

The main staple of food here—as indeed throughout Africa—is ugali, a sort of porridge. It is made by boiling water and then mixing in flour and stirring until the mixture becomes a stiff and heavy mass. It is then turned out and the superfluous moisture is allowed to drain away.

Meat is so rarely obtained that it is most voraciously devoured. When game is plentiful, however, they sometimes exercise a little forethought and smoke the flesh for keeping. This process consists of cutting it into strips and placing on branches over a fire of green wood.

The clothing of the Wanyamwési is usually of cloth obtained in trade, but the poorer people have to content themselves with native cloth made from the inner bark of a species of fig-tree.

The outer covering of this tree is stripped off in the rainy season and the trunk swathed with banana leaves until the inner bark becomes sufficiently soft and tender for manufacture. It is then removed and steeped in water, after which it is laid on a plank and tapped gently with mallets, usually made of rhinoceros horn grooved on the face. At each tap the piece of bark grows larger and larger, and when finished has something the appearance of a felted corduroy.

December, 1873.

Kaffir corn on being first gathered is threshed on floors of trodden clay with long curved sticks —sometimes having a small piece of board like the blade of an oar at the striking end—and when separated from the rougher part of the chaff is stowed away in the lindo.

On being required for use it is beaten in a mortar to remove any chaff that may still remain and then ground into flour between two stones. The larger of these is fixed in the earth, and a woman kneeling down works the small one upon it. Altogether it is a rough operation resulting in a large proportion of the flour being composed of sand and grit.

Whilst employed in this labour women often have babies lashed on their backs, and their pendulous and flaccid breasts may frequently be seen swinging to and fro, with each motion of the body, amongst the slowly accumulating heap of flour.

The distinguishing tribal marks of the Wanyamwési are a tattooed line down the centre of the forehead and on each temple, the two upper front teeth chipped so as to show a chevron-shaped gap, and a small triangular piece of hippotamus ivory or

December, 1873. of shell, ground down white and polished, hung round the neck.

Their ornaments consist principally of beads and brass and iron wire.

Chiefs and headmen wear enormous cylindrical bracelets of ivory extending from wrist to elbow, which are also used as signals in warfare. The noise occasioned by striking them together is heard at a long distance and is used by chiefs as a call for their men to rally round them.

The men usually shave the crown of the head and wear their hair twisted into innumerable small strings, lengthened artificially by plaiting long fibres of bark cloth with the hair. This is often carried to such an extent as to make it hang down to the small of the back, and when on the road this mixture of bark and hair is usually tied into a sort of club-tail.

Others, who only want to appear smart on occasions, have wigs of string and keep their wool shaved or clipped close.

The women follow no particular fashion in dressing their hair. Sometimes they allow it to remain in its native frizziness, often using it to stick a knife, pipe, or other small article into. Others have their hair dressed in innumerable small plaits, lying close to the head and having something the appearance of the ridges of a field; and occasionally they make it into large cushion-like masses, padded out with bark-fibres.

The two latter methods of hair-dressing occupy two or three days, but when the work of art is finished it remains undisturbed for six months or even longer.

Mrima Ngombé, being engaged in making a royal progress through his dominions, called on me here. He was dressed in a scarlet burnous trimmed with gold embroidery which looked rather odd over his greasy waist cloth, his only other garment. He was much displeased with the headman of Hisinéné, and reprimanded him for not having paid me sufficient attention or supplied me with pombé.

On the 28th of December Asmani arrived with the welcome news that a settlement of the misunderstanding had been accomplished, and that we could now pass through Ugara without let or hindrance. But since the embassy had remained behind on the spree, we were advised to make a détour to avoid their village, otherwise we might be suspected of having murdered them.

With Asmani came some of Said ibn Salim's men, bringing a few of my deserters and a hint to beware of Mirambo, as one of the Watosi—a tribe of herdsmen, of whom many are settled at Unyanyembé—had been detected conveying to him information of the route we proposed to follow.

They expressed the hope that I should be pleased on hearing that the unfortunate Mtosi had been shot for carrying the news to Mirambo. This act

December, 1873. was doubtless intended as a piece of civility but it was one with which I could well have dispensed.

Nothing further had been done towards perfecting a plan for the campaign against Mirambo, owing to a difference of opinion as to the selection of a leader.

The officer who had brought the reinforcements from the coast wished to take chief command, civil and military; but this Said ibn Salim and Abdallah ibn Nassib refused to allow as they were both senior to him in the Sultan's service. The new troops stood by their own commanding officer, whilst the Balooches and others who had been serving under Said ibn Salim and Abdallah ibn Nassib refused to recognise the new comer.

And whilst divided councils prevailed at the Arab head-quarters, their native allies were daily leaving them and Mirambo was increasing in power and strength.

Asmani had neither seen nor heard of my servant Mohammed Malim, but believing I could trust him to follow me I made ready for starting at once.

The men refused to march, and Bombay, instead of assisting me, supported them by asserting that it was necessary to wait to enable them to clean their corn. This was nothing less than a gratuitous falsehood and idle excuse. On the 30th of December, after a deal of trouble, I marched through a pelting rain to another

Kwikuruh, a large and populous place ruled over by the mother of Mrima Ngombé.

December, 1873.

The old lady was remarkably civil, sending me eggs and pombé and declining to receive anything in return, saying she had been requested by her son to look after me as I was his friend, and that everything she possessed was at my disposal.

Upon starting the next morning Asmani tried a short cut he had heard of, and managed to miss it, and led us north-east, south-west, east, west, south, and north, in rapid succession.

A sore heel prevented my getting to the head of the caravan to put matters right; for my riding donkeys were away with Mohammed Malim and the old steed, Jenny Lind, which I had ridden from the coast, was left behind at Hisiméné on account of illness. To add to our miseries it was raining the greater part of the time, the mud in many places being knee-deep.

Right glad was I when we sighted the clearing surrounding a village, and soon I was seated under a verandah of the chief's house.

All my clothing except that required for decency I at once hung up to dry; for a box containing a change of clothes was as usual behind. But a fire and a cup of hot coffee provided by Sambo soon pulled me together somewhat.

In the evening I tried for lunars and latitudes, but bad sight prevented my obtaining any.

Here I decided to wait for Mohammed to over-

December, 1873.

take us, which he did the following evening, bringing in Jasmin with a sore back caused by his villanous riding.

From some men who accompanied him from Said ibn Salim I learnt that Murphy was well away on his return journey, having been heard of past Jiwé la Singa.

During the day I had an opportunity of watching a man engaged in the peculiar process of making a sack for carrying corn.

Taking a pole about fourteen feet long, the outer thick bark which had been previously loosened by soaking in water for some days was removed by tapping with a small mallet. He next put a strong seizing round the pole at about three feet from one end, and began at the other to turn the inner tough bark inside out, using for this purpose an instrument made of a bent branch cut to an edge at one end and forming a kind of adze.

The man then cut the pole short off above the lashing, and turning the bark back again increased its size by beating it out with a hammer very like that used in making native cloth, which also rendered it soft and more pliant.

He afterwards put corn into this bark sack, ramming it well in, and when it was perfectly full tied up the open end and wound wide strips of bark around the package.

It now resembled a hard bolster about six or

seven feet long—the lateral expansion having shortened the bag—with a short pole projecting at one end. <small>January, 1874.</small>

This serves to keep the contents from becoming wet when the baggage is stacked against a tree. Larger packages of this kind are used as granaries, being carefully thatched and then planted by the projecting pole in an open place in the village.

On the 2nd of January, 1874, we broke up from Shikuruh (which, by the way, is the village called Kwikuruh by Stanley), after being detained by some men going out for the carcase of a buffalo they had shot.

I here ascertained that a donkey which was supposed to have strayed at Unyanyembé had actually been sold by Umbari and one of Livingstone's men named Manua Sera whom I had sent for it. Upon this discovery I turned Umbari out of the caravan, as, in addition to being a rogue, he was a grumbling, troublesome fellow, who was constantly stirring up a spirit of dissatisfaction amongst the men.

Asmani seemed doubtful about the road for the next day's journey so I steered a course by compass, and, after five hours through trackless jungle full of game, camped by some pools in an open space.

I went out with my gun and saw numerous tracks of giraffe, and stalked one large antelope for a considerable distance; but before getting

January, 1874. within range, Leo, who had been left in camp, found me, and testified his delight so noisily that the antelope was frightened and my chance of a shot was spoiled.

On returning I found a party of Said ibn Salim's men had arrived in search of three women slaves, reported to have accompanied the men sent by me to Unyanyembé with Mohammed Malim, and on their being discovered I ordered them to be immediately handed over.

During the night two more pagazi ran away, but a hunter whom we found in the woods fortunately volunteered his services.

Guided by compass we continued our march through jungle—where Leo startled a herd of antelope and the caravan found a sounder of pig, of which I bagged one little squeaker—and following this course for some hours came amongst a number of barked trees which denoted our approach to a village.

Shortly afterwards we struck a path leading through freshly cleared plantations, where the stumps of trees which had been felled were left about four feet high, having a most curious appearance. This brought us to the last village in Ugunda, and although it was still early I decided to halt, as three long marches lay between us and the first village we should arrive at in Ugala.

Food was plentiful, and enough corn for four

days being purchased I directed that it should be cleaned at once instead of allowing the men to take a whole day about the business. *January, 1874.*

The village was large and strongly built and additions had evidently been made at various times. The oldest portion, in which the headman lived, was almost entirely under the shade of one enormous banyan-tree.

In addition to the usual stockade this one was surrounded with a ditch and embankment loopholed for musketry on the inside, and the entrances consisted of narrow passages with two or three doors in each.

The different state of the country to that which prevailed when Burton was here was particularly noticeable. In his time a musket was an heirloom for a chief and the happy possessors were few and far between; but when I passed nearly every village could turn out at least half of its men armed with muskets.

In consequence of the disturbances between Mirambo and the Arabs, trade had suffered much and the whole country was very unsettled. The lawless inhabitants of villages took advantage of the disorder which existed, and formed parties, from forty to fifty strong, to loot and destroy their weaker neighbours. These they attacked indiscriminately, calling themselves friends of Mirambo or of the Arabs according to which party they were at the time intent on plundering.

January, 1874.

As water was reported to be scarce and there was some danger of not finding any if steering by compass, we took the road pointed out by Asmani. Soon we were clear of jungle and entered an apparently illimitable plain covered with long grass and having numerous small mounds crowned with wood, as also solitary trees scattered over its surface. We halted near a pool of muddy water, and camped on one of the little wooded knolls.

Game was wonderfully plentiful. We saw quail and secretary-birds, startled a large herd of antelope, and crossed a buffalo track—about twenty yards wide and trampled into the semblance of a ploughed field—running in a dead straight line from north to south.

Soon after starting from here for the South Ngombé nullah we passed some shallow swampy pools surrounded by trees and thick jungle.

I was in front and happened unfortunately to be without my gun, when a huge white rhinoceros waddled past me, grunting. He failed to notice me as I quietly slipped behind a tree, but the shouts of the porters who now sighted him warned him off and he turned into the jungle. I followed directly my rifle arrived and tracked him for some way, but was brought to a standstill by a bed of swamp.

The remainder of our road to the South Ngombé was swamp, followed by a piece of the most beautiful plain that it is possible to imagine.

Clumps of magnificent trees were grouped with an effect which could not have been surpassed had they been arranged by the art of the landscape gardener; while wooded knolls and stretches of green grass, and a background of heavy timber along the banks of the nullah completed the scene.

January, 1874.

The South Ngombé—not to be confounded with the Northern Ngombé which drains the country to the north of Taborah—is one of the southern affluents of the Malagarazi river, and is joined by the Walé nullah which rises a few miles west of Itumvi. Near the point at which we crossed it lay in long reaches of four or five miles in length divided from each other only by sand bars about fifty yards wide.

Its waters afford a home to numerous hippopotami and crocodiles, and are covered with a profusion of immense waterlilies. In times of flood it spreads about three miles on either side and pours a vast quantity of water into the Malagarazi.

Our camp was pitched on its western bank, in a clear space of grassy turf surrounded by gigantic trees festooned to their topmost branches by enormous creepers.

The men being tired after our two long marches I decided on a day's halt and gave them leave to go out shooting. The surrounding country was full of game, but I found it very wild and so frightened by the number of my own people as

January, 1874.

well as hunting parties of Wagara who were about, that I only shot a boar, which, being an unclean animal, none of my men would bring in.

During my ramble I noticed the remains of a lion, buffalo, and crocodile, lying together in a heap, and was told a curious story to account for this strange sight. It was said that when the buffalo came to drink a lion sprang upon him, and, both rolling into the water together, they were seized by a crocodile. He in his turn was dragged about twenty yards from the bank by the struggles of the two beasts, and there the trio perished in an inextricable entanglement.

I also saw an enormous crane of a bluish-grey colour, looking a king amongst birds, being by far the largest I had ever seen with the exception of the ostrich.

ANTS' NEST.

CHAPTER XII.

UGARA.—A LUDICROUS SIGHT.—MIRAMBO'S HEAD-QUARTERS.—DESTRUCTION AND DESOLATION.—THE HAVOC OF THE SLAVE-TRADE.—A FIELD FOR ENGLAND'S LABOURS.—LEO SURPRISES THE NATIVES.—LEG ORNAMENTS.—LIOWA.—MY PETS.—A LAWLESS SET OF RUFFIANS.—HEAVY RAINS.—BEE-NESTING.—A STAMPEDE.—LOST IN JUNGLE.—A PANIC.—ROCKY RESIDENCES.—AN ATTEMPT AT EXTORTION.—I GIVE A LECTURE ON HOSPITALITY.—ITS GOOD EFFECT.—NOTHING TO EAT.—JASMIN DIES.—TAMENESS OF MY GOAT.—UNFRIENDLY VILLAGES.—A BUFFALO CHARGE.

UGARA, in which we were now, is not recognised as being part of Unyamwési proper, although owing to the people having the same manners and tribal marks, and their language being nearly identical, they are not to be easily distinguished from their neighbours. *January, 1874.*

On the 8th of January we moved from the banks of the South Ngombé towards Téwéré; but were shortly met by about twenty people sent by Taka—chief of the easternmost of the three portions into which Ugara is divided—to enquire our reasons for having entered his territory without sending to apprise him of our approach. Matters being soon explained, they returned with us and showed us where to halt, but we were not allowed to camp in Téwéré.

This village was a perfect mass of vegetation,

January, 1874.

the trees within it growing so thickly and closely together that nothing could be seen of the huts; and even the palisades, constructed of poles of the bark-cloth tree, had taken root and sprouted and had thus become like the fortifications of Robinson Crusoe.

Taka's own village was some seven miles to the northward of us, and would have lain on our route had we been allowed to follow the road taken by us on making our first journey from Hisinéné.

We had scarcely camped when emissaries arrived from Taka and demanded twenty doti and two guns as mhongo. The guns I could not spare and would not give, so compromised the matter by paying twenty-two doti. A present was then asked for Taka's mother; but I refused to give anything, expressing my opinion that he was fully able to take care of his own mother.

The messengers informed me that if I visited Taka he would give me some provisions; but as this would have entailed a delay of two or three days I declined the invitation.

Guides were placed at our disposal and we marched across a perfectly level country until just at the close of the day's journey, when we breasted a small hill close to a village named Kwatosi and camped on its summit.

I was greatly amused by one of the guides who displayed much pride at possessing an umbrella.

He kept it open the whole day, continually spinning it round and round in a most ludicrous fashion; and when we came to some jungle he added to the absurdity of his appearance by taking off his only article of clothing—his loin cloth—and placing it on his head after having carefully folded it. The sight of a perfectly naked negro walking under an umbrella was too much for my gravity, and I fairly exploded with laughter.

Nothing but boundless plain covered with jungle was to be seen from the camp, the only break on the horizon being two small hills far away to the N.N.W.

These were said to be Mirambo's head-quarters which the Arabs had never attacked, the strength of the position being so great that it was felt that to make the attempt would be to court defeat.

We passed the sites of many deserted villages which had been destroyed quite lately in the war; and after camping one night in the jungle arrived at the capital of Utendé, the central district of Ugara.

The chief was moderate in his demands for mhongo, and would have been satisfied with six doti had not a son of Taka who unfortunately arrived at that moment said to him, "Don't be a fool! my father got twenty-two, you ask the same." This caused much haggling and arguing as I was greatly averse to complying with his increased claim. Still he managed to get the twenty-two doti

January, 1874. in the end by prohibiting his people from selling food to us until he was paid.

In the village there were many of Mirambo's men who graciously informed us that they would certainly have attacked us had we been Arabs; but being English we were allowed to pass, because they knew we had not come for slaves. I have a strong suspicion that this was "bunkum," for Mirambo is as much a slave-dealer as any Arab in the country. But I suppose these men had heard something of the English from my people, and not being strong enough to rob us considered it advisable to appear friendly.

The chief proved a curious sort of fellow, frequently withdrawing permission for us to buy food and then restoring it. By taking advantage of the permission when granted we procured enough in two days and went on our way.

The rains were now exceedingly heavy and at times came down with a roar that made sleep almost impossible. The following note in my journal was evidently entered on one of these occasions: "Thunder and lightning; lying awake listening to the rain. If the blessed old Tanganyika gets all this it *must* burst out somewhere."

Our next halt was at the village of Liowa, chief of Western Ugara. The country before this had been dead level but now began to get rather broken and the road was across undulating country. The valleys were swamps with deep and stiff black mud that, in everything but extent, put the stories of the dreaded Makata altogether into the shade.

Passing through the ruins of so many deserted villages, once the homes of happy and contented people, was indescribably saddening. Where now were those who built them and cultivated the surrounding fields? Where? Driven off as slaves, massacred by villains engaged in a war in which these poor wretches had no interest, or dead of starvation and disease in the jungle.

Africa is bleeding out her life-blood at every pore. A rich country, requiring labour only to render it one of the greatest producers in the world, is having its population—already far too scanty for its needs—daily depleted by the slave-trade and internecine war.

Should the present state of affairs be allowed to continue, the country will gradually relapse into jungles and wilds and will become more and more impenetrable to the merchant and traveller.

That this should be a possibility is a blot on the boasted civilisation of the nineteenth century. And should England, with her mills working half-time and with distress in the manufacturing districts, neglect the opportunity of opening a market which would give employment to thousands of the working classes, it will ever remain an inexplicable enigma.

Let us hope that the Anglo-Saxon race will allow

January, 1874.

no other nation to outstrip it in the efforts to rescue thousands, nay, millions of fellow-creatures from the misery and degradation which must otherwise infallibly fall to their lot.

At Liowa's village the whole population turned out to stare at us, and their astonishment at beholding a European was far less than that displayed at the sight of old Leo. This was in no way diminished by the wonderful stories related of him by my men, who declared that single-handed he was a match for any two lions in Africa.

These people were a fine, manly, warlike race, well armed with guns and spears, the blades of the latter being sometimes two feet in length and more than four inches wide in their broadest part.

Two ornaments which I had hitherto rarely seen now became common. One, the sambo, consisting of a quantity of small circles of elephant's hair or hide neatly bound round with very fine wire, was worn on the legs. Natives of high degree frequently wore such a mass of these as to give them the appearance of being afflicted with elephantiasis; and though I had no means of ascertaining the exact number on each leg, I may safely affirm that in some instances three hundred would be under rather than over the mark.

The other ornament to which I allude was composed of fringes of long goat's hair, also worn round the leg, commencing just above the swell of the calf and reaching well-nigh to the ground.

To both these ornaments there were often appended small bells and pieces of tin and other metal, and the happy possessor of such extra decorations was never inclined to let them pass unnoticed but would stamp and strut about like a lunatic in order to make them jingle and herald his approach.

January, 1874.

Whilst we were at Liowa's, a party belonging to Mrima Ngombé arrived *en route* to Simba, a chief of the Warori, who, having lately been successful in looting a quantity of ivory from his neighbours, had sent out circulars stating that he had on hand a very large stock of a superior article which must be sold at a ruinous sacrifice to effect a clearance before removing from the premises.

Liowa's father, who bore the same name, was chief of all Ugara, and having had a tiff with some Arabs set out with the intention of destroying Bagamoyo; but his vaulting ambition o'erleaped itself and he and most of his followers perished on the road.

The feudatory chiefs of the two other divisions of Ugara taking advantage of the youth of the present Liowa on his succeeding his father, declared themselves independent and thus robbed him of more than two-thirds of his patrimony.

Liowa presented me with a small goat which became so greatly attached to me that I had not the heart to kill her but decided on keeping her as a pet, and she soon knew me and learned to answer to her name, Dinah. She and Leo were

January, 1874. inseparable, and both used to follow close upon my heels on the march.

News now reached me that the direct road to the Malagarazi ferry was blocked by large bodies of escaped Arabs' slaves, who were well armed and had turned their hand against everybody. They had been armed by their masters to fight against Mirambo, but had deserted and joined a number of runaways who infested the vicinity of Unyanyembé. And now they were doing their utmost to harm their former masters.

Many of the atrocities ascribed to Mirambo should properly be placed to the account of these ruffians, who, bound by no laws human or divine, placed no limits upon the brutalities in which they indulged.

Liowa's was left on the 17th of January, and soon after starting we met Mrima Ngombé's men who had gone on the day before, and had turned back to place themselves under our protection being afraid to proceed alone.

Three miles downhill and half a mile through swamp was all we managed before being fairly stopped by the rain which came down like a waterfall, and the difficulty in getting the men and donkeys to face it and cross the swamp to a dry place for camping was very great. The rain approached us like a moving wall of water, and some time before the storm reached us the sound resembled the roar of a cataract.

Fortunately the tents were quickly pitched and the stores were kept fairly dry. I fully appreciated Murphy's waterproof coat; but the men were drenched, and most of them adopted the costume of Adam in the early days of the Garden of Eden.

January, 1874.

When the rain ceased some of the men took a bees' nest which had been discovered in a tree overhanging the camp. I watched their proceedings with interest, for it seemed marvellous that the naked fellows up in the tree should be able to hack away at the hole where the nest was with infuriated bees swarming around them. Yet they only stopped occasionally to brush them away from their faces, or to pull out a sting. The fellows' skins must have been somewhat like that of the honey-guide, impervious to the sting of the bee; but after all their labour no honey was forthcoming, dead and rotten combs only being found.

On resuming our march we passed through an open forest of fine trees with little or no undergrowth, where I succeeded in rolling over a large antelope. We then came to a precipitous ravine with numerous streams gushing down its rocky sides, sometimes hidden by bushes and at others forming miniature waterfalls.

We rounded the southern end of this dip and reached the river Mtambo flowing at the bottom of a rocky valley. It was two or three feet deep

January, 1874.

with many cascades, the bed being so full of rocks that we found an easy path of stepping-stones across it, the only difficulty being the work of getting the donkeys over.

The next day's attempt at a journey was a failure. After a couple of hours on the move some buffalo were seen, and down went every load immediately, some men running away and others going in pursuit of the beasts. The runaways soon recovered their lost nerve, and returned; but as the hunters did not put in an appearance there was no option but to camp. I was crippled by a painful wound in my leg, caused, I think, by the bite of a centipede, and was quite unable to do any shooting.

The sporting men found their way back during the evening, excepting a few who remained in charge of a rhinoceros and an eland which Asmani had shot; and the next day they refused to move before the meat was brought in and divided, for which purpose a halt became necessary.

To add to the annoyance of this delay the road was lost on setting out, and my leg had meanwhile become so troublesome that I was unable to take the lead of the caravan and steer by compass.

For three days we wandered round and round, going along a track perhaps for half an hour only to find it end abruptly, while the scouts sent forward to discover the right road declared that impassable swamps and "muds" lay in the direction I wanted to travel.

During all this time we were toiling through jungle, and passed several streams; two of which were so deep that it was necessary to use the indiarubber boat and to haul some of the donkeys over, until one, bolder than his fellows, jumped in and swam across and was followed by the rest.

January, 1874.

Soon after we camped on the evening of the third day I was startled by the report of firearms in all directions.

Hobbling out of my tent I met a man with his hair standing as straight on end as its woolly nature would allow and with fright depicted on every feature, crying out, "Master! master! Ruga-Ruga! Shika Bunduki!" (Master, master! Robbers! Get your gun!)

Only about twenty of my men could I find, their first impulse having been, as usual, to look to their own safety by taking to their heels; and where the enemy was, none could tell me.

At last I ascertained that one of my followers, on meeting an old native in the jungle, had fired his gun as a signal that we were near a village. The other men being thoroughly intimidated by the stories of Mirambo, Ruga-Ruga, and escaped slaves, had immediately imagined that we were attacked. Hence the fright and general stampede.

Upon the native being brought to me I learnt from him that the village of Mân Komo, chief of part of Kawendi, could easily be reached the following day. He further volunteered to conduct some of my men there at once, in order that they might return the next morning and show us the road.

January, 1874.

This old man had been engaged in cutting bark to make clothing for himself and his wife; and judging from appearances he had not undertaken the task before it was needed. I rewarded him with a shukkah for his civility and he departed perfectly delighted.

The men whom I sent to the village did not return till after mid-day. Others then absent on a hunting expedition afterwards brought in a zebra, and the consequent feasting extinguished all hope of marching until the following day, when we passed through a marsh and crossed the river flowing by the village of Mân Komo.

Mân Komo is protected in front by this river, which was twenty-five feet wide and eight deep, and at the rear by a precipitous rocky hill, on the side of which the principal portion of the place is built.

Many of the people have appropriated holes and caves in the rocks as residences; and so difficult of access and easily defended is the village, that even Mirambo has been beaten off by the inhabitants on his attempting to plunder them.

Representatives from Mân Komo, whose errand was to demand a mhongo of fifty doti, soon waited upon me, he having heard from Mrima Ngombé's men that similar payments had been made in Ugara.

Knowing full well that this demand was an attempt at extortion, Mân Komo having never before been given mhongo, I refused to pay anything and lectured his messengers on hospitality.

January, 1874.

I told them that since they were well aware that we had been wandering for a considerable time in the jungle they should properly have brought us a present of food. Had they done so I should have made Mân Komo a handsome present, but now I assured them he would not receive from me even an inch of cloth.

Two villagers offered for a small payment to direct me to the capital of Uvinza, our next stage, on the road to which they said we should have no difficulty in obtaining supplies. I therefore decided on going forward, and early in the morning when the guides came, faithful to their promise, we started at once.

My leg had become so much worse that I was utterly unable to move, and poor Jasmin was so weakened by the want of proper food that he could not bear my weight; so I slung my iron chair to a pole and was carried by askari.

The lecture given to Mân Komo, coupled with my speedy departure from his place, seemed to have had some effect; for soon after leaving we were overtaken by one of his sons who promised that if I would return I should receive a present of a goat, some corn, and pombé. But being fairly under way I refused to turn back.

January, 1874.

Following the road along a small flat lying between the stream and the foot of the hill—the northern end of which we rounded—brought us to another mountain with so sharp an ascent that the men were unable to carry me, and I had literally to be dragged up by my arms.

From the summit there was a most extensive view of meadows, woods, and valleys spreading at our feet, surrounded by mountains presenting every variety of outline and size. The most distant, I was told, overhung the Tanganyika.

We had ascended this hill at the only accessible point in the direction from which we approached it, and the sides in many places went down so sheer that huge stones rolled over the edge crashed through the branches of projecting trees without touching earth till they landed in the valley below.

A blinding rain now set in and drenched everybody and everything and covered the hillsides with running water, much to our discomfort, and in the afternoon we were glad to camp near a small assemblage of huts with about a dozen inhabitants.

No provisions were obtainable here; and the men, instead of pushing on at once, started away on a foraging expedition which detained us for three days. They then returned without having met with any success.

During these days I was so seedy from the

drenching on the hills and the pain my leg gave me that it quite prevented my feeling any hunger.

January, 1874.

And this was rather fortunate, for there was nothing to eat excepting one plum-pudding which I had kept thus far on the chance of seeing another Christmas in Africa.

Poor Jasmin was thoroughly broken down from want of corn. His last effort was to drag himself to my tent-door, where he lay down exhausted and utterly unable to move. Having no food whatever to give the poor beast I thought it a merciful act to put a bullet through his brain, for I could not bear to witness his sufferings any longer.

The only riding donkey now remaining was a half-bred one which also showed symptoms of being beaten by starvation.

My goat had become extraordinarily tame and would persist in sleeping on the foot of my bed. If she were tied up elsewhere she disturbed the camp by continual bleating until allowed to come back to me.

The men managed to find roots and mushrooms for themselves and I believe a certain amount of corn and flour; but I did not get anything until the evening of the third day.

On the 31st of January we gladly left this inhospitable place, and made our way down a steep descent and along a narrow valley through which

January, 1874.

there ran a winding stream with numerous fenced-in patches of cultivation on each side.

The villages were perched among the rocks, and the inhabitants refused to have any intercourse with us.

The cause of this unfriendly behaviour was that they mistrusted our honesty of purpose, having suffered much from the slave-trade by being preyed upon by neighbouring tribes who sell them to the Arabs. This they are enabled to do in consequence of there being no friendship amongst the villages, each little hamlet of perhaps only half-a-dozen families asserting its independence.

Emerging from this valley we passed through open forest along the slope of a hill. Suddenly I found myself most unceremoniously dropped by my carriers who bolted right away, and immediately afterwards a general stampede took place all along the line, the men in their panic throwing down guns, loads, and everything, while scampering off to ensconce themselves behind the nearest trees.

"What is it? thieves, wild beasts, or what? Bring me my gun!" shouted I, as I lay on my side, jammed in the chair by the pole to which it was slung and perfectly unable to move.

The only answer I received was a personal explanation from the cause of all this terror—a solitary buffalo—which came charging along with head down. A black, vicious "varmint" he looked as he passed within twenty yards of me; but luckily he did not see me, or in all probability February, 1874. he would have sent me flying into the air, chair and all.

That evening we camped in a wide ravine in the hillside which proved rather an unhappy selection, for a heavy downpour of rain in the middle of the night converted our quarters into a stream two feet deep, by which boxes of books, cartridges, and stores in general were flooded.

We arrived the following day on the banks of the Sindi, a large affluent of the Malagarazi, having passed on the march a wide stretch of country under water varying from one to three feet in depth. Across the deeper places the dog and goat swam in loving company, close alongside my chair.

BUFFALO CHARGING CARAVAN.

CHAPTER XIII.

FLOATING ISLANDS.—THEIR ORIGIN AND GROWTH.—CROSSING THE SINDI.—UVINZA.—A CORDIAL RECEPTION.—STRANGE ECONOMY.—A BOY CHIEF.—CURIOUS VISITORS.—CEREMONIOUS SALUTATION.—TATTOOING.—UGAGA.—APPROACH OF MIRAMBO.—ON OUR DEFENCE.—DESTRUCTION OF SEVERAL VILLAGES.—FERRY CHARGES.—A HOST OF CLAIMANTS.—THE MALAGARAZI FERRY.—SAMBO'S COOKERY.—SALT-MAKING.—A CONSIDERABLE TRADE.—LIQUID SNUFF.—A DROLL SIGHT.—MY FAITHFUL LEO DIES.—A WILD BEAST IN CAMP.—SIGHTING TANGANYIKA.—ARRIVAL AT KAWÉLÉ.

February, 1874.

THE Sindi was crossed on the 2nd of February on a mass of floating vegetation, one of the peculiarities of intertropical Africa. Many rivers for a great portion of their courses are studded with these islands, which, when in good condition, are frequently used both by man and beast as natural floating bridges.

At the point where we crossed there was only a clear channel about two feet wide on each side, the remaining hundred yards of the river's width being covered with this vegetable growth, which extended about three-quarters of a mile down the stream.

Stepping on these islands is accompanied with much the same sensation as walking on a quaking bog overgrown with rushes and grass. On boring with a pole through about three feet of closely matted vegetation mixed with soil the river is found, and the hippopotami pass underneath.

These masses vary in thickness and stability from year to year. They owe their origin to the rushes growing in the bed of the river impeding the course of floating débris and causing it to accumulate and form soil for vegetation.

Plants quickly spring up and flourish, and, interlacing their roots, a compact mass is the result. This continues to increase for about six years, when the limit is reached. Then the island begins to decay and disappears altogether in about four years.

Caravans sometimes pass over them when the stage of decay has already set in, and several have been lost in the attempt. Consequently it was not without many prophecies of disaster befalling us that the men ventured to trust themselves on this floating vegetation. However, we found ourselves across it without any accident having happened, and passing through cultivated grounds and habitations, soon reached the village of Itambara, the head-quarters of the chief of Uvinza.

Looking back towards the hills we had traversed, their likeness to an archipelago could not fail to occur to me, the islands being represented by numerous hills detached from each other by narrow gorges, with bluffs, promontories, and cliffs.

Many of them had such precipitous sides as to

February, 1874. appear from this distance quite inaccessible; but the curling faint blue smoke betokened the presence of villages nestling under the rocky crags. Taking it all in all the scene was one of marvellous beauty.

In Uvinza food of different kinds was plentiful and we saw many plantations of Indian corn, matama, sweet potatoes, beans growing on a sort of bush, and tobacco.

At Itambara we were cordially welcomed by the headman, who offered us the use of some huts and, remarking that we must be hungry, brought a goat and some fowls for myself and flour for my men.

Mhongo was paid here for permission to cross the Malagarazi. The amount was very heavy, but I was assured it would clear us with the Mutwalé at Ugaga—where the ferry is—and that I should only have to reward the canoe-men.

Mutwalé is the title given throughout Uvinza and some of the neighbouring districts to the chief of a single village.

A day was consumed in arranging this matter and drying clothing and stores which had suffered much from the rains we had experienced; and another was lost by the obstinacy of Bombay who would not get the men together.

My lameness prevented my moving about amongst the men and forcing them to start, and Bombay, as an excuse for his folly, continually reiterated,

"Food cheap here, master; better stop another day." And stop we did, though for the life of me I could not understand the economy of remaining an extra day in a place doing nothing simply to save about one-sixth of our ordinary daily expenses.

February, 1874.

The headman brought the chief, a boy about eight years of age, to visit me. He was in a terrible fright and cried bitterly at the first sight of a white man. But I soon pacified him, and amused him with pictures in Dallas's "Natural History," and finally sent him away perfectly happy with some pages of the *Illustrated London News* which had been used in packing.

Ugaga was reached on the 5th of February, by a road leading through jungle and past many villages and plantations, and then descending diagonally the face of a cliff which divided the uplands from the plain of the Malagarazi.

Far and wide stretched the green plain and in the distance in the north were the blue hills of Uhha, while close to the foot of the cliff was Ugaga in which we halted.

The Mutwalé, to my disgust, demanded a heavy toll for our passage over the Malagarazi. The mhongo already exacted at Itambara would, we had been assured, free us from all further demands. Yet the Mutwalé declared that we had paid only for permission to cross the river, and that he, as lord of the ferry, besides the chief of the canoe-

February, 1874. men and various other officials, all expected their fees. Otherwise no canoes whatever would be forthcoming for our service.

The Mutwalé was a good-looking young fellow of five and twenty and very civil, though he would do no business on the day of our arrival and was politely firm on the mhongo question.

When he called on me I was lying on my bed without boots or stockings, waiting for my bath. I showed him my guns, books, and other curiosities to occupy his attention; but in the midst of his examination of these things he suddenly caught hold of my toes and looked at them most carefully, remarking that my feet were much too white and soft for walking. Then he transferred his attention to my hands which certainly could not be called white, having been tanned to the colour of a dirty dogskin glove; but after inspection he arrived at the conclusion that I had done very little work and therefore must be an important personage in my own country.

The mode of salutation here is very ceremonious, and varies according to the ranks of the performers.

When two "grandees" meet, the junior leans forward, bends his knees, and places the palms of his hands on the ground on each side of his feet, whilst the senior claps his hands six or seven times. They then change rounds, and the junior slaps himself first under the left armpit and then under the right. But when a "swell" meets an inferior, the superior only claps his hands and does not fully return the salutation by following the motions of the one who first salutes.

February, 1874.

On two commoners meeting they pat their stomachs, then clap hands at each other, and finally shake hands. These greetings are observed to an unlimited extent, and the sound of patting and clapping is almost unceasing.

The people are most extensively tattooed with small cuts forming spirals, circles, and straight lines, and they wear their hair shaved in patches or clipped close.

Their ornaments are wire bracelets, sambo, beads, and little iron bells. A very small amount of trade cloth is worn, most of the people being dressed in bark cloth and skins.

In the afternoon some fugitives brought the news that the village to which they belonged had been destroyed by Mirambo who was then only eight miles distant, and that five people had been killed and many more, with some cattle, driven off.

This so fully occupied the Mutwalé's attention that we did not commence the palaver about payment for crossing the Malagarazi until late in the afternoon. And almost immediately afterwards an alarm was raised that Mirambo was coming to attack the place. The bearer of this disquieting intelligence asserted that he was the sole survivor of a large village about five miles distant.

Of course we cut short our conference and pre-

February, 1874.

pared to confront our redoubtable foe. On going outside the village I saw several columns of smoke rising to the east and south-east of us, and more fugitives came running in stating that Mirambo had parties in all directions, looting and destroying.

Everything was arranged for meeting the anticipated attack, and as we were enjoying the hospitality of Ugaga I told the Mutwalé we were ready to assist him to the utmost. He smiled and said that as Mirambo had been beaten off with the loss of many people—including his son and brother—when he attacked the village some four years before, it was probable he would not try it again.

The Mutwalé was right, for Mirambo left the neighbourhood during the night after having destroyed and looted seven or eight villages.

The excitement having subsided, we again turned our attention to the knotty question of the amount to be paid for crossing the river. And knotty it was, for no sooner had I settled one demand than others were brought forward.

The people must have exercised their ingenuity to the utmost, for I received claims from the following officials, their wives and relations:—

1st, The Mutwalé; 2nd, his wife; 3rd, head Mtéko or councillor; 4th, his wife; 5th, Mwari, or head canoe-man; 6th, his wife; 7th, Mutwalé's relations; 8th, people who make the palaver; 9th, to buy rope; 10th, canoe paddlers.

I objected strongly to the charge for rope as it

had been specially mentioned and paid for at Itambara—although when or why it was required I could not ascertain. I also made a stand against many other items, especially wives and relatives.

At last, being thoroughly tired of argument, I rose and said, "If we go on like this, we shall remain here till the end of the world;" and went

CROSSING THE MALAGARAZI.

away, leaving them in a state best described by the last word of the marriage service.

My action brought the claimants to their senses, and the Mutwalé and Mtéko soon followed me offering to settle the whole business for less than I had already consented to pay, and promising that canoes should be at the ferry early the next morning.

February, 1874.

At the appointed time I went down to the river, a swift, swirling, brown stream, running between four and five knots and about thirty yards wide. But not a canoe was there.

Summoning my patience, already sorely tried, I sat down a short distance from the stream, when presently a head and shoulders appeared gliding along just above the grassy river-bank, and then another and another.

These were the all-important canoes, six in all. Four were the roughest specimens of naval architecture I ever came across, being merely hollow logs about eighteen feet long by two wide; the others were constructed of a single strip of bark sewn up at the ends, and were rather narrower and longer than the logs. They were each manned by two men, one of whom squatted down and used a paddle whilst the other stood up and punted along with a pole.

When the whole of the men and loads had been ferried over, an altercation arose about the donkeys, the canoe-men refusing to tow them across until a fetish man had made medicine.

This, of course, entailed an extra fee. But it was inadvisable to refuse, especially as Bombay swore that it was owing to the neglect of this precaution that Stanley lost a donkey on crossing this river.

So much time was occupied here that we were compelled to halt at Mpeta, the village of the other chief of the ferry, who fleeces travellers from Ujiji in the same way as his *confrère* does those from Unyanyembé. The Mutwalé here, a small boy, was unwell, and I therefore escaped a visit from him, which I did not regret since it would have obliged me to make him a present.

At Mpeta I got sights for latitude which agreed to within fifteen seconds with those taken by Captain Speke at the same place, a difference caused possibly by our position not being exactly the same, and which may therefore be regarded as practically giving the same result.

Leaving Mpeta we traversed a level country, just above the heads of many valleys and ravines running down to the Malagarazi which lay some little distance to the southward and much below us, on account of the rapid descent of its bed. Beyond the valley of the Malagarazi were high and rocky hills similar to those we had passed before crossing the river.

At Itaga we halted a day to buy food and partly because I was ill with fever and was also suffering from the effects of Sambo having mixed the dough for my breakfast cakes with castor-oil.

Whilst here two more villages were reported to have been destroyed by Mirambo, yet by all accounts he had no more than a hundred and fifty fighting men with him. Had the people banded together they could easily have thrashed him; but they were perpetually squabbling amongst themselves

February, 1874. and could therefore be attacked and destroyed piecemeal.

Our next station was Lugowa, to reach which we had to pass several villages and some muddy swamps, whence salt is procured in the following manner.

A quantity of mud is placed in a trough having at the bottom a square hole partially stopped with shreds of bark, beneath which about half-a-dozen similar vessels are placed, the upper one only containing mud. Hot water is then poured into this topmost trough to dissolve the salt with which the mud is impregnated, and the liquid being filtered by passing through the bark in the holes of the lower troughs, runs out of the bottom one nearly clear.

It is then boiled and evaporated, leaving as a sediment a very good white salt, the best of any I have seen in Africa. If the first boiling does not produce a sufficiently pure salt, it is again dissolved and filtered until the requisite purity is attained.

This salt is carried far and wide. The whole district from Lake Victoria Nyanza, round the south of Tanganyika, much of Manyuéma, and south to the Ruaha, is supplied by the pans of Uvinza.

There are some other places in these districts where salt is produced, but that of Uvinza is so superior that it always finds a ready sale.

At parting the old chief presented me with a load of salt, which I acknowledged by a gift in return.

At Lugowa I witnessed for the first time a curious method of using tobacco which prevails to a great extent at Ujiji. Instead of taking dry powdered snuff according to the ordinary custom, the people carry tobacco in a small gourd, and when they wish to indulge in a "sneeshin" fill it with water, and after allowing the leaf to soak for a few moments they press out the juice and sniff it up their nostrils.

February, 1874.

The pungent liquid snuff is retained in the nostrils for many minutes, being prevented from escaping either by holding the nose with the fingers or with a small pair of metal nippers. The after performance will not bear description.

It is indescribably droll to see half-a-dozen men sitting gravely round a fire trying to talk with nippers on their noses.

Another touch of fever came upon me at Lugowa, but I managed to continue the journey the next morning although still very lame and scarcely able to walk, which was a terrible hindrance in every way.

After marching four miles a man named Sungoro declared he was too ill to proceed any further, so I determined to leave him in charge of a coast negro who had settled in a village of salt-makers. I paid the negro to attend to the wants of the invalid and to forward him to Ujiji by caravan when he became convalescent.

Rain coming on heavily made it advisable to

February, 1874. camp earlier than I had intended, and on looking round for Leo I missed him. I immediately sent men to search for him, and they quickly returned carrying the poor animal.

To my sorrow I found he was nearly dead, and had only strength left to lick my hand and try to wag his tail, when he lay down and died at my feet. I believe he must have been bitten by a snake, for he was running about near me, well and full of life, only a short time before I lost sight of him.

Few can imagine how great was the loss of my faithful dog to me in my solitude, the sad blank which his death made in my everyday life.

One of the Mnyamwési donkeys gave birth to a foal here, and the little creature was carried for a few days until it grew strong enough to march with the caravan.

Five hours from this brought us to the Rusugi, which flows into the Malagarazi along a valley flanked by rocky hills on either side. And it was remarkable that though flowing through a soil impregnated with salt the water tasted perfectly fresh. On both banks of the Rusugi there were temporary villages now quite deserted, innumerable broken pots, stone fireplaces, and small pits where people make salt in the season.

During the night we were disturbed by a great noise amongst the donkeys, and found that one had been pinned by the nose by some wild beast, but luckily without doing much damage, the donkey being more frightened than hurt. *February, 1874.*

The next three marches were through a mixture of jungle, long grass, and occasional outcrops of granite. On the first we passed ten small streams besides the Ruguvu, which was twenty feet wide

CROSSING THE RUSUGI.

and four feet six inches deep; on the second one more, and on the third the Masungwé.

There were many tracks of buffalo and elephants, and we several times heard the latter trumpeting in the jungle.

In some places the grass was of great length, far above our heads, and the pouring rain made the work of forcing our way through this wet and heavy grass most laborious and unpleasant.

February, 1874.

After arriving in camp on the third day I had a general inspection of the men's private loads and found that ten had been guilty of stealing my beads. This I had long suspected, but Bombay always persisted that nothing of the sort was going on.

I firmly believe the whole caravan had been systematically robbing me and that those I detected with the stolen goods were really not more guilty, but only more unfortunate, than the rest. I took possession of the beads thus recovered, and made prisoners of the thieves.

From this I sent forward two men to Ujiji to deliver letters of introduction which had been given me by Said ibn Salim at Unyanyembé; also to request that boats might be provided at the mouth of the Ruché river to convey us to Kawélé, the chief town of Ujiji.

Near the camp I noticed several nutmeg-trees and picked up some very good nutmegs. The country about here was much broken up, and there were many small streams and rivulets, and brakes of bamboo.

The next morning I moved to Niamtaga, in Ukaranga, a good-sized palisaded village with many skulls bleaching on poles close to the entrance, and surrounded by fields neatly fenced in with bamboo.

The people proved an inhospitable set and would not allow us inside the village, so we camped by a large brake of bamboo which afforded admirable material for huts.

Anxious as I was to push forward to Ujiji, now so near at hand, I found it impossible to get the men on by hook or crook. Everything I tried, even to pulling down their huts; but it was altogether useless, and Bombay and the askari were quite as troublesome as the pagazi.

February, 1874.

However, on the 18th of February, fifteen years and five days from the time Burton discovered it, my eyes rested on the vast Tanganyika.

At first I could barely realise it. Lying at the bottom of a steep descent was a bright blue patch about a mile long, then some trees, and beyond them a great grey expanse having the appearance of sky with floating clouds.

"That the lake?" said I in disdain, looking at the small blue patch below me. "Nonsense."

"It is the lake, master," persisted my men.

It then dawned on me that the vast grey expanse was the Tanganyika, and that which I had supposed to be clouds was the distant mountains of Ugoma, whilst the blue patch was only an inlet lighted up by a passing ray of sun.

Hurrying down the descent and across the flat at the bottom—which was covered with cane-grass and bamboo intersected by paths made by hippopotami—we reached the shore and found two large canoes sent for us by the Arabs at Ujiji. Both were quickly filled with stores and men, and after an hour's pull Kawélé was reached.

The scenery was grand. To the west were the

February, 1874. gigantic mountains of Ugoma, while on the eastern shore was a dense growth of cane-grass of a bright green. Occasional open spaces disclosed yellow sandy beaches and bright red miniature cliffs with palm-trees and villages close to the water's edge. Numerous canoes moving about, and gulls, divers and darters, gave life to the scene; and distant floating islands of grass had very much the appearance of boats under sail.

At Kawélé I was most warmly welcomed by the traders who turned out to meet me, and with them I sat in state until the house placed at my disposal was ready to receive me.

This ceremonious sitting took place under the verandah of Mohammed ibn Salib who, with his compatriots, was full of anxiety to hear any news from Unyanyembé and the coast, as none had been received at Ujiji for a long time previous to my coming. Especially anxious were they to learn particulars of Mirambo's proceedings, and were greatly annoyed and disgusted to hear of his continued activity. The prevailing feeling amongst them did not seem to be one of fear that they might be robbed by him on the road to Unyanyembé, but rather that they should be compelled by Said ibn Salim to remain there instead of going on to Zanzibar, so as to increase the numerical strength at his disposal. However, they were rejoiced to hear that the journey had been accomplished, and began almost immediately to discuss means of sending to Unyanyembé. I found this long waiting and conversation rather purgatorial, for having had nothing to eat that day I was very hungry, besides being thoroughly tired and wet from wading through a swamp just before reaching the boats. My patience was rewarded, however, for after enjoying a comfortable wash and shift into dry clothes, I found prepared for me such a meal as I had not seen since partaking of Said ibn Salim's hospitality.

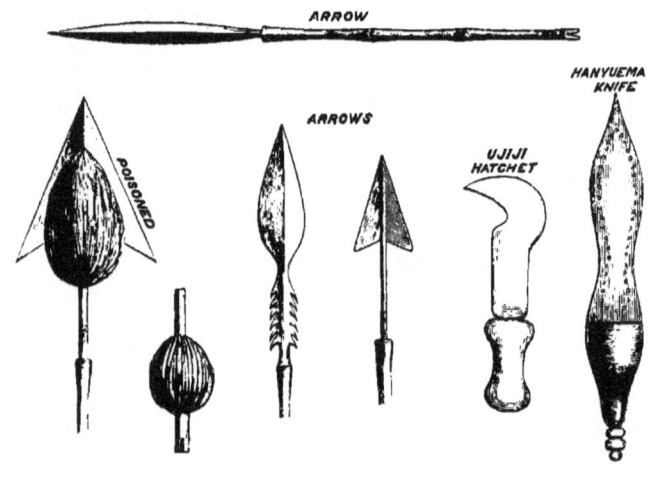

ARMS.

CHAPTER XIV.

RECOVERY OF LIVINGSTONE'S PAPERS.—ROBBERY OF MY STORES.—PUNISHMENT OF A THIEF.—DIFFICULTY IN SENDING THE JOURNALS TO THE EAST COAST.—THE TRADERS OF KAWÉLÉ.—THE NATIVE DRESS AND ORNAMENTS.—THEIR MARKETS.—WARUNDI BODY-COLOURING.—PRODUCTS OF THE DISTRICT.—THEIR CURRENCY.—HIRING BOATS.—CURIOUS MODE OF PAYMENT.—FITTING OUT.—I AM THOUGHT "UNLUCKY."—MY GUIDES DESERT ME.—"NEGRO MELODISTS."—SAILING AWAY ON THE TANGANYIKA.—DEVILS' DWELLINGS.—PROPITIATING THE SPIRITS.—SLAVE-HUNTERS.

February, 1874.

I FOUND it impossible to remain in the house which the Arabs had lent me at Kawélé. It was very wretched, and the only place where I could stand my bed was under a verandah open to the market-place and exposed to the gaze of the whole population. I therefore moved into another which I rented for two doti a month.

This house, though not so large as the one I occupied at Unyanyembé was much more comfortable, and a table placed under the verandah enabled one to work at ease.

My first enquiries were for Dr. Livingstone's papers, and I was greatly rejoiced to find them safe in the charge of Mohammed ibn Salib, who—although holding no authority from Syud Burghash—was looked upon by the traders here as their practical head to whom they always referred in any matter of dispute.

February, 1874.

I now took the opportunity of overhauling my loads to discover what I had lost by theft, and found that no fewer than thirty-two frasilah of beads, weighing thirty-five pounds each and equal to sixteen loads, had been stolen.

Only one load remained intact and that had been carried the whole way by a pagazi named Suliman, who was a very good, honest fellow.

Owing to the frequent desertions and my many illnesses, I had been unable to keep the men to the same loads throughout the journey, and therefore could not detect the thieves unless I actually found the stolen property in their possession. But I had little or no doubt that there were barely half-a-dozen men in the caravan who had not robbed me at one time or another.

I discharged those whom I had caught thieving and gave notice that I would flog the next offender.

And scarcely had I said the words when I detected a man coming out of the store-room—which had been left open by Bombay with his usual carelessness—having several strings of my most valuable beads and three coloured cloths partially hidden under his loin cloth. Instantly I ordered him to be seized up and given the flogging I had promised, and discharged him on the spot with a warning that if he or any other de-

February, 1874. tected thief came near my house he should receive similar treatment.

The result of enquiries as to the prospects of continuing my journey on the other side of the lake, and the best method of sending Livingstone's papers safely to the coast was not encouraging.

I was assured that no travelling would be possible to the west of Tanganyika for at least three months, and that it would be most unsafe for a small party carrying the box of papers to leave Ujiji for the East Coast on account of the disturbances on the road to Unyanyembé. It therefore appeared better to wait until the convoy of a caravan could be obtained.

I then turned my thoughts to the subject of a cruise round the Tanganyika, and immediately set about making preparations.

Before proceeding with my narrative I will endeavour to describe Kawélé and its residents, both native and foreign.

Giving precedence to the traders, there was first Mohammed ibn Salib, a fine portly old half-caste Arab with a very good presence, who had not been to the east of Ujiji since the year 1842. Trading at that time in Ma Kasembé's country he had been detained prisoner for more than twenty years, most of which he passed either in chains or with a slave fork round his neck. He had now settled permanently at Ujiji.

The next in importance were Muinyi Heri, a

rich Mrima trader who married the daughter of the chief of Ujiji during my stay; Mohammed ibn Gharib, a great friend of Livingstone, whom he had often assisted, and who, as a token of friendship, had presented him with a gun; and his brother Hassani.

February, 1874.

These were the principal traders; but there were also Syde Mezrui, a half-caste, and as it afterwards turned out, a bankrupt; Abdallah ibn Habib, a Mrima trader, and several men who acted as agents for large merchants, besides blacksmiths, carpenters, and sandal-makers.

The natives are rather a fine-looking race, but have the reputation of being a very drunken and thieving lot, yet I scarcely think they are as bad in either respect as the lower orders of the coast natives. They are good smiths and porters and expert fishermen and canoe-men.

Their dress usually consists of a single piece of bark cloth with two corners tied in a knot over one shoulder and passing under the opposite armpit. It is often dyed in stripes and spots of black and yellow and cut to imitate the shape of a leopard's skin. It leaves one side of the body perfectly naked, and in a breeze flaps about in such a manner that it barely satisfies the commonest requirements of decency.

Their special ornaments are made of beautifully white and wonderfully polished hippopotamus ivory. In shape and size they represent the blade of a sickle and are worn hung round the neck. They also wear a profusion of sambo, small bells and wire bracelets. The men usually carry a spear.

Their hair is clipped and shaved into most peculiar patterns, such as spirals, zigzags, tufts left on a bare scalp or round patches shaven in the centre of the crown of the head, and, in short, every conceivable vagary in shaving in fancy devices.

The chiefs among them may be distinguished by their wearing coloured trade cloths—after the same fashion as their poorer countrymen wear their bark cloth—and by having heavy penannular bracelets with a projection at the back.

The head chief or Mtémé of Ujiji lives in a village in the mountains some distance from the lake; but every small district is ruled over by a Mutwalé or headman, whose office is often hereditary, assisted by three or four Watéko or elders.

These people arrange disputes, collect all tributes, and remit the proceeds to the Mtémé after deducting a certain amount for their trouble.

One of the sights at Kawélé is the market held daily, between half-past seven and ten in the morning and again in the afternoon, in an open space in the town close to the shore. The more important is that in the morning, which presents an interesting and lively scene.

It is attended by the people of Uguhha, Uvira, Urundi, and many tribes dwelling on the shores of the lake.

SOKO AT KAWÉLÉ.

The Waguhha are easily distinguished by the elaborate manner in which both sexes dress their hair and the fanciful and extensive tattooing of the women; while the Warundi may be known by their being smeared with red earth and oil, giving their bodies a bright bronze colour. They are called by the Arab traders a "red people," meaning light-coloured.

February, 1874.

Women of Kawélé and surrounding hamlets bring baskets of flour, sweet potatoes, yams, fruit of the oil-palm—which is here seen for the first time—bananas, tobacco, tomatoes, cucumbers, and a great variety of vegetable products, besides pottery and huge gourds of pombé and palm wine.

The men sell fish—both dried and fresh—meat, goats, sugar-canes, nets, baskets, spear and bow staves, and bark cloth.

The Warundi principally deal in corn and canoe paddles, and from the island of Ubwari is brought a species of hemp used by the Wagogo in making their nets; while Uvira furnishes pottery and ironwork, Uvinza salt, and various other places large gourds of palm oil.

Each vendor takes up the same position daily, and many build small arbours of palm-fronds to shelter them from the burning rays of the sun.

Amongst the crowd of buyers and sellers there circulate parties who have travelled from a distance to this central mart to endeavour to dispose of their slaves and ivory; and the whole of the bargaining

February, 1874. being carried on at the top of the voice the noise is almost deafening.

A curious currency is in vogue here, everything being priced in beads called sofi, something in appearance like small pieces of broken pipe-stem.

At the commencement of the market, men with wallets full of these beads deal them out in exchange for others with people desirous of making purchases; and when the mart is closed they receive again from the market-people and make a profit on both transactions, after the manner usual amongst money-changers.

To obtain boats to proceed on my Tanganyika cruise was my first consideration; but the owners of two promised me by Said ibn Salim at Unyanyembé were away, and therefore I could not procure them. I discovered a good one, however, belonging to Syde ibn Habib—who had met Livingstone both in Sékélétu's country and in Manyuéma—and managed to hire it from his agent though at an extortionate rate.

The arrangement at the hiring was rather amusing. Syde's agent wished to be paid in ivory, of which I had none; but I found that Mohammed ibn Salib had ivory, and wanted cloth. Still, as I had no cloth, this did not assist me greatly until I heard that Mohammed ibn Gharib had cloth and wanted wire. This I fortunately possessed. So I gave Mohammed ibn Gharib the requisite amount in wire, upon which he handed over cloth to

Mohammed ibn Salib, who in his turn gave Syde ibn Habib's agent the wished-for ivory. Then he allowed me to have the boat.

February, 1874.

The agreement was that she should be handed over to me fit for sea, and having been a long time hauled up she required caulking, which was a tedious business.

A sail was supposed to be forthcoming, but all that appeared was a few tattered rags of cloth which they informed me would be quite sufficient for all sailing purposes. I could get nothing better out of this agent, who, not contented with having received as hire quite enough to buy two or three canoes in honest trade, now wanted to cheat me in every petty detail.

In addition to his impudence in calling these rags a sail, he stated that the oars were not included in the bargain and I must give a further amount for them.

But I appealed to Mohammed ibn Salib in this matter, and he decided that I was to have the oars without payment. The question of the sail he gave against me.

I therefore set to work cutting out and making a lateen sail which frightened nearly every one in the place out of their senses owing to what they considered its enormous size; but the boat was a great lumbering craft and needed a large sail, so I held to my own ideas.

Whilst these matters were progressing I

February, 1874. learnt that a small party were going to Unyanyembé in company with a caravan of Waguhha, intending to travel by night through the unsettled districts. I determined to seize this opportunity to despatch three men to Said ibn Salim with letters for the coast, and to urge on him the immediate necessity of forwarding at the earliest opportunity the beads I had left at Mrima Ngombé's.

I did not venture to trust Dr. Livingstone's papers to such a poor chance of arriving at Unyanyembé.

My first trip was to Bangwé, a small island which is the northernmost land on the eastern shore visible from Kawélé, though owing to the lay of the lake it only bears N.W. by W. $\frac{3}{4}$ W. from that place.

Here I got a set of bearings, and having carefully calculated the distance from another point of observation at Kawélé, I was able by crossbearings to plot in the principal points visible from both points with considerable accuracy so as to serve as a base for my survey of the lake.

Just before starting on a surveying cruise I heard by chance that the wife of one of those men who, according to Said ibn Salim, would readily lend me a boat, was at Ujiji. And on making my request known to her she immediately complied, giving me one in good order, but without a sail. The first boat I named *Betsy*, and the second, which was to be the tender, *Pickle*.

It now became necessary to engage men from whom I might learn the names of the different places round the lake, and to point out the nightly camps and act as interpreters.

February, 1874.

Two who went to the north end with Livingstone and Stanley were brought to me. But in the weighty matter of engaging them, the Mutwalé and Watéko of course had a finger and charged more for their fees than the men received as hire.

In consequence of my being attacked with fever, which lasted two or three days, these fellows, in the belief that I was unlucky, threw up their engagement and refused to accompany me.

Their pay and the elders' fees were returned, on the principle of "no work, no pay;" and three days afterwards I obtained the services of two very decent men, Parla and Régwé, of whom the last-named was the principal but by no means the better.

The amount they were to receive for the journey was seventeen and a half dollars each, whilst the fees to the elders amounted to thirty-four.

It was rather a long price to pay two naked fellows for about a couple of months; but it must be remembered that uncivilised countries are always the most expensive for the traveller, though they may not be for the settler.

Whilst at Ujiji I met with great civility from the traders who frequently sent me cooked food, and Mohammed ibn Salib gave me a bullock and half-a-dozen sheep. I naturally made them presents in return, and was the more inclined to do so from having heard that they had befriended Livingstone.

Syde Mezrui was expecting a caravan from Unyanyembé with stores exchanged for ivory; but was good enough to say that, whether it had arrived or not when I returned, he would be ready to show me the way to Nyangwé.

I should mention that I was visited here by three mountebanks or minstrels who were walking about the country much after the fashion of Italian organ-grinders in England, seeking whom they might render miserable with their noise.

They were furnished with enormous rattles made of gourds filled with pebbles, and with these they accented their songs and dances. The noise was something deafening when all three rattled away at once; for these instruments were far more powerful and effective than the bones of Christy Minstrels.

They treated me to break-downs and walk-rounds which might well be the original of our music-hall style; while the songs, solos with chorus, had the "yah yah" accompaniment precisely as given by the stage nigger.

At last, on the 13th of March, I managed to get away with Bombay and thirty-seven men, leaving Bilâl in charge of the remainder and some stores. But having served out beads to enable the crews to buy five days' rations in advance, all hands took the opportunity of getting drunk early in the morning, and it was afternoon before I could collect them or they could collect their senses.

March, 1874.

I selected the *Betsy* for my flag-ship, and over a sort of poop of which she boasted, fitted up a waggon-roof awning, hoping it would serve for me to live under altogether; but it proved anything but weather-proof, and it was fortunate I took my tent on board.

A light, fair wind enabled us to make sail, and that evening we ran down past the settlement of Jumah Merikani—of whom I shall have to speak hereafter — in Ukaranga, and camped at Point Mfomdo.

After proceeding a short distance the next day, passing lovely country with small cliffs and hanging woods reminding me very much of Mount Edgcumbe, I made for the shore for the purpose of beaching the *Betsy*, as water was leaking through a considerable hole in her stern and damaging cargo. Defects having been made good, we again got under way and camped near Ugunya.

The beauty of the scenery along the shores of the lake requires to be seen to be believed. The vivid greens of various shades amongst the foliage of the trees, the bright red sandstone cliffs and blue water, formed a combination of colour seeming gaudy in description, but which was in reality harmonious in the extreme.

March, 1874.

Birds of various species—white gulls with grey backs and red legs and beaks, long-necked black darters, divers, grey and white kingfishers, and chocolate-coloured fishhawks with white heads and necks, were most numerous; whilst the occasional snort of a hippopotamus, the sight of the long back of a crocodile looking like a half-tide rock, and the jumping of fish, reminded one that the water as well as the air was thickly populated.

During the night I was knocked over by a severe attack of fever, but tried to go on the next day. However, I soon found my head and compass spinning in opposite directions, so was compelled to give in and camped at Kabongo, a short way south of the Malagarazi, where I remained two days before I was sufficiently recovered to take a bearing.

Some very curious sensations were experienced by me whilst laid up with this attack. One night I thought I was at least twenty people, all of whom were in pain, and that each one had the same feeling as all the rest.

Another night the fancies were more distinct and I experienced a complete sense of duality. I imagined that another person, a second self, was lying on the opposite side of the boat, and I was perfectly conscious of every shake of ague and pang of headache that he suffered. I thought, too, that the teapot full of cold tea which had been placed on that side of the boat was for his sole benefit. And when in my tossing about I rolled over to that side I seized the teapot and drank like a whale and chuckled at the idea of the other thirsty mortal having been done out of some of his tipple.

March, 1874.

Notwithstanding being so incoherent in my ideas whilst alone, yet whenever my servant came to me I managed to pull myself together and talk to him somewhat sensibly, although feeling decidedly dazed. When I began to recover we moved again and camped at Ras Kébwé.

My boats' crews were not a plucky order of men, for a thunderstorm and a little squall so frightened them in the morning that they refused to stir till it had passed off, when an hour's pulling brought us to Machachézi, a deep inlet.

The pilots now showed the white feather, and made me camp because they would not pass Ras Kabogo—where a devil and his wife were supposed to reside—until the next day, and the men being equally superstitious believed every word of this story.

Here three small canoes of Wajiji going south to exchange goats for slaves joined us; and when I found that Régwé's father was of the party I arrived at the conclusion that family affection as well as superstition might have had something to do with our stopping.

Ras Kabogo was passed on the following day without either the he or she devil being visible;

March, 1874.

but the pilots stood together in the bow of the canoe to make an offering to these evil spirits.

One held out a paddle on the blade of which a few common beads had been placed and both said together, as nearly as it can be translated, "You big man, you big devil, you great king, you take all men, you kill all men, you now let us go all right," and after a little bowing and gesticulation the beads were dropped into the water and the dreaded devil propitiated.

There is a kind of double cape at this place, one being the supposed residence of the male devil and the other that of his wife, and the spot is therefore believed to be doubly dangerous.

Having rounded Ras Kabogo we skirted a large bay lying between it and Ras Kungwé—the southernmost point visible from Kawélé—then passed along the base of fine bold hills sloping down to the water, and put up for the night in a splendid little harbour into which two rivers fell.

I now began to regain my appetite and directed Sambo to kill and cook a fowl, when, to my astonishment, I found there was not one in the boat although I had given him beads and cloth to lay in a stock. To save himself trouble he bought a couple of goats instead, as they could easily be procured in the market while fowls could only be obtained by a house to house visitation.

One would scarcely have thought that his stupidity would have led him into still further errors. But he explained that one goat was killed the day fever attacked me, and that on the meat turning bad he killed the other, in order to have something ready for me if I got better. That having also become too "high" to eat, it was plain that of the two goats not a single mouthful would fall to my share.

March, 1874.

Happily the Wajiji were persuaded to sell me a good milch goat; and her milk was as nourishing and good for me at that time as meat would have been.

The next two days saw us nearly round the bay. On the first night we camped at the mouth of a river, close to the spot where Stanley landed when he came south from Ujiji with Livingstone on his return to Unyamyembé.

Here we met a few wretched natives who declared themselves to be in great fear of a party of Wanyamwési slave-hunters who had built a village on the shore, from which they used to sally forth and harass the whole surrounding country.

On the second day I received a visit from the chief of these slave-traders, and he seemed quite annoyed at my not having brought corn and goats to trade for slaves. The natives then at my camp ran away in abject terror directly they saw his canoes approaching, although I assured them that they should not be harmed whilst I was there.

I have not mentioned the numerous rivers we passed on this cruise, for a glance at the map will

March, 1874.

suffice to show that to do so would render this account monotonous in the extreme. They bring an enormous quantity of water into the lake and many floating islands, principally composed of vegetation like that by which we crossed the Sindi; but a few had bushes and even trees upon them.

Their appearance is most peculiar, as many as fifty or sixty being sometimes in sight; and at a distance they bear a striking resemblance to vessels under sail.

On the 23rd of March we rounded Ras Kungwé, and entered upon that part of the lake which had hitherto been unexplored, and indeed unseen, by any white man.

UJIJI POTTERY.

CHAPTER XV.

PROFITABLE SLAVE-BUYING. — STREET ACROBATS. — WAR-PAINT. — A BAD NIGHT.—COWARDLY BOATS' CREWS.—KABOGO.—A PUBLIC ENTERTAINMENT. — STEALING MEN'S BRAINS. — COAL. — A HONEY DEMON. — A PLAGUE OF FROGS.—ENLARGEMENT OF THE LAKE.—MASSI KAMBI.—AN OPTICAL ILLUSION.—MANY DEVILS.—ONE OF MY MEN SHOOTS HIMSELF.—DOCTORS DIFFER.—CURIOUS HAIR-OIL.—THE CHIEF OF MAKUKIRA.—HIS DRESS.—WIVES.—DOLLS.—INFANTINE TASTE FOR DRINK.—COTTON MANUFACTURE. —SPREAD OF THE SLAVE-TRADE. — THE WATUTA. —CUSTOMS AND DRESS. —TWINS.

RAS KUNGWÉ is situated near the narrowest part of the lake, where it is not more than fifteen miles across, and after rounding that point we passed under enormous hills clothed with trees, and having crystal torrents and waterfalls flashing down their sides. March, 1874.

At the bottom of these hills, especially near the mouth of the torrents, were many small beaches, some of fine sand and others of coarse angular shingle of granite, quartz and iron ore.

Patches of corn amongst the jungle denoted the haunts of wretched fugitives from the slave-hunters. These poor creatures were doomed to a miserable existence owing to the few strong villages hunting down their weaker neighbours, to exchange them with traders from Ujiji for food which they are too lazy to produce themselves.

VOL. I.   S

March, 1874.

For the night we remained in the river Luuluga near the village Kinyari, where the Wajiji who coasted down with us sold their corn, oil, and goats for slaves—the only product of the place—and then turned homewards.

The price of a slave was from four to six doti, or two goats; and as a goat could be bought for a shukkah at Ujiji, where slaves were worth twenty doti, the profits of the Wajiji must have been enormous.

I took occasion to visit the village and found it of moderate size, composed of conical huts surrounded by a heavy palisade and a ditch, a single slippery plank across which led to the only entrance. Above the entrance and at each corner of the palisade were heavy crows'-nests well supplied with large stones in readiness to hurl at an enemy; while the palisade was lined with horizontal logs to a height of seven feet above the ground, rendering it nearly musket-proof.

Tobacco was grown in small quantities—that being the only attempt at cultivation—and the men sometimes went fishing if the fancy took them, but for *trade* and *support* the place depended upon nothing but the traffic in *slaves*.

At the moment of my entering the village a dance was being performed by two men, with a variety of pantomimic action, jumping, and somersault turning, but their efforts as a whole were very tame and lacked spirit and energy.

When they considered they had exercised themselves sufficiently for the amusement of the bystanders they dragged themselves along the ground as if utterly exhausted, and, pretending to be dying of hunger, threw themselves at the feet of some person who was expected to give them a handful or two of corn. Having received their reward they then continued their performance.

They were accompanied by half-a-dozen men beating drums, and another who droned through a sort of recitative.

One native obligingly turned out in war-paint for me to admire him. He wore a cap and particularly hideous mask of zebra-skin and carried two spears and a shield. The latter was five feet six inches long and ten inches wide, with a cane handle in the centre, and was made of the wood of a palm-tree, and though he declared it was strong enough to resist anything he declined to submit it to the test of a rifle bullet.

In the night there were such heavy squalls, with thunder and lightning, that I turned out to make certain that my boat was properly secured. All the men except Bombay were quartered on shore and had utilised the oars for the framework of their huts, and I did not fancy going for a cruise on such a night without either men or oars.

While thus engaged the rain fell fast and furious, half-filling the boats with water; so I

March, 1874. roused up the men to bale them out and then returned to my crib in the stern of the *Betsy*.

But what a sorry sight met my view. My awning had nearly blown away, and bed, charts, books, and guns, were all soaking wet.

After surveying for a moment these dismal ruins I gathered together what I could under my waterproof, and putting my head between my knees sat like a hen on a brood of chickens.

The lightning and thunder were almost appalling. One flash struck the water close to the boat, and was so quickly followed by the thunder-clap that they seemed simultaneous. I was quite stunned by the crash and at first thought I had been struck, being so dazzled by the glare that my sight did not properly return for more than half an hour.

The morning was very uncomfortable as may be supposed, and the men being rather unnerved refused to move because of a little sea being on; but late in the afternoon we got away and passing close under the hills—from which many torrents were falling into the lake—camped in the river Lubugwe.

On the 26th we were under way early and passed the small island Kililo, river Lufungu, and Ras Katimba, where we camped intending to move again in the afternoon if the weather cleared.

But a slight swell frightened my brave Jack tars. They said, "Lake bad, and canoes break again;"

and persuade them to go on I could not. Even the Wajiji who had lived all their lives by the lake were quite as bad, for they brought their hire to me, saying, "Let us go back. We don't want to die."

What would I not have given for a man-of-war's whaler and crew for six weeks! I should then have been able to have done something thoroughly satisfactory instead of creeping in and out of the bays and getting no cross-bearings.

All the danger we ran arose from the habit of going along almost touching the rocks. They will persist in following this course, and if there is a sudden squall, on shore they go. Their extreme timidity actually brings them into danger, though they cannot see it. But it is often noticeable that cowards really run more risks and come oftener to grief than those who face things manfully.

The hills were now getting lower and running further back from the lake; and on the 28th we ran between the island of Kabogo and the mainland.

The strait is about two and a half miles long and three hundred yards wide at the entrance—where there are sand-bars—and widens to a mile and a half in the middle.

We landed on the island and obtained some fish from the inhabitants in exchange for palm oil, of which they are very fond. It is very thickly populated, fertile and well cultivated, and the huts standing alone in their own provision grounds

March, 1874.

and shaded by a sycamore or some other giant of the forest, gave a look of peaceful security which had been wanting since leaving Kawélé.

Opposite on the mainland there was only the village of the chief; but on both the island and the main the fan-palm was very plentiful.

Birds of many kinds were numerous, and a handsome pencilled brown lily-trotter with white head and neck walked about on the floating leaves of the lilies—with which much of the surface of the water was covered—looking amongst the blossoms for its meal of insects.

At the end of the strait a sandspit almost joins the island to the main, and here amongst a mass of reeds was the landing-place. Several narrow passages admitted the small canoes of the natives, numbers of which were flitting about from point to point. Our large boats, however, could only reach the shore by dint of shoving and hauling and breaking down the reeds on either side, and so thickly did they grow that the men were able to get out and shove the boat along while standing on the broken-down reeds.

Ponda was the name of the chief, and Karyan Gwina that of the village. Ponda was one of two sons of a chief who formerly ruled, or claimed to rule, over the whole of Kawendi; but on the old man's death it was divided into many factions and the sons contented themselves with settling on the shores of the lake.

A PUBLIC ENTERTAINMENT.

After a time they quarrelled and Ponda, being the weaker, left his brother in possession and founded this village which was large and strongly fortified with ditches and palisades.

March, 1874.

The people were very jealous about allowing strangers inside. Indeed, a party of Wanyamwési sent by Mkasiwah, chief of Unyanyembé with a present of cattle for his daughter who had married Ponda, were obliged to camp outside. Perhaps this was partly owing to the Wanyamwési having unfortunately had the present stolen from them on the road by the Warori.

Having obtained permission to enter I went to the village, and found it well kept and divided into several sections by interior palisades radiating from an open space in the centre.

On each side of the gate leading to the chief's quarters a couple of logs were placed as seats for the convenience of persons waiting an audience, and above them were about forty skulls of men and half-a-dozen of wild beasts.

A crowd was assembled in the village, looking at two hideously ugly old hags dancing to the sound of large drums beaten by men. This performance was very disgusting, the principal feature being a sort of convulsive trembling and twitching of the body and limbs, while the shrivelled and wrinkled breasts of the dancers shook about like a couple of empty leather bottles.

They howled a song, and at any particularly hard

March, 1874. shake the women standing round joined in the chorus.

Their dress consisted of most scanty waist cloths of bark, bunches of long hair (zebra's tails) tied to their knees and elbows, and rings of bells round their ankles.

The chief sent me a little sour milk and some flour, and I made him a small return while expressing a hope that he would either visit me or that I might call upon him. But he refused any intercourse, because, as I afterwards heard, he believed me to be a magician capable of stealing his little mind and leaving him a complete idiot if given the opportunity of looking upon him.

Here I met a young Msuahili whose acquaintance I had made at Unyanyembé. He had come to trade, ivory being very cheap. A frasilah could ordinarily be bought for twelve doti, but by hard bargaining he had obtained two frasilah for eighteen doti.

Bitterly did he complain of the high price of slaves, twelve doti for a young girl and five or six for a child being to his mind an exorbitant price!

Being unwilling to remain here until he had disposed of all his goods, he wanted me to buy his cloth and other stores and give him a passage to Ujiji, his men being afraid of the road to Unyanyembé—by which he had come—on account of its being infested by robbers. I did not require his cloth, but told him he was welcome to a passage in my boat; but when we got away the next day we left the Msuahili behind, for his Wanyamwési porters were more afraid of the perils of the lake than the danger of being attacked by banditti on shore.

After clearing the reeds we skirted along a beach under Karyan Gwina crowded with people bathing, filling water-pots, looking after their fishing gear, or staring at the passing boats.

We then came to low cliffs formed of granite, porphyry and sandstone, and rotten clay—with many landslips and caves caused by the beating of the waves—and ran into the Luguvu under more cliffs formed by a line of large hills.

My men's dread of facing a little wind and sea detained us here a whole day; for, if forced to go on, they were just in the humour to have done their utmost to make difficulties in order to prove that they were right in objecting to start.

Hippopotami, crocodiles and monkeys were here in abundance, and but for my lameness this halt would not have been so tiresome. My feet and legs were, however, covered with boils that prevented my going out shooting or even leaving the boat.

Getting away from here we passed close under nearly vertical cliffs of sandstone and black marble streaked with white, and after a time a great patch of what, from the appearance of the cleavage, I believe to have been coal.

March, 1874.

When the East Coast men saw it, they called out, "*Makaa Marikébu*"—ship coal. The thickness of the principal seam, which lay on the top of synclinal curves of rock of which the anticlinal curves had been worn away, was between fifteen and eighteen feet.

Although unable to obtain a specimen of coal from this particular spot, some was afterwards given me which came from Itawa, in the same latitude and a short distance to the westward of the lake. This was undoubtedly a light bituminous coal.

Passing several streams and torrents we came to the termination of the cliffs at river Makanyazi. Here the guides said there were large quantities of honey; but as it was under the protection of an evil spirit none was to be collected lest he should do us some injury, and not one of the men could be persuaded to gather any.

Just as we landed I noticed the scaly back of a crocodile amongst the grass, and seizing my rifle put two bullets into him killing him at once. On clearing away the grass round him he turned out to be only a small one about four feet long.

Hippopotami blowing and snorting kept us awake all night, but our fires prevented their venturing into the camp. Judging from the number of their footmarks we must have pitched upon a favourite landing-place, whence their tracks led straight up a steep hill which one would have thought it impossible for such unwieldy beasts to scale.

Besides the disturbance caused by river-horses there was quite a plague of frogs incessantly croaking the livelong night. The noise of some resembled that made by caulkers or riveters, while others, larger or nearer, sounded more like smiths

CAMP ON SPIT.

forging, and a few made a croak like a ratchet drill, so that with a little imagination it was not difficult to fancy oneself in a ship-building yard.

We passed the village of Ponda's brother the following morning, and upon a heavy squall coming up behind, ran inside a small sandy spit with half-a-dozen huts on it.

The inhabitants bolted with their goods and

April, 1874.

chattels when they saw us coming; for although a very heavy palisade was built across the spit as a protection on the land side, it was perfectly open to the water.

After the squall a steady soaking rain set in and we lay up for the night. Some of the men went to a neighbouring village in search of food and found there the people who had been frightened at our approach, believing that we were Arabs' slaves employed to hunt for slaves.

Food was not obtained here, nor indeed for some days afterwards, and the stock of corn laid in at Ujiji being spoilt by the continuous rains we began to feel hungry.

At the mouth of the river Musamwira—which drains the Likwa into the Tanganyika—we next halted amongst a group of sandy grass-covered islands. Some people engaged here in fishing made an attempt to run away on seeing us. For on this occasion we were thought to be followers of Mirambo, whose dreaded name had reached this remote spot.

A few years previously these islands had been part of a large, cultivated, and inhabited plain; and during the day we pulled through stumps of trees and over sites of many old villages.

According to the accounts given me by the guides, the lake is constantly encroaching upon its shores and increasing in size. And at Kawélé I remarked that since Burton was there a strip more than six hundred yards wide appeared to have been washed away for a distance of three or four miles.

April, 1874.

Although there were many large fishing traps lying about we could get nothing to eat, the few fishermen telling us that all the people had gone elsewhere owing to the constant washing away of the shores of the lake. Indeed the errand which had now brought them to the island was merely to collect fishing gear which had been left behind when the flitting took place.

Another devil's habitation was passed on the next day's cruise. The guides made the usual offering and oration with the addition of putting salt on their heads besides throwing some into the water.

The name of the demon was Musamwira, and on enquiring why he did not haunt the river of that name I was told he sometimes went there, but his usual dwelling-place was just behind a hill where the offering was made.

We made sail the next morning to run down to Massi Kambi, where we hoped to be able to get some food. But it being rather squally my men became so nervous that I had to allow the sail to be lowered. They then persisted in going close in shore, and in the end had to pull head to wind instead of running right across with a fair breeze.

All the entrances of Massi Kambi were closed and the crows'-nests manned on our drawing near;

April, 1874.

so we camped on a small sand-bank, having on it a few fishermen's huts built on piles. The wind and sea increased to such an extent that we were subsequently obliged to move to the mainland.

Here we remained a day to procure food, but a few sweet potatoes and beans were our only reward. In the afternoon I shot a large Lepidosiren, called by the natives, Singa; but it was so loathsome to look at that no one would touch it, and the people declared it was poisonous.

Leaving this place we rounded Ras Mpimbwe, a promontory formed of enormous masses of granite piled on each other in the wildest confusion and looking as though some race of Titans had commenced building a breakwater.

In the early morning just after we started there was a most curious optical illusion. The summits of the mountains on the west of the lake had the exact appearance of being covered with snow, and while I was wondering and looking at them steadily

AN INHABITANT OF MASSI KAMBI.

through the glasses the white began to disappear and then I discovered the cause of the illusion.

April, 1874.

The almost horizontal rays of the rising sun had been reflected by the lower sides of the clouds down on the tops of the mountains, which consequently looked quite white in contrast to the lower parts which were still in deep shadow. It is just possible that many reports of snow-capped mountains might be ascribed to this cause.

Off Ras Mpimbwe there were very many rocks in all directions just half a-wash, and dangerous work it was passing through them.

About noon we camped on the north side of Ras Kambemba—off which lies a small island of the same name—and shortly after settling down I heard a cry that some game was in camp. On going out with my rifle I found that some buffalo had been near but had been completely scared by the noise.

In returning my rifle to its place against the tent-pole, my fowling-piece which was also strapped to the pole was accidentally discharged. My head being close to the muzzle, the fire and report naturally made me spring backwards, when I tumbled right over my bed and cut my head severely and half-stunned myself.

I confess I rather thought I was shot, but on hearing my servant sing out, "Bwana amepigwa" (Master's shot), I roused myself and found only a scalp wound resulting from my fall.

April, 1874.

My servant on seeing me lying in a heap with my head bleeding made certain I was killed; but the only damage done was a hole through the top of the tent where the charge of shot made its exit.

The country here was composed of great masses of granite and hardened sandstone chiefly imbedded in very soft red sandstone, which, being easily washed away leaves the hard rocks standing out by themselves.

Tanganyika seems to have more than its proper share of devils, for at Kamasanga we arrived at the dwelling of another. The Wajiji, as usual, paid their respects, saying, "Oh! devil, give us good lake, little wind, little rain; let canoes go well, go quick."

There were many islands brought down by the rivers, more like those of the Mississippi than the ordinary masses of floating vegetation, and one about a quarter of a mile in diameter had some small trees on it.

Signs of recent cultivation and marks where a few huts had stood were noticeable at our camping-place. I enquired where the people were; "killed, slaves, or runaways," was as usual the answer.

Ras Katanki, with small rocky points inside it, and the village of Massanga being passed, the east and west of the lake closes in. And this, I expect, is the narrowing of Livingstone's Lake Liemba.

A cowardly panic arose amongst all hands because I made sail to the breeze before a thunderstorm, in order to reach to camp Chakuola before rain came on. *April, 1874.*

Two canoes of natives were in a horrid fright at our arrival and while a few stopped and prepared for action the majority bolted off into the jungle; but we soon restored confidence and bought some fish of them.

The Wajiji guides now asked for what they termed a customary present of cloth to dress in; and although they were already well paid I complied with their request, for they were very good and useful men.

Passing Ras Chakuola on the 9th of April—the rocks near which were composed of a sort of pudding-stone looking as though it had originally been liquid clay and had become mixed with small stones—we came to the river Chakuola, and Makakomo islands, which the guides informed me had been a portion of the mainland within their remembrance. Kapoopia, the sultan of the islands, was a chief of some importance.

At Ras Makurungwe the rocks consisted of masses of granite seventy or eighty feet high with perpendicular sides; and at Kowenga island there were huge blocks strewn about in the utmost confusion.

When we landed the women and children ran into the jungle and the men cleared for action, each having his bow and half-a-dozen arrows ready and about twenty more arrows in his quiver.

April, 1874.

Squalls and rain during the night and a wild-looking morning delayed our start, and on beginning to pack up one of the askari accidentally shot himself in getting into the boat. The bullet entered under the right arm, and passing either close in front of, or behind, the shoulder-blade, came out at the lower inner angle. He was so fat that it

BROTHER ROCKS.

was difficult to determine which course it took; but the lung was not injured and there was no escape of air.

I made a couple of pads of a cambric handkerchief and bound him up, lashing his arm so that he could not move it, and though he lost much blood it was all venous, and soon stopped.

After I had given him some morphia to induce

VILLAGE OF KITATA, TANGANYIKA LAKE.

sleep, his chums differed from my treatment and gave him hot water to drink in order, as they said, to remove any bad blood in his stomach. He consequently retched most violently and the bleeding burst out again.

April, 1874.

I constantly cautioned the men against keeping their guns loaded, yet this fool used his rifle as a boat-hook, holding it by the muzzle and clawing at the gunwale of the boat with the hammer!

No imported cloth was to be seen at the village of Kitata, the people wearing skins, bark cloth, or cotton of their own manufacture.

The people suspend their clothing round the waist by rope as thick as the little finger, bound neatly with brass wire.

Their wool is sometimes anointed with oil in which red earth has been mixed, giving them the appearance of having dipped their heads in blood.

We next camped at Makukira on a river of the same name, as I was suffering from a severe pain in my eyes and was too ill to take bearings. Makukira was a large place with a ditch and stockade banked up on the outside.

The chief was profusely greased, had a patch of lampblack on his chest and forehead and wore a tiara of leopard-claws with the roots dyed red, and behind it a tuft of coarse whitish hair. A pair of leopard-skin aprons, a few circles of yellow grass below his knees, a ring of sofi on each ankle and a fly-flapper with the handle covered with beads,

April, 1874.

completed his attire—if we except the lampblack which was rubbed into all his tattoo marks.

His wives, one of whom was very good-looking, were busy getting pombé ready for him; and having poured some into a calabash and filled it up with hot water, one of them sat on a stool alongside him. Then taking the calabash on her lap she held it while he sucked the contents through a reed. He kindly sent me some of this beverage, but I was much too unwell to taste it.

Girls without children often make dolls of a calabash ornamented with beads and lash it to the back in the same manner as infants are usually carried in their country.

Children are reared at the breast until two or three years of age, and I saw one alternately sucking at nature's fount and a pombé reed; so that they may literally be said to imbibe the taste for pombé with their mother's milk.

Long knobbed walking-sticks were used by the chief and his wives, and beads and wire were common.

We went on to Kirumbu on the Mivito, where cotton is manufactured, nearly a third of the population wearing clothes of native make. It is coarse stuff something like superior gunney-bag, and the patterns are checks after the style of large shepherd's plaid with black stripes near the border, all having fringe.

As I sighted land at the end of the lake, I hoped

another day's pulling would be all that was necessary before turning.

April, 1874.

But we wanted food, the small villages not supplying enough and even Makukira being drawn almost blank. Camping that night near a village in the river Kisungi, we were again disappointed at finding food scarce and expensive.

Yet when Dr. Livingstone was here on his last journey, only about fifteen or sixteen months previously, I am told provisions were plentiful and the people had many goats. Parties of Wanyamwési and others had, however, carried off not only the goats but many people also.

The slave-trade is spreading in the interior, and will continue to do so until it is either put down with a strong hand or dies a natural death from the total destruction of the population. At present events are tending towards depopulation; for the Arabs, who had only penetrated Manyuéma a few years, already had a settlement close to Nyangwé from which parties are able to go slave-hunting still further afield.

The head chief of this place lives four days' journey inland; but at Mikisungi there was a chief named Mpara Gwina whom I called upon.

He was old and perfectly white-haired, and his office did not seem profitable for he was certainly the worst dressed of the people. His forehead and hair were daubed with vermilion, yellow, and white powder, the pollen of flowers. A tribal mark of

April, 1874. raised cuts formed a blotch on each temple, and he wore a frontlet of beads.

When I called he was busy spinning cotton with another man, while their wives and daughters sat near picking the seeds out of freshly gathered pods. The fibre was laid in heaps by the side of the chief and his friend, who—spindles in hand—were making it into yarn.

Their wooden spindles were about fourteen inches long and half an inch in diameter, with a piece of curved wood as a weight, half an inch from the top, where a small wire hook was fixed.

The cotton was first worked between the forefinger and thumb into a sort of rough tape about half a yard long, and then hooked to the spindle, which was rolled along the right thigh to give it a rapid spinning motion. The yarn was held in the left hand—the spindle hanging from it—and the right forefinger and thumb were used to prevent any irregularities in the size of the thread. As soon as a length was spun it was unhooked and wound round the spindle, and more cotton was prepared, hooked on and spun in the same manner.

The yarn turned out by these means, though coarse, is fairly strong and wonderfully regular in size. It is afterwards wound on sticks about four feet long used as shuttles in weaving.

The profile of the people was good, their noses being Roman; but all have the spreading *alæ nasi*.

The heads of some were completely covered with sofi or pipe-stem beads, each strung on a separate tuft of hair, an arrangement which must be very uncomfortable and is not at all prepossessing, having too much the appearance of scales.

April, 1874.

Those who cannot afford beads imitate the fashion by making their wool into blobs and greasing it until one cannot detect the separate fibres.

Grass leglets and bracelets made from the Upindha (brab) very neatly twisted or plaited, were very commonly worn.

Their bows were provided with a fringe of long hair at one or both ends, and were sewed over besides having the spare string wound round them. Arrows were of various lengths, not feathered or poisoned, and all knives were shaped like spear-heads.

The people had at one time grown a considerable amount of corn but the Watuta killed most of the men, and a few of that tribe who still remained in the jungle hereabouts — neither cultivating nor building huts — subsisted entirely by the chase and plunder. The hoes I saw were very large, exceeding the size of an ordinary garden spade.

I may mention that here the prefix "Ba" is used instead of "Wa" by the different tribes, such as Bafipa, Batuta.

Arabs occasionally pass inland, but no large

April, 1874. boats had been here for years and the people never saw a sail before the *Betsy* arrived.

Leaving early on the morning of the 15th of April, and passing the rivers Mundewli and Muomeesa and the villages of Kasangalowa and Mambema, we began to lose sight of the land of rocks.

On the outside of Polungo island were enormous masses, scattered and piled in the most fantastic manner—vast overhanging blocks, rocking-stones, obelisks, pyramids, and every form imaginable. The whole was overgrown with trees jutting out from every crevice or spot where soil had lodged, and from them hung creepers fifty or sixty feet long, while through this fringe there were occasional glimpses of hollows and caves.

The glorious lake with its heaving bosom lay bathed in tropical sunshine and one could scarcely imagine the scene to be a reality. It seemed as if designed for some grand transformation in a pantomime, and one almost expected the rocks to open and sprites and fairies to appear.

As I paused to gaze at the wondrous sight—all being still, without a sign of life—suddenly the long creepers began to move as some brown object quickly followed by another and another was seen. This was a party of monkeys, swinging themselves along and outdoing Leotard on the flying trapeze; and then, stopping and hanging by one paw, they chattered and gibbered at the strange sight of a boat. A shout, and they were gone more rapidly than they came, whilst the rolling echo almost equalled thunder in its intensity.

April, 1874.

In places the slightest shock of earthquake would cause masses of thousands of tons to topple down from their lofty sites and carry ruin and destruction before them.

Large cotton-plants were apparently growing wild at the camping-place, but possibly this had formerly been a clearing. The cliffs were of chalk or very white limestone split vertically, the lines as sharp as though cut with a knife.

I found it extremely difficult to keep my map correctly, as the guides changed the names most perplexingly and called an island a cape and a cape an island; while my ideas were not the clearest after so much fever and quinine.

We now came to the debatable ground between Ufipa and Ulungu.

On starting on the 16th we rounded a low point with cliffs looking exactly as though built by man. It was only at the point that this peculiarity existed, inside the cliffs were quite different. The courses, too, were as regular as possible, and where bared at top they were in a perfectly level unbroken surface, so I suppose they are innumerable small strata.

There was a deserted village here, and I saw several others which had been abandoned owing to deaths having occurred in them.

April, 1874.

Industrial settlements after the pattern of the French mission at Bagamoyo, to teach trades and cultivation, would seem to be the proper line for missionary work in this country.

In the afternoon the eclipse commenced while we were camped at Lungu. The sun was hidden in clouds, and when it became clear again rain was falling and two very perfect rainbows were formed. These faded away for three minutes from the eclipse and occurred again for a few minutes before sunset.

The diminution of light was very perceptible, and some of my men took this opportunity of stealing seven goats belonging to people living near.

There were too many concerned in the theft to discover the real offenders; but I sent the goats back with a present of beads for the owner. If one only had been stolen it would probably have been killed and eaten outside the camp. I should have known nothing of it, and no very flattering opinion of white men would have been left on the minds of the people.

Land now lay right across on the west side and we were apparently at the end of the lake. But there was a narrow arm running up about twenty miles, ending in a mass of grass through which boats cannot pass, and a river called Kirumbwé here falls into the lake.

On sighting a village all hands immediately

wanted to halt for food although a week's provisions had been laid in two days before. We were only two days out, and the boats were regularly lumbered up with bags of corn, sweet potatoes and bananas, so I would not yield to this laziness and idle excuse.

April, 1874.

We passed Ras Yamini with high cliffs having the appearance of ruined ramparts. There is no doubt they are natural formations, as enormous irregular blocks occasionally showed out; but the ruined cities of Central America have much the same appearance, as they are not of any great extent and are succeeded by masses of rocks.

A large village in front ought to have been reached on this day; but the men persisted in pulling so badly that I could no longer remain in the boat, but camped.

Small worries add immensely to the hardships of travelling. Real troubles and difficulties one faces as a matter of course. But lazy men wanting to stop when there is everything in favour of a good day's work, a cook who says that there is no dinner when one is hungry, and being constantly thwarted, annoy one and try the temper more than enough.

My pipe was, however, a great consolation, and I told my servant to bring it to me whenever he heard me pitching into any one.

Since leaving Ujiji the work had been very wearying owing to the constant, never-ceasing attention required to prevent mistakes between the different points and to make people understand my questions. And I was obliged to prove everything after all by my own observation—being so frequently told that islands were points and points islands.

As an instance of the haziness of these people's ideas I may mention that, on first seeing high land at the south end I was informed it was a large island named Kahapiongo, and I tried to fix it by bearings. On nearing the islands of that name I found them quite small, with about half-a-dozen people on them.

The guides were never able to name a place until close to it, and had very little conception of the lay of the land they had coasted along many times. Local knowledge is wonderfully good, but they seem incapable of grasping anything like a general idea.

They stared at my map and thought it a most wonderful performance; and when I said that people in England would know the shape and size of Tanganyika and the names and situation of rivers and villages by means of it, I am inclined to fancy they thought me a magician.

My telling them of the eclipse before it happened impressed them greatly.

The supposed "long arm" I found to be a myth, but I believe a river of considerable size with a very grassy mouth flows into the lake at the bottom.

Tingi-tingi is the name given to grassy places at the mouths of rivers and elsewhere if the grass is too thick for boats to pass through but not thick enough for men to walk on: *Sindi* is the name given when it will bear a man's weight. From this cause the river near Ugaga is called Sindi; but they also talk of other rivers as sindi, *e.g.* the Kirumbwé is said to be tingi-tingi with a little sindi.

Shortly after starting again we came to Kasangalowa in the Kowa—Kongono being the name of the sultan—and here saw Michikichi or palm-oil trees for the first time since leaving Ujiji.

The village was in the possession of the Watuta, the lawful inhabitants having fled to the hills.

All the Watuta men carry bows and arrows, short spears either for throwing or close quarters, a knobstick, small axe, and an oval shield of skin four feet by two feet six inches. Even the little boys carry a heavy knobstick.

They turned out in great numbers, very black and naked, to see what our business might be and seemed very friendly to us notwithstanding their character is that of universal robbers.

They enlarge the lobes of the ears like the Wagogo, carrying in them pieces of gourd and wood sometimes ornamented with beads.

The women wear a small skin apron and dispose another skin behind in a manner more fanciful than decorous; for while covering the upper part of their legs it leaves another portion of their body most fully exposed. These stern aprons are cut so as to turn down a flap—occasionally decorated with beads—to allow of a full and open rear view. It must therefore be the fashion to show that part. Perhaps their object is to prove they have no tails.

WATUTA WOMAN.

Those who can afford it wear a broad band of parti-coloured beads round the head and another round the waist.

In some cases the hair is shaven away underneath the band of beads worn round the head while allowed to grow bushy above, having exactly the appearance of a fur cap or Kilmarnock bonnet.

The people universally chip the two upper front incisors, and some chip the whole of them and extract the two centre ones in the lower jaw. The tribal mark seemed to be a line down the centre of the forehead and two on the temples, sometimes continued to the chin.

Some of the men had enormously heavy spears, generally used in elephant-hunting. The butt was larger than the rest of the haft and was made of black wood or ebony to give weight.

Wapimbwe and Watongwe live in Ufipa mixed with Bafipa. Watuta and Wapimbwe live in Ulungu as a wild people, with different chiefs, but allies of the Watuta. Kitimba is chief of all Watuta.

April, 1874.

The Watuta obtain their livelihood by the chase and settle down in any village, as they had in this one, until all their victims' food is consumed and the huts are burnt as fuel. They then make a foray on another and repeat this little game. None of the regular inhabitants attempt resistance but seek safety in flight, for Watuta fighting means indiscriminate slaughter.

Here, for the first time in Africa, I saw a woman with twins.

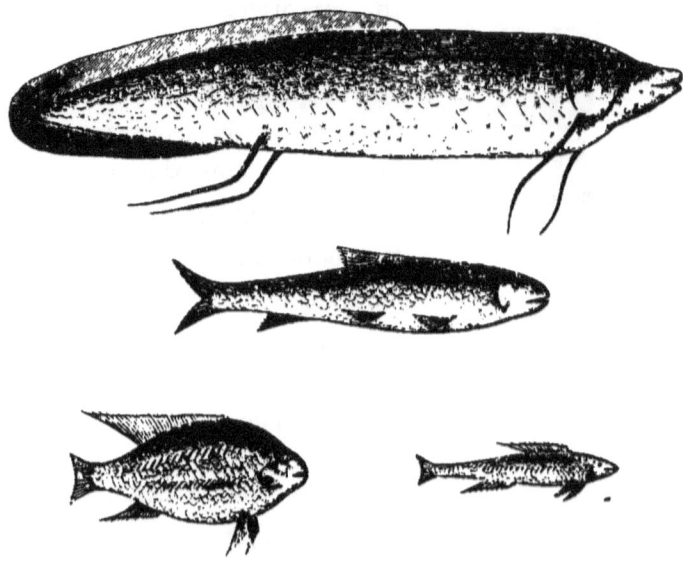

TANGANYIKA FISHES.

CHAPTER XVI.

THE ART OF POTTERY.—MY MEN GROW BOLDER.—AKALUNGA.—THE CHIEF.—A NATIVE NOTION OF PORTUGAL.—GRANARIES.—STRANGE MUTILATION BY WOMEN.—ORNAMENTS.—THE LUWAZIWA.—GORILLAS.—HILLSIDE CULTIVATION.—SPIDERS.—MOSQUITOS, BOILS, AND SORE FEET.—A STRIKE.—HOT-WATER SPRING.—WAGUHHA HAIR-DRESSING.—IDOLS.—THE LUKUGA.—RETURN TO UJIJI.—LETTERS FROM HOME.—MY MEN INDULGE FREELY.—ARAB OPINION OF THE LUALABA.—FEAR OF OPPOSITION TRADERS.—BOMBAY'S JEALOUSY.—COST OF CUTTING THE SOD IN THE LUKUGA.—I GIVE READINGS.—ARSON.—DOMESTIC JARS.—MORE ORGIES.—OFF AGAIN.

April, 1874.

IT was with pleasure that I learnt on leaving Kasangalowa on the 19th of April—for the purpose of crossing the lake and working northwards along the other shore—that there was no camping-place within an easy distance. The men would therefore be obliged to do a good day's pulling whether they wished it or not.

There was trouble in getting away on account of tingi-tingi, the boats being jammed one hundred yards from land and the water deep. We had to go backwards and forwards in small canoes—several of which were capsized causing more amusement than harm—and then to pole out for some distance.

The mountains on the south-west were so precipitous as almost to be cliffs; and many gorges

RAWLINSON MOUNTAINS.

formed by landslips and waterfalls were amongst the hills.

April, 1874.

We camped on very rough ground evidently overflowed by streams when in flood; but a place where hippopotami had been rolling afforded a smooth spot for my tent. The cliffs were red sandstone on the top and light-coloured granite towards the base.

The rains now appeared to be passing although I still saw showers amongst the hills and heard occasional thunder, and the nights were cloudy for sights.

I was much interested at Kisungi by watching a potter at her work. She first pounded with a pestle, such as they use in beating corn, enough earth and water for making one pot, until it formed a perfectly homogeneous mass. Then putting it on a flat stone she gave it a blow with her fist to form a hollow in the middle, and worked it roughly into a shape with her hands, keeping them constantly wet. She then smoothed out the finger-marks with a corn cob and polished the pot with pieces of gourd and wood—the gourd giving it the proper curves—finally ornamenting it with a sharp-pointed stick.

I went to examine this work, wondering how it would be taken off the stone and the bottom shaped, and found that no bottom had yet been formed. But after the vessel had been drying four or five hours in a shady place it was sufficiently stiff to

April, 1874.

be handled carefully, and a bottom was then worked in.

From beginning to pound the clay till the pot—holding about three gallons—was put aside to dry, occupied thirty-five minutes and providing it with a bottom might take ten minutes more.

The shapes are very graceful and wonderfully truly formed, many being like the amphora in Villa Diomed at Pompeii.

Soon after leaving camp we passed the mouth of the Luguvu, a considerable stream with a good current discolouring the water a considerable distance from its mouth; and there were numerous small landslips and water oozing from the sides of the hills.

This exceptional day's work had, according to the men's statement, quite exhausted them; so I camped early at a spot evidently much resorted to by elephants, some of the trees being quite polished from their rubbing themselves against them after bathing.

And while running along under sail close to the shore we sighted an elephant on the beach, having evidently come down to bathe. I loaded my rifle with hardened bullets and ordered all the men to get below the gunwale and keep silence, leaving a man asleep on the forecastle because I was afraid he would make some noise if aroused. But before we got within range this fellow most provokingly awoke, and catching sight of the elephant yelled out at the top of his voice, "Tembo Bwana" (Elephant, master), and away went the tembo into the jungle flapping his big ears like a rabbit bolting into his burrow.

April, 1874.

There was very heavy thunder during the night and the echoes exceeded anything I have ever heard.

TEMBO BWANA.

I managed to make a move for Kipimbwé although there was a heavier sea and surf than I had previously seen, for it blew hard right on the shore—an open beach with no grass. Happily the men no longer heeded that which would have given them a terrific fright at starting.

On visiting Akalunga I found it one of the largest villages I had seen in Africa. The chief, Miriro, was a very old man with a large white

April, 1874.

beard, but whiskers and moustaches shaved. A number of Arab slaves and Wangwana were here for trade; also one Mrima man who left Bagamoyo soon after us and Unyanyembé at the same time. He came direct here by crossing the lake at Makakomo's, and had arrived about a month.

Many of the women dressed in the same fashion as at Kasangalowa, but the traders import a quantity of cloth. Some of the people wore small skull caps made of beads.

Old Miriro paid me a visit, putting on a fez cap instead of the greasy handkerchief he usually wore, and a robe of red and black Joho. He was much astonished at the breech-loaders and revolvers, and wanted me to present him with a gun and to remain to mend a musical box.

Although a king he did not act royally, and made no return present for a very good cloth I sent him. However, he seemed friendly and assured me that the year in which the first white man had come there would always be remembered as a great year.

Food for the men was plentiful, but I could obtain no eggs, fowls, milk, or ripe bananas, the latter being cooked and eaten when green.

One of the Wanyamwési began talking of the Portuguese, saying they were a people like the Wazungu and lived on the coast and had two kings. The chief one was a woman called "Maria," —evidently the Blessed Virgin—and they had

GRANARIES.

houses with her figure in it. The other king was Moeneputo, the African name for the King of Portugal. *April, 1874*

The granaries of these parts deserve notice. They are built on posts raising the floors about

KING MIRIRO AND HIS GRANARY.

three feet from the ground, and are from four to twelve feet in diameter, while some of the larger may be twenty feet high exclusive of the conical roof. Those for old corn are plastered and have under the eaves a small hole for access, reached by a notched trunk used as a ladder. Those for fresh

April, 1874.

corn are made of canes about eleven feet long and two inches apart with hoops of the same material at every two or three feet, thus allowing the air to pass through freely and prevent heating.

Many of the women here and at Kasangalowa had not even the usual negro apology for a nipple to their breasts, but only a hole. I was rather astonished and was told that they scar themselves thus for ornament. I should have thought it too painful to willingly mutilate themselves in this manner, and had supposed that it might be a punishment and still have my doubts on the subject. I may remark that it was usually the best-looking that were thus deformed.

Pretty little ivory combs are made here for the small price of four strings of beads, and when not in use are worn in the hair as an ornament and look rather well.

Solid bracelets and anklets of iron and brass like the Indian bangle are common, besides the ordinary beads and sambo; and the majority band the leg below the knee with small circles of plaited grass which take the place of wire and other ornaments with those who cannot afford the latter. The ropes for suspending the loin cloth are often covered with beads of various colours instead of wire, and many men wear broad leather belts.

As a fair wind favoured us the next day we made sail, the *Pickle* using a mat and loin cloths.

I went into the stream of the Luwaziwa to determine its course, and found that it flowed into the lake. It is said to have its source in the country of Maubembé and to wind very much, caravans from Kasengé having to cross it three times on their way to Akalunga. I at first thought that it ran out of the lake, it looked so like a clear entrance, but when we opened it properly there was the regular grass mouth and sand-banks.

I believe the lake to be fed by springs in its bed in addition to the numerous rivers and torrents; as in several places where landslips had occurred the water was bursting out between the stones and trickling down into the lake. The country was like a huge sponge full of water.

Game was very plentiful; but I was so lame as to be obliged to be carried to and from the boat and consequently could not go out shooting. The boil which lamed me on the road to Ujiji had formed a large sluggish sore, and in addition I had prickly heat rather badly.

Numerous small streams and torrents were to be seen as we came along and the hills were bold but not very high—from four hundred to six hundred feet. No villages were in sight, as all the people lived inland behind the hills; but some canoes were hauled up in one or two places and their owners could not have been far off.

On the 24th of April a good breeze again helped us along, though it was rather puffy in the vicinity of the hills. An hour was lost through the men

April, 1874.

stopping to land, when they looted a fisherman's hut and I had the greatest trouble to get the things returned. Bombay was amongst them eating the stolen fish.

Passed Runangwa Ras and river of the same name—much smaller than the Malagarazi—flowing into the lake; very rocky, high hills, a thousand feet and more, covered with trees to their summits. The rocks were granite, and light-coloured soft sandstone.

Here I saw some gorillas (Soko), black fellows looking larger than men. Before I could get a shot the boat slipped round a point which covered them, and on putting back to have another look at them they had vanished. They are said by the natives to build a fresh house every day.

For three hours we were searching for a camping-place, but with a multiplicity of rocks and no beach or place where it was possible to lay up the boats, we met with constant disappointments. I was greatly consoled at knowing that we were getting over the ground more quickly than if camps were easily found, although an hour's daylight would have been valuable to me for working at my map after lying up for the night.

The next day we camped at Katupi village where ivory was ten doti a frasilah and good slaves five doti each. A Mngwana trading there told me that from Chakuola they get to Unyanyembé in about twenty days.

From this place we passed many small villages and shambas with cultivation on the sides of hills as steep as Swiss terraces; only instead of being regularly terraced, there were irregular retaining walls of loose stones at intervals, and the soil was left nearly at its natural slope. The people working there looked like flies on a wall.

April, 1874.

Five large canoes from Ujiji were reported to be in front, and the people seemed less afraid than formerly to hold intercourse with us. A large and crowded canoe came off to look at us, and some man of importance going the other way in a canoe with twelve paddlers was also brave enough to venture a few hundred yards from the shore in order to have a stare.

Much cultivation and small villages without stockades and huts being seen in all directions, I inferred that we were entering a more peaceful country.

As we slipped along before a good south-easterly breeze I took in a reef by twisting the tack of the sail into a rope for a couple of feet and lashing it, and a second reef by a lashing round the yard-arm. With a good sea running and the wind aft, the boat rolled about like a porpoise and prevented my getting bearings.

Indeed, I became rather anxious to find a good camping-place, for with such a breeze and sea the boats would have come to grief at once had they touched the rocks. We therefore pulled in close

April, 1874.

to Kanenda and settled down for the night near the village Mona Kalumwe.

A great disturbance was caused during the night by some natives quarrelling with my men about a stolen cloth which was now claimed by the rightful owner. On being found it was returned, but the thief had bolted into the jungle. Still that did not save him, for I had punishment parade in the morning and gave him a thrashing, and young Bilâl, who was mixed up with the affair, received the same.

I was unable to make any reparation to the man from whom the cloth was stolen for the trouble and annoyance he had suffered, as he did not wait for the small present I intended to have made him, but disappeared from the camp immediately he recovered his property.

The breeze now seemed inclined to fall light although there was a considerable sea; but we rounded Ras Mirrumbi and passed several torrents and villages.

I here noticed enormous spiders' webs on some of the trees, a few being almost covered with them.

The *Pickle* did not come up with us that evening and I became rather anxious about her safety; and, on nothing being seen of her the next morning (April 28th), began to think of turning back in search of her. But in the afternoon she hove in sight, and it appeared that her crew being frightened at the sea had camped before Kapoppo.

In a deep inlet near the mouth of Lovuma river I found the remains of a large Arab camp, and also two very large boats—one pulling twenty and the other eighteen oars and fitted with masts—hauled up under a shed. They were the property of Jumah Merikani, who had gone into Msama's country to trade.

April, 1874.

Jumah Merikani first began trading past here when Burton was at Ujiji, and had now been fifteen years at it. He is said to keep a permanent gang of Wanyamwési porters, and only to stay at Ujiji long enough to sell and despatch his ivory and lay in a fresh stock of trade goods.

The people seemed very friendly, and one jolly-looking old fellow who was doing duty as chief while the latter was away on a tour of inspection came and salaamed most profoundly to me and rubbed dust on his chest and arms, that being the customary way of paying homage.

Heads and tails were adorned here much the same as before.

Large mosquitoes were constantly biting in the daytime and my back was covered with boils. I could neither sit nor lie down in comfort, and the soreness of my feet prevented my making much use of them. My stay was not altogether enjoyable.

I should mention that I met wild grapes here for the first time on my journey.

The night of the 29th of April promised to be so fine that I decided to sleep in the boat in a little land-locked bay, instead of under canvas, and the men lay out in the open air without building any huts. A sudden change to rain consequently brought with it some hours of discomfort and misery. The boats were half-filled with water and the men's spare gear was all swamped.

I gave them two hours to dry their clothing and do their cooking, and seeing no signs of a move at the expiration of that time I sung out, "Paka, Paka" (Pack up). The reply I received was, "Kesho" (To-morrow). On looking for Bombay to ascertain what this meant I found him quietly sitting in the other boat under an awning, doing nothing.

He excused himself by saying, "What can I do? The men say they won't go; they are afraid." I replied, "Bring me one who says no, and I'll punish him;" but his answer was, "I can't; they all say they won't."

This was too much to bear, so, bad legs or not, I was quickly out of the boat, and picking up the first bit of wood I saw told the men to pack. They began while I stood by them, but immediately I went to others stopped again. It was evidently time for action, so I struck out right and left and soon made them clear out. Bombay was of no more service than a log of wood; indeed, not half so useful as the persuasive piece I had just fisted.

After getting away the men seemed in a very good-humour and much more jolly than usual and

I began to think they enjoyed their thrashing although one or two got some shrewd knocks.

April, 1874.

Later in the day I ascertained the reason of the men not wishing to move. They had heard of a trading party on the other side of the neck of land between Ras Tembwé and the main and wanted to exchange visits. We saw the canoe of the traders, and also a small party who had been away from Ujiji for about six months to shoot elephants.

The land about here was low, and the bearings I took were not of much value.

My expectations and hopes were now greatly raised by the guides promising to show me the outlet of the lake on the following day.

It appears that Speke did not get quite far enough down; and Livingstone, coming from Ma Kazembé's town, passed its mouth in a canoe without noticing it and on going to Manyuéma did not come sufficiently far south.

No Arab at Ujiji seemed to have any knowledge of this outlet, which appears to lie just between two of their routes and out of both. I thought, however, that the Wajiji had made no mistake about my questions, for they had noticed how particular I was in ascertaining the direction in which a stream flowed whenever there was any doubt on the matter.

We now passed Ras Kalomwe, and the river Kavagwé, two hundred yards wide and two

May, 1874.

fathoms deep in the middle, having an almost imperceptible outward current.

May-day broke upon us most gloriously. The surrounding country was also very beautiful, with small cliffs and some open park-like spaces with clumps of fine trees.

On rounding Ras Niongo, we shortened sail and went on shore to look at a reported hot-water spring. After half an hour's tramp through very long thick grass—which to me was pain and grief—we arrived at the swampy edge of the lake, where a few bubbles were rising.

The thermometer showed the same temperature in this water as in the shade—96°—and I arrived at the conclusion that the hot spring had only a slight foundation in fact. But I afterwards heard from others who had visited it, that when in full activity the spring has been sufficiently hot to scald one. It had, perhaps, a slight flavour as of soda-water.

The man who conducted us to this bubbling water, asked for some beads that he might make an offering to the spirit of the place. He evidently thought the spirit was easily satisfied, for he only threw a bead or two into the water and retained the remainder as his own reward.

No reliance whatever could be placed in the guides, for having heard from the people that a large river called Lukuga flows into the lake near Kasengé they at once said the same, though they had hitherto declared that it was an outflow. The chief, Luliki—who, by the way, was so excessively fat that at the first glance I thought he was of the other sex owing to his pendent breasts—cheered me on my visiting him by asserting that the Lukuga ran out from the lake.

May, 1874.

HEADS OF WAGUHHA AND OTHER LAKE TRIBES.

The Waguhha dress their heads very elaborately, dividing their hair into four parts, drawing it over pads, and making the ends into four plaits with the assistance of false hair when necessary. These plaits are disposed in a cross, and numerous skewers or pins of polished iron are thrust into the hair, and some wear a double row of cowries.

They also carry in their hair the knives used for tattooing and wear polished iron strips, crossed to form an arch as in a royal crown. Little extinguisher-shaped ornaments are attached to the ends of the plaits; and flat-headed iron, ivory, and shell-headed pins are used.

The plaits are plastered and smoothed with red earth and oil, and although the effect is striking the fashion is dirty. Some twist their hair into the form of four ram's horns, the one in front being turned backwards.

This was the first place where I had seen any likeness to idols. And here several men wore round their necks a little figure with a carved head—the body being a sort of cone with rings and two or three feet—and a hole through the neck for the string by which it was hung.

On the 3rd of May there was a slashing breeze freshening up from the eastward, and I made sail with many a hope that I might in a few hours find myself in the outflowing Lukuga.

Shortly before noon I arrived at its entrance, more than a mile across but closed by a grass-grown sand-bank, with the exception of a channel three hundred or four hundred yards wide. Across this there is a sill where the surf breaks heavily at times, although there is more than a fathom of water at its most shallow part.

The chief visited me and informed me that the river was well known to his people, who often travelled for more than a month along its banks, until it fell into a larger river, the Lualaba; and that in its course it received the Lulumbiji and many small streams. No Arab, the chief said, had been down the river, and traders did not visit this place, all beads and cloth required being obtained by sending to Ujiji.

May, 1874.

It rained very hard in the morning, but, in

ENTRANCE TO LUKUGA, OR MARIE ALEXANDROVNA.

company with the chief I went four or five miles down the river until navigation was rendered impossible owing to the masses of floating vegetation. It might be possible, however, to cut passages for canoes.

Here the depth was three fathoms; breadth, six hundred yards; current, one knot and a half, and sufficiently strong to drive us well into the edge of the vegetation.

May, 1874.

This first block was said to continue for four or five miles, when an open channel of about the same length would be found; and that for a very great distance alternate choked and clear portions existed.

I noticed that the embouchures of some small streams flowing into the river were unmistakably turned from the lake, and that the weed set in the same direction. Wild date-palms grew thickly down the river.

Early the following day I continued my observations of the entrance to the river. Inside the bar or sill already mentioned there were three, four, and five fathoms obtained; and three fathoms close alongside the grass which barred our progress.

I wanted the chief to commence cutting a passage through the grass, offering to leave beads to pay the men. He did not wish to have anything left with him, for he remarked his people would say, "You take all these things from the white man and only give us a little and make us work for it."

His proposal was that when I returned I should pay the people who worked, daily, and then they would understand. He said he wished a trade road passed by his village to bring traders there.

After pulling an hour and a half the breeze freshened up almost in our teeth, so I put into a convenient little inlet, which I discovered to be part of the other river. It was all swamp, marsh, or low flat plains inside a long bank with some small openings; deep water in places, shoals, sand-banks, long grass, &c.

May, 1874.

I suppose the drift matter of the lake which gravitates towards this outlet forms the banks and morass owing to the want of a passage for it.

A fair instance of this was given during the seven or eight hours we were here; a large quantity of drift-wood having come in and worked away into the grass without leaving any sign of its passage. The inlet in which we lay was only a break in the bank, and the water works through the grass into the Lukuga.

I entertained strong hopes of being enabled to undertake the work I so much desired, of tracing the course of the Lukuga. But at Ujiji not a guide or interpreter could be obtained for that route, and not a man would follow me alone.

And when I began to estimate the cost of cutting a channel through the grass and of buying canoes, I found the necessary expenditure so heavy that I confess I did not feel myself justified in incurring it. For I firmly believed that the stream was too considerable to be lost in marshes or be merely a backwater. I had also the word of the chief who accompanied me on entering the river that his people had travelled for months along its banks.

The entrance is situated in the only break in the hills that surround the lake, the mountains of Ugoma ending abruptly ten or twelve miles north

May, 1874.

of Kasengé, whilst those that encircle the southern end trend away to the westward from Ras Mirrumbi, leaving a large undulating valley between the two ranges.

When passing down south on the eastern shore of the lake, near Ras Kungwé, the guides pointed to this gap in the mountains and asserted that there the outlet of the lake was to be found.

At various points on my journey afterwards I obtained corroborative evidence—to which I shall make further allusion—of the river joining the Lualaba from people who asserted they had travelled great distances along its banks.

Leaving the inlet we made for Ras Mulango and camped there, touching the following day at Kasengé on the mainland. We then went on to a deep inlet in the eastern side of Kivira island to prepare for crossing the lake, which we did the next day and arrived at Machachézi, where we found a large party bound for Manyuéma, under charge of Muinyi Hassani, a Mrima and a slave of Syde ibn Habib's.

Another day took us beyond Jumah Merikani's settlement, and the next, May 9th, to Ujiji.

On arrival I was gladdened by the receipt of letters from home, nearly a year old; and the packet having been opened by Murphy at Mpanga Sanga on January 12th, he enclosed a message that he was getting on well.

These letters had a curious escape. The caravan

by which they were forwarded from Unyanyembé by Said ibn Salim was dispersed by a party of robbers who afterwards attacked another and stronger caravan and were beaten off with the loss of some of their numbers. On the body of one of the killed this packet of letters was found and brought on to me at Ujiji.

May, 1874.

All hands managed to get drunk on their return, and a complaint reached me that they entered a woman's house and appropriated her pombé. Bilâl the younger made himself particularly offensive outside my verandah. And when I sent for Bombay in the morning he replied that he was sick; the truth being that he had a terribly bad head from over-indulgence in pombé. How they made themselves drunk on that liquor I could never understand.

Amongst the news which reached me was that the men I sent to Unyanyembé were in the vicinity of Uvinza in company with an Arab caravan. They had been attacked by Mirambo's men (or heard of them) on their way to Unyanyembé, and went round by Kawendi instead of taking the direct route.

The donkeys had reduced themselves to four during my absence, my riding donkey being unfortunately amongst the defunct ones.

I had many long yarns with the Arabs who knew these parts—Mohammed ibn Salib, Mohammed ibn Gharib, Syde Mezrui, Abdallah ibn Habib, and Hassan ibn Gharib—and learned that in their opinion the Lualaba is the Kongo, though whence they got this idea I could not ascertain.

One man said he went due north (!) fifty-five marches and came to where the water was salt and ships came from the sea, and white men lived there who traded much in palm oil and had large houses.

Fifty-five marches, say five hundred miles + three hundred to Nyangwé=eight hundred, gives about the distance to the Yellala cataracts.

This looks something like the Kongo and West Coast merchants, although the direction is evidently wrong.

Abdallah ibn Habib and Syde Mezrui said palm oil and cowries were mentioned as being amongst the trade articles, with ivory, brass wire and beads.

I tried to get a map drawn amongst them, but north and south, east and west, and all distances were irretrievably lost in a couple of minutes.

The Lukuga tastes the same as the Tanganyika, not salt, but peculiar, and *not* sweet and light like the other rivers; but the further I enquired the more contradictory the answers became.

I expect that in the dry season, or when the lake is at its lowest level, very little water leaves by the Lukuga. Some Arabs said it joined the Lualaba between Moero and Kamalondo. Below Nyangwé the Lualaba is called Ugarowwa, and is said to be in places "as wide as the Tanganyika," and full of islands, some having five hundred or six hundred men living on them together with their wives and families.

May, 1874.

They said they did not wish to give any information about it here, and that which I had received was wrong and intended to mislead; for finding I had some defined ideas on the subject they were anxious I should not know too much.

They promised to tell everything when on the road, but they are afraid of opposition traders making an appearance. Already it is getting too crowded and they know not where to make fresh openings. The Egyptians to the north, or, as they call them, Toorkis, are known to them and they wish to avoid clashing with them.

Hassan ibn Gharib said he offered to take Livingstone from Nyangwé to the place where ships come—as he was about to make the journey —for one thousand dollars, but he refused.

They also told me that a large canoe might be obtained near Nyangwé to go the whole way from there by water. It was enough to puzzle the clearest mind.

As Bombay and my servant could never agree the latter now wanted to leave me on that account. Bombay was very well in his peculiar way, but neither the "Angel" of Colonel Grant nor the "Devil" of Mr. Stanley. I generally found after yielding to him that I should have done far better to have adhered to my first intention. He did not like any one to have my ear but himself; and was as jealous as the green-eyed monster itself. He slandered Issa, and made accusations against Mohammed Malim which I found to be false. However, I was compelled to put up with his failings, for I should have lost a number of men if I had sent him away.

In that part of the lake explored by me I found ninety-six rivers flowing in besides torrents and springs, and one, the Lukuga, going out.

The more I enquired into the matter the more laborious and costly the work of cutting away the vegetation on the Lukuga was represented to be; for in some parts the floating sod is said to be six feet thick, and no sooner is the surface cut away than a further quantity floats up from underneath the adjoining grass.

I was now only waiting for the men from Unyanyembé; and each evening I spent some hours reading "Suahili Tales" to the Arabs—having shown the book to Syde Mezrui in a thoughtless moment. A large audience always awaited me, and as they enjoyed it thoroughly I felt it repaid them somewhat for the kindness they had shown me, and I was therefore pleased to do it though it was very tiring work.

On the 15th of May some people—by way of amusement or more probably with the object of thieving in the confusion caused—set fire to Bilâl's house during the night. Worse still the door was fastened outside; but fortunately the men who usually slept in the house were not there on this occasion. I was not able to discover the perpetrators of this outrage.

May, 1874.

The next day I held a sale of my Joho and large cloths, and the commoner kinds went very well. To provide my men with some clothes I then purchased fifteen pieces of other cloth of nine doti each, at twenty-eight dollars apiece. And to prevent the *certainty* of starving and to pay Wajiji for bringing back canoes from the other side I bought twenty frasilah of beads at fifty dollars a frasilah—a large price, but it was a case of "give it, or give up the work."

If I had not been robbed these purchases might have been avoided; but theft and the non-arrival of stores left behind compelled me to make them.

When on the other side I intended—metaphorically speaking—to "burn my boats," so that there should be no retreating or looking back.

Several men pretended to be too ill to start, the fact being that they were afraid, so I gave these timid ones their discharge.

All my men seemed inclined to celebrate their last days at Ujiji by a series of drunken orgies, and Bombay being annoyed, on returning home one night from some festivities, at finding that Mrs. Bombay had only just arrived from a tea party tried to "reorganize her," but with much the same result as befell Artemus Ward.

314　　　　　　　ACROSS AFRICA.　　　　　[Chap.

May, 1874.

During the domestic struggle they upset a box of singo-mazzi beads—made of opal-glass and the size of pigeons' eggs—and rendered the greater portion of them worthless by cracks and stars.

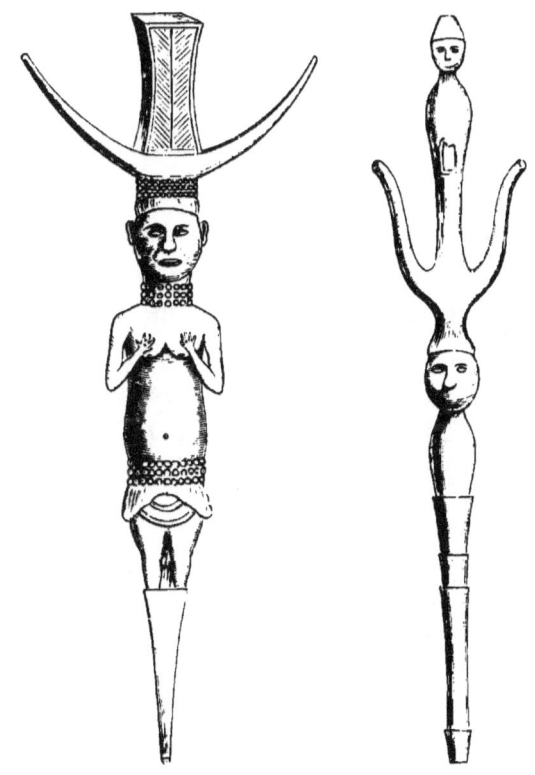

BOW STANDS OF WAGUHHA.

Some other drunken rascals ripped all the caulking out of the canoes to occasion delay, and four days were wasted in re-caulking them although the work might have been completed in a day.

And when the canoes were ready the Wajiji who were to bring them back from Kasengé were not forthcoming.

May, 1874.

Thus it was the 22nd of May before we made a move. Even then I was obliged to put in behind the first point and send back for several missing men and rifles, and to collect the return crew of Wajiji.

My servant Mohammed Malim and Bombay were so perpetually fighting that for the sake of peace I gave Mohammed charge of the box containing Livingstone's and my own journals, selecting Jumah Wadi Nassib for the office of valet and factotum. And most invaluable he proved.

The men were so fearfully lazy and shaky in consequence of their debauch at Ujiji that four days were occupied in getting to Ras Kabogo. They then complained that the sun was too powerful for the long pull across the lake in the daytime, and I had to wait until after sunset.

When day dawned we were a long way to leeward of the Kabengé islands, and it was blowing strong from the S.E., with a heavy sea running, but we reached Kivira in the *Betsy* during the forenoon. The *Pickle*, however, was not in sight, so I camped on the mainland the following morning to await her arrival.

There the Wajiji crews deserted with the *Betsy* and Syde's boat, and when the *Pickle* arrived on the evening of the 29th her return crew had also bolted,

May, 1874. and I was obliged to engage a crew of Waguhha to take her back.

Absentees and making arrangements for serving out loads, &c., detained me here until Sunday, the 31st of May.

BAY IN KIVIRA ISLAND.

CHAPTER XVII.

HOPEFUL PROSPECTS.—RUANDA.—COPPER.—BOMBAY'S INGENUITY.—AN ACCIDENT.—LAST VIEW OF TANGANYIKA.—DISHONEST FELLOW-TRAVELLERS.—MÉKÉTO.—A BRUTAL SLAVE-DEALER.—DRESS AND ORNAMENTS.—WEAPONS.—FISH-DEALERS.—RIVER-SIDE SCENERY.—GAME.—SKULKING CARRIERS.—BOWL-MAKING.—INDIARUBBER.—A TRYING MARCH.—FETISH HUTS.—A GOOD SAMARITAN.—MY MEN WANT TO TURN BACK.—"MAKING BROTHERS."—AN ARTIST IN OILS.—FEARFUL IMPRECATIONS.—MUSICAL INSTRUMENTS.—MRS. PAKWANYWA.—PERFORATION OF UPPER LIPS.—DRESS.—TATTOOING.—CHARMS.—A HOT STREAM.—A MIXED CARAVAN.

THE cheering hope of getting boats at Nyangwé and of floating down the unknown waters of the Kongo to the West Coast in two or three months, rallied my spirits to the highest pitch as I started on my first journey west of Tanganyika.

May, 1874.

Syde Mezrui had assured me that he could procure canoes almost immediately on my arrival at Nyangwé, as he was friendly with chiefs who possessed many. This was, I considered, a great point in his favour when I engaged him as a guide, because none of my men would have followed me west unless accompanied by some person well acquainted with the road.

Passing over very steep hills—the last spurs of the mountains of Ugoma which end abruptly over the lake—and across some small torrents we reached Ruanda, the capital of Uguhha. It is a

May, 1874. considerable town situated on a very fertile, flat, alluvial plain extending from the mountains of Ugoma to the river Lukuga, and intersected by the Lugumba and smaller streams flowing into the lake.

The populace turned out to stare at me, the

HEAD OF UGUHHA WOMAN.

crowd forming quite a lane as I passed through the place; and an unfortunate sheep getting hemmed in just before me heralded my approach by a frantic baaing which gave rather a ludicrous aspect to the scene.

On leaving the town I sat down to allow the caravan to overtake me, and then continuing the march for a short distance went into camp after crossing a stream which must be of a considerable size in the rains.

May, 1874.

In the afternoon a messenger informed me that the chief would call on me. But soon afterwards I heard with some regret that he and S.P.Q.R. were so greatly under the influence of the rosy god that any attempt at reaching my camp would be attended with very serious difficulty. The visit was therefore abandoned.

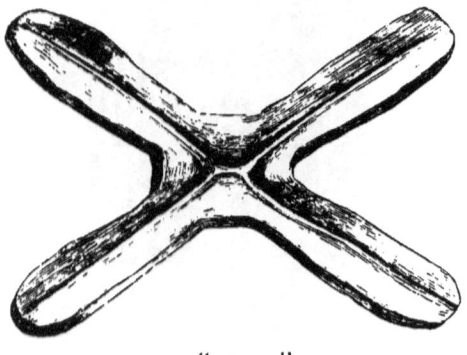

A "HANDA."

My efforts at obtaining copper in exchange for singo-mazzi were somewhat hampered by the discovery that in the free fight arising between Mr. and Mrs. Bombay, on the attempted re-organization of the lady, most of them had been rendered unmarketable. But four or five pieces of copper and some goats were given for those that remained undamaged.

This copper comes from Urua in pieces called "handa," varying in weight from two and a half to three pounds. They are cast in the rough shape of a St. Andrew's cross, and the diagonal measurement is from fifteen to sixteen inches, while the arms are about two inches wide and half an inch thick. Many of them have a raised rib along the centre of the arms.

These were said to be in great demand in Manyuéma and singo-mazzi were useless beyond Uguhha.

To avoid the necessity of employing extra men to assist further in carrying our stores, as on the road from Kasengé, I distributed a load of beads as a month's rations in advance and opened and issued a box of cartridges.

What the men did with their ammunition it was difficult to understand. At Bagamoyo I served out a hundred and thirty rounds of ball cartridge, and at Unyanyembé twenty-five per gun besides blank, yet now many had not even a single cartridge. They seemed to think themselves remarkably clever in getting rid of them, and came with a grin on their faces, saying, "Hapana Bwana" (There are none, master).

By this reduction of loads I thought it would be possible to get along without further trouble, but Bombay exercised an almost fiendish ingenuity in making work and upsetting my plans.

Out of loads which I had broken up and distributed amongst the askari, and of shot, wads, and cartridges belonging to my own guns which I put into the lighter loads in order to equalise the weight of all, he made extra ones. And when I ordered the start in the morning he reported that four loads were unprovided with carriers!

June, 1874.

Rearranging matters delayed our moving, and our next camp was not reached until nearly two o'clock after a heavy march under a most powerful sun. The thermometer, in partial shade under a tree, registered 131°.

It was all the more trying from our having to walk through stinking fœtid mud at some marshy spots.

At noon we forded the Lugumba forty yards wide and mid-thigh deep, running two and a half knots, with the water glittering in the sun from the number of particles of quartz held in suspension.

Thus far we had skirted the base of the landward spurs of the southern end of the mountains of Ugoma; but now they were left and a small independent line of hills was before us, forming the watershed between the Lugumba and Lukuga.

A painful accident occurred to one of the pagazi when crossing a deep but narrow nullah. He unfortunately stumbled, and in falling forward one of the sticks forming the cradle of his load ran into his eye, completely destroying the eyeball and lacerating the lid. I wished to apply a cold-water dressing, but he said he wanted "stronger medicine" than water; so I handed him over to the care of a native doctor in a village near the camp. His treatment consisted of a plaister of mud and dirt, and his fee was forty strings of beads.

As this poor fellow was totally incapacitated from carrying a load and some other men were suffering from the effects of excesses at Ujiji, I tried to procure the services of some Waguhha as carriers to Mékéto, where our next halt was to be. Some volunteered to go but afterwards hauled off, so I served out more beads as rations—making an advance till the end of July—and redistributed loads, giving the sick men light weights according to their powers.

A sharp touch of fever, brought on by exposure to the sun on the march from Ruanda, added greatly to the worry and trouble I experienced in managing matters.

From this place we moved on the 5th of June for Mékéto. On our two days' journey we passed over many hills and crossed rivulets flowing into the Lugumba and Lukuga, the valley of which could be plainly seen running away to the W.S.W. From the highest of these hills—the day before reaching Mékéto—I had a last view of the Tanganyika, a patch of bright blue backed by sombre masses of mountains near Ras Kungwé.

We saw many tracks of big game, and where a large herd of elephants had passed the scene of destruction was amazing.

CAMP AT MÉKÉTO.

A small but dishonest party of Warua, carrying oil to the lake to exchange for the salt of Uvinza, camped near us, and in the morning all my goats excepting Dinah and one given me at Ujiji were missing. The Warua had also departed.

June, 1874.

Mékéto lies in a broad, deep valley, drained by the Kaça, an affluent of the Lukuga, and viewed

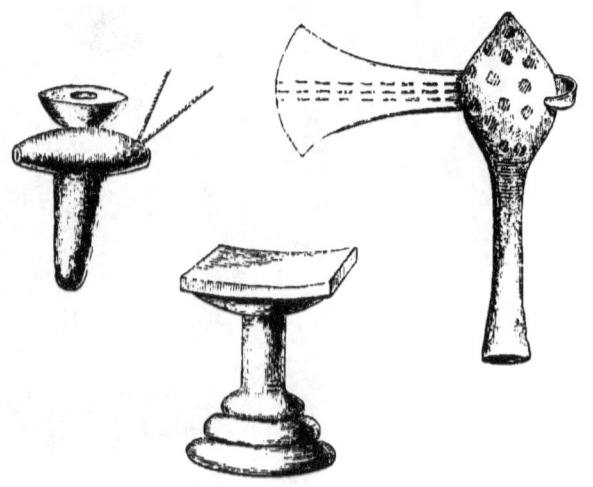

WHISTLE, HATCHET, AND PILLOW.

from the hill which forms its eastern side is almost perfect in its rural beauty. Many fields of green matama and cassava, contrasting with the already sun-dried yellow grass; tiny hamlets of thatched huts clustering at the foot of groves of fine trees, with wreathes of pale blue smoke curling up from the fires; and in the foreground a line of heavy vegetation along the Kaça which here and there

June, 1874.

reflected a ray of the sun as from a surface of burnished silver, combined in making a most beautiful scene.

Here we remained three days to obtain supplies and carriers for the journey to Kwamrora Kaséa, five marches off, as a number of the men pleaded illness to avoid carrying their loads.

During the stay the chief sent civil messages with excuses for not coming to see me on account of the distance. I also received from him a fat goat for which I, of course, sent a present in return and paid his messengers. He did me further good service in providing carriers.

A native slave-dealer brought into camp a little boy of ten or eleven with his neck in a slave-fork, and wanted to sell him. The poor child had evidently been brutally used, and was crying so bitterly that my first impulse was to set him free and give his master a sound thrashing. Yet, knowing that directly my back was turned any punishment would be repaid to the child with interest, I had to content myself with ordering off the brutal dealer.

People thronged the camp, bringing groundnuts, corn, sweet potatoes, and other articles of food for sale.

They were chiefly women, the men being away on journeys; for, like the Warua of whom they are a branch, they are a travelling and trading race.

DRESS AND ORNAMENTS.

June, 1874.

The women wore their hair after the fashion of those at the entrance of the Lukuga already described. Their ornaments consisted of coiled bracelets of brass wire, bangles of iron, brass, and copper round their ankles, strings of large singomazzi round their necks and waists, and a band of cowries or small beads bound around their heads.

The upper part of the forehead was often painted in stripes of vermilion and black, which had not such an unpleasing effect as might be supposed.

Round the waist was a piece of fringed grass cloth about eighteen inches deep and open in front, but in the hiatus they wore a narrow apron reaching to the knees and frequently ornamented by lines of cowries or beads down the centre.

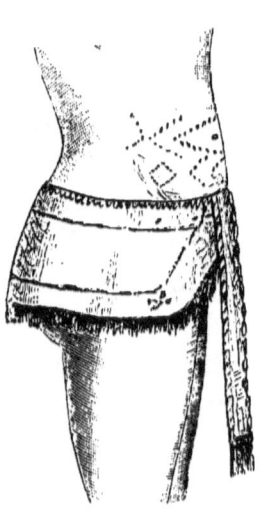

DRESS AND TATTOOING OF WOMAN OF UGUHHA.

The hoes used in this district are large and heavy, but their hatchets are the smallest and most useless I ever saw, the blade being only an inch and a half wide. Their arrows are, however, broad-headed, deeply barbed, and poisoned.

All the men carry whistles with which they signal to each other on the road.

Some Warua arrived whilst we were here,

June, 1874.
having dried fish and the scented oil of the mpafu-tree for sale; and it occurred to me as curious that although the Tanganyika abounds in fish, the people dry only the small minnow-like "dagaa,"

MRUA FISHMONGER.

and are always ready to buy that brought a distance of a hundred and fifty miles or more by the Warua.

After leaving Mékéto we did not make another halt until the 16th of June, when we reached the

CROSSING THE LUGUNGWA RIVER.

[PAGE 327, Vol. I.

village of Pakwanywa, chief of Ubûdjwa, one long march beyond Kwamrora Kaséa.

June, 1874.

Streams without number were passed during this march. The principal, the Rubumba—one of the most important affluents of Luama and often confused with the Lugumba—we crossed twice, and found it so wide and deep that it was necessary to throw a rope of creepers across for the men to hold on by to prevent their being swept away.

Many of the streams were particularly beautiful, especially the Lugungwa, a short way below the ford, where it had cut a channel fully fifty feet deep in the soft sandstone and not more than eight feet wide at the top. On the projections of its cliff-like sides most lovely ferns and mosses grew, and large trees on both banks mingled their branches and formed a perfect arch of verdure over the river.

The hills along which we had been marching now joined the Ugoma mountains, having hitherto been separated by the valley of the Lugumba.

Tracks of all kinds of large game—except giraffes, which do not exist much to the westward of Unyanyembé—were very numerous; and on a sandy island the tracks of buffalo were so thick as to give the appearance of a large herd having been penned there. The grass on each side of the path was almost too thick and heavy to penetrate in search of sport.

And it was also needful for me to keep in rear

of the caravan in order to prevent my men from straggling. With all my care they often eluded me and lay hidden in the jungle till I had passed in order to indulge in skulking.

The men carrying my tent and bath were especially prone to this habit although their loads were light, and I frequently waited long after camp was reached for these necessary appliances to come to the front.

On this march I first saw the mpafu, from which the scented oil is obtained. It is a magnificent tree, often thirty feet and more in circumference and rising to eighty or a hundred feet before spreading and forming a head, the branches of which are immense. The oil is obtained by soaking the fruit—which has some resemblance to an olive—for a few days in large pits of water, and when the oil collects on the surface it is skimmed off. It is usually of a reddish colour, very pure and clear, with an agreeable smell.

Under the bark are great masses of scented gum, used by the natives in fumigating themselves.

Besides the mpafu there were several other trees perfectly new to me, one having a soft dense wood out of which the natives make beautifully finished bowls.

A man whom I watched at this work had felled two or three trees and cut them into logs of about the same length as the diameter of the trunk, *i.e.* from one to two feet. These he split into halves, and with a very sharp and small single-handed adze made them into bowls as truly formed as though he had been a master-turner.

June, 1874.

At this stage of their manufacture they are rubbed with a rough leaf, which answers the purpose of sandpaper, until the marks of the adze are perfectly smoothed down. In many instances lips are hollowed out with a knife and patterns are also occasionally carved on them.

Staining the outside a dark red is the finishing

DRUM AND IDOL.

touch, and when new this effectively contrasts with the white of the inside; but with use they become perfectly black from dirt and grease.

I also saw a peculiarly shaped wooden drum hollowed out from a solid block of wood, the outside being modelled with adzes like those used in bowl-making, and the inside by chisel-shaped pieces of iron with wooden handles three feet long.

We passed through many strips of thick and intricate tangled jungle. The creepers were principally indiarubber vines with stems the thickness

June, 1874.

of a man's thigh; and in cutting them away in order to clear a passage we were well bedaubed with the sap, which was very plentiful. Indeed, sufficient indiarubber to supply the wants of the civilised world might easily be collected here.

All the villages possessed fetish huts with little carved idols, under whose protection they were supposed to be; and in fields rougher idols were

IDOLS.

placed to watch over the crops. Offerings of pombé and corn were often made to these images, and on occasions of harvesting or sowing a goat or a fowl was sometimes lavished upon them.

The last march before arriving at Pakwanywa's village was one of the most exhausting and trying I had up to that time experienced. The road led us over a succession of small hills, and the sun beat down upon us from a cloudless sky.

The heat of the parched ground scorched my feet through thick boots, knitted stockings and socks. Drawing a breath was like inhaling the fumes of a heated furnace.

June, 1874.

On entering the village I was thoroughly beaten by heat and thirst, and the agony was increased by the people crowding round to stare at me.

Water seemed to be unattainable. But at last a kind-hearted old man pushed through the crowd and handed me a large calabash full, and if ever I blessed a man it was that one. With a continuous draught I drained the calabash, large as it was, and the friendly old native sent for more; and when I offered him a small present of beads for his thoughtfulness and trouble he declined to accept any reward whatever.

At Pakwanywa's I heard that a large caravan under the leadership of Muinyi Hassani was waiting for us a few days in front, and although I had no desire to join them it was better to yield and avoid opposition on their part.

The men engaged at Mékéto declined to go any further with us, nor would other natives volunteer to assist; so I issued two more loads of beads as rations instead of abandoning them for lack of carriers.

Others of my followers were malingering, and Bombay and Bilâl instead of assisting me in the slightest were ever ready to throw difficulties in my way in the vain hope of inducing me to turn back and abandon the expedition.

June, 1874.

Syde Mezrui "made brothers" with Pakwanywa, and I went into the village to witness the interesting ceremony.

Pakwanywa I found sitting out in the open superintending the painting of his wife's forehead, and a serious matter it seemed to be. The artist, having the different colours prepared with oil—each in a separate leaf—plastered them on with a knife and then carefully scraped the edges of the various tints till they were exactly true and formed the required pattern.

This being finished, Pakwanywa invited me into his hut, which was about twenty feet square and smoothly plastered on the inside to the height of four feet. The walls were ornamented with squares of red, white, and yellow, bordered with black and white stripes, some left plain and others profusely dotted with white finger-marks.

On two sides of the building a raised earthen bench three feet wide and covered with mats served as a divan.

A pile of large logs out of which the wooden bowls are made was placed in one corner to season; and in another was a sunken fireplace for use at night or in rainy weather. The sole means of obtaining light, air, and ventilation was by the doorway, consequently the inside of the roof, where bows and spear-staves were seasoning, was black and shiny with soot. The floor was of clay and was perfectly smooth.

On entering it was with difficulty I could distinguish anything, but as my eyes became accustomed to the absence of light I noticed gourds and cooking pots hanging up, and everything appeared to be in its place, showing Mrs. Pakwanywa to be a "notable housewife."

After a certain amount of palaver Syde and Pakwanywa exchanged presents, much to the advantage of the former—more especially as he borrowed the beads from me and afterwards forgot to repay me. Pakwanywa then played a tune on his harmonium, or whatever the instrument might be called, and the business of fraternising was proceeded with.

Pakwanywa's headman acted as his sponsor, and one of my askari assumed the like office for Syde.

The first operation consisted of making an incision on each of their right wrists just sufficient to draw blood, a little of which was scraped off and smeared on the other's cut, after which gunpowder was rubbed in.

The concluding part of the ceremony was performed by Pakwanywa's sponsor holding a sword resting on his (Pakwanywa's) shoulder, whilst he who acted for Syde went through the motions of sharpening a knife on it. Both sponsors meanwhile made a speech, calling down imprecations on

June, 1874.

Pakwanywa and all his relations, past, present, and future, and praying that their graves might be defiled by pigs if he broke the brotherhood in word, thought, or deed. The same form having been gone through with respect to Syde, the sponsors changing duties, the brother-making was complete.

This custom of "making brothers" I believe to be really of Semitic origin, and to have been introduced into Africa by the heathen Arabs trading there before the time of Mahomet; and this idea is strengthened by the fact that when the first traders from Zanzibar crossed the Tanganyika the ceremony was unknown to the westward of that lake.

That which I have termed Pakwanywa's harmonium, for want of a better name, was composed of a board to which were attached a number of springy iron keys of different lengths and breadths to give variety to their tone, and a gourd was placed behind to act as a sounding board. The keys are played on by the thumbs, and a fair amount of music can be extracted from this instrument by a clever performer. They are called Kinanda by the natives, but Kinanda is a generic term for almost all musical instruments.

The following is the description of Mrs. Pakwanywa as I wrote it at the time of my visit:—

"She is a merry sort of person and really ladylike in her manners. It was great fun showing her a looking-glass, she had never seen one before, and was half-afraid of it and ashamed to show she was afraid. She is a very dressy body, double row of cowries round her head, besides copper, iron, and ivory ornaments stuck in her hair, and just above and in front of each ear a little tassel of red and white beads. A large necklace of shells (viongwa) round her neck, and round her waist a string of opal coloured singo-mazzi, and a roll (or rope) made of strings of a dull, red-coloured bead. Her front apron was a leopard-skin, and the rear one of coloured grass cloth, with its fringe strung with beads and cowries sewn on it in a pattern; bright iron rings round her ankles, and copper and ivory bracelets on her arms. Her hair was shaved a little back from her forehead, and three lines, each about a quarter of an inch wide, painted below it. The one nearest the hair was red, the next black, and the next white, and to crown all she was freshly anointed with mpafu oil, and looked sleek and shiny."

June, 1874.

The upper classes of Ubûdjwa wear similar dresses, ornaments and tattoo marks to those of the Waguhha and Warua, and are apparently of the same race.

The lower orders, whom I believe to be the aborigines, are quite different in features and dress. Their women perforate their upper lips and insert a piece of stone or wood which is gradually increased in size until the lip frequently protrudes an inch and a half or two inches, giving a particu-

June, 1874.

larly hideous expression and making their articulation very indistinct.

Their clothing consists of from one to three leather cushions, very much like buffaloes' horns in shape, the thickest parts being placed behind and the tapering points in front. A small piece of bark cloth, about six inches wide by eight or ten deep, is tucked into the front part to serve as an apron. Skin aprons are worn by the men,

WOMEN OF UBÛDJWA.

who smear the unclipped wool with red clay and grease.

They also tattoo their faces and rub in lampblack after a fashion that gives them the appearance of having been badly scratched by a cat, black blood having been drawn instead of red.

Both sexes of all classes carry little carved images round their necks or tied to the upper part of their arms as a charm against evil spirits. They are usually hollow and filled with filth by the fetish man.

We left Pakwanywa's on the 19th of June for Pakhûndi; and directly after starting passed a stream rising in a hot spring, the water where we crossed being 107° Fahrenheit, whilst the air was only 70°. At the spring the water bubbled up in a sort of fountain, and there the heat must have been much greater, but it was impossible to reach it on

CHARMS.

account of mud and weeds. Notwithstanding the temperature of the water, trees, plants and frogs flourished in it.

To Pakhûndi the road lay across fairly level country, partly jungle and partly clearing, and one sandy plain with many palms. There were several small streams all flowing towards the Rubumba,

June, 1874.

excepting the last—the Katamba—which ran south, towards the valley of the Lukuga.

Near some villages were small iron foundries, and in dangerous proximity to the path there were many pits from which the ore, a kind of red hæmatite, is obtained.

The caravan awaiting us at Pakhûndi consisted of Muinyi Hassani and his people; a party under charge of a slave of Syde ibn Habib; and two small traders, Muinyi Brahim and Muinyi Bokhari. The two latter had each only about a dozen men, whilst the remainder, about two hundred and fifty in number, were equally divided between Muinyi Hassani and Syde ibn Habib's slave. There were also a few freedmen, smiths and carpenters, travelling on their own account with one or two slaves.

CARVED STICK.

CHAPTER XVIII.

PAKHÛNDI.—FOUNDRIES.—DUST AND ASHES.—SLAVE GAGGING.—FREEDMEN THE HARSHEST MASTERS.— SALUTATIONS.— DISOBLIGING PEOPLE.— HAIR, DRESS, TATTOOING.—NAKED PEOPLE.—NATURAL STOMACHERS.—BUILDING OPERATIONS.—NO VENTILATION.—UVINZA.—CLAY IDOLS.—CARVING.—ARMS. —THE ARABS' KIRANGOSI.—HIS IMPERTINENCE.—CLIMBING OIL-PALMS.— MY SHOWMAN.— THE BAMBARRÉ MOUNTAINS.— MAGNIFICENT TREES.— A DARK RAVINE.—MANYUÉMA.—DRESS AND ARMS.—THE WOMEN.—ECONOMY IN CLOTHING.—LIVINGSTONE'S INFLUENCE.—AN ENLIGHTENED CHIEF.— DWARFS.—MUSICAL INSTRUMENTS.— FEARFUL CANNIBALS.— DANCING.—NO SHOOTING ALLOWED.

ON joining the caravan we were welcomed with all outward civility, but little else. The traders were naturally glad that a well-armed party should accompany them across Manyuéma, as they had barely sixty guns amongst them, many of those being useless Tower and other flint guns while the best were merely French trade percussion single barrels.

June, 1874.

Of course we could not expect to start from Pakhûndi without wasting a day for the men of the two caravans to enjoy their gossip; but on the 22nd of June we marched, and passing through a hilly and diversified country watered by a few streams — some working to the Rubumba, now about twenty miles north of us, and others flowing away to the Lukuga—arrived at Kwaséré.

June, 1874.

Here a prosperous village once stood, but it had evidently been destroyed in some recent fight, together with others lying near.

Stools, pots, mortars and other articles of household furniture were lying about in confusion, instead of being removed as would have been the case had the flitting been premeditated; and growing crops were left standing.

I firmly believe the traders had something to do with this work of destruction, for they now took the precaution of building a very strong fence round their camp, although they had not previously done so since leaving the Tanganyika. But in answer to my enquiries they asserted that no disturbance whatever had occurred here.

In Kwaséré there were two or three small foundries about twelve feet square with a raised bank round the sides, the centre of the floor sloping towards a deep trough which was placed to receive the molten metal. The remains of a furnace lay in one corner, and 'clay nozzles for the wooden bellows were scattered about in all directions. The whole of the floors of these foundries were well plastered with smooth and polished clay burnt quite red in many places.

This day the thermometer at half-past one registered 100° in complete shade, and 142° in the sun.

The grass through which we forced our way had grown to such an extent as to be almost impenetrable. In many places it was upwards of twelve feet in height and so dense that leaning against it scarcely made any impression, the stalks of the main stems being often thicker than my thumb.

June, 1874.

Even where the grass had been burnt down these stems remained four or five feet high and scratched one's face and hands in a most horrid manner.

And in addition to this the ashes, blown about by the slightest breeze, filled eyes, nose, mouth, hair and ears. After marching an hour or two through a strip of burnt country one had much the appearance and feeling of having been in a coal-pit.

For some days we marched in company with the Arabs through well-watered, fertile, and fairly populated country, with crops of matama growing in luxuriance.

But along the whole route a very hollow peace seemed to reign, the traders owing their security to the fear inspired by their guns. Yet the inhabitants constantly came into camp with slaves and ivory for sale, as well as flour and other provisions.

Slaves were usually gagged by having a piece of wood, like a snaffle, tied into their mouths. Heavy slave-forks were placed round their necks and their hands were fastened behind their backs. They were then attached by a cord to the vendor's waist.

June, 1874.

I believe that as a general rule they were much better treated when bought by the traders than whilst they remained in the hands of their native owners.

They were mostly captives, surprised when in the woods a short way from their own villages, and had of course to be kept in chains by their masters to prevent their escaping; otherwise they were not really badly used, being fairly fed and not overloaded.

In the few cases of bad treatment which came under my notice the owners were either slaves themselves, or freedmen who on beginning to taste the delights of freedom seemed anxious to prevent any one lower in the scale from rising to a like state of happiness.

Many of the villages through which we passed had their "public parks"—large open spaces preserved in their centres and shaded by fine trees. Large trunks of the fan-palm were laid upon the ground and on these we usually found the male population seated for a stare when we went by, whilst the women and children, though kept in the background, rivalled them in curiosity.

The men saluted the principal people of the caravan as they passed by singing, "Maji muko," in chorus, and clapping their hands; and on being answered in the same manner they vociferated, "Eh hân."

Notwithstanding this apparent desire to be civil

they were churlish and disobliging. If asked for a drink of water or a light for a pipe, they would reply that the river would be found near or that the fire was their own; although had they been more obliging they would have received a small present of beads, or a pinch of salt, of which they are inordinately covetous, having none in their own country.

We were now passing through Uhiya, and the people differed materially from their neighbours in dress and habits.

Many adopted the horrid practice of chipping all their teeth to points, giving them the appearance of wild beasts, and their head-dresses were both hideous and curious.

Some wore a huge bowl-shaped leather chignon having a hole in the centre out of which hung a kind of leather tongue. Others plastered their hair with mud and oil, and so frizzed and trained it as to present a certain resemblance to a judge's wig, and others divided it into crests and ridges.

Tattooing was common amongst both sexes, but there was no beauty or design in the patterns as amongst the Waguhha; indeed, the appearance of the ghastly scars left by some of the gashes was most abhorrent. Amongst the most favourite marks were rude attempts at crescents, Maltese crosses, and a trellis-work formed of deep cuts disposed irregularly over the body.

The clothing of the men usually consisted of a

short kilt of skins or bark cloth. The women wore leather belts—divided into two or three strips—which supported a small square of cloth behind and a very minute apron in front. Some were even more scantily attired, having only a string round the waist with a small leather apron, about three inches wide and four or five deep, cut into strips no wider than a boot-lace.

I heard that a short distance further west the people were perfectly nude, but that they managed, by constant manipulation when the children were very young, to cause the fatty covering of the lower part of their bellies to hang down like an apron almost to the middle of the thigh. And this was allowed to answer the purpose of dress.

On mentioning this to H.E. the Governor-General of Angola, Admiral Andradé, on my arrival at Loanda, he informed me that he had witnessed a similar peculiarity amongst tribes in the interior near Mozambique.

Instead of pounding their corn in mortars, the people here made use of trunks of trees let flush into floors of hardened earth, and in consequence of their having small holes in them, the flour they made was even more gritty than that prepared in wooden mortars.

Close to the western end of Uhiya we crossed the Luwika, a considerable stream falling into the Lukuga according to the evidence of a travelled Mguhha who had settled in Uhiya as chief of a village. The latter river he said he had traced to its confluence with the Lualaba.

Just before leaving Uhiya we camped in a deserted village, the whilom inhabitants of which had, in accordance with a very common custom, flitted on account of the death of their chief and were now busily engaged in building a new village not far from their former habitation.

They had planted young bark-cloth trees round the site of their new home and had erected the frame-work of their huts and granaries. These they were now plastering with red clay obtained from the large ant-hills. This clay is also used for making pottery.

The huts were square, and were constructed of stakes four feet in height planted in the ground and kept secure by a couple of binders wattled in.

To the head of each of these stakes, which were about eight inches apart, a long tapering flexible wand was tied. These were bound together at the top, and horizontal rings of small sticks were fastened to them at every three feet. In this stage the huts looked exactly like huge birdcages.

The walls were then filled in with mud, and the roof thatched with long grass, the eaves reaching nearly to the ground. A couple of stout logs were planted on each side of the doorway and, with some extra sticks worked in and the thatch trimmed, formed a sort of porch.

In the interior, the floor, walls and lower part

of the roof were plastered over smoothly with clay, while the remainder of the roof was lined with a spiral wisp of grass something after the manner of a straw beehive.

The only aperture by which smoke could escape or light enter was the door, and at night this was most jealously kept shut and a whole family of six

HUTS IN UHIYA.

or eight people—together with fowls, goats, dogs and sheep—with a fire burning in their midst, remain hermetically closed until the morning. How they manage to exist without a better supply of oxygen is a mystery to me.

The granaries are circular, of hurdle-work daubed with clay, and stand eight feet high and four in diameter, being placed on small platforms two feet from the ground. They have movable, conical, thatched roofs.

June, 1874.

In the deserted village there were many very fine bark-cloth trees, and the late inhabitants sent people over to prevent our injuring them when making our camp.

From this place we crossed a level plain along which the Luwika ran, lying between two almost cliff-like ranges of hills, but on arriving at a village our road suddenly turned to the right and we had to clamber up the face of so steep a cliff that hands and knees were used almost more than feet.

At the summit we had about ten yards level walking and then an equally steep descent into a rich and fertile valley full of villages.

This was the commencement of a second Uvinza, which must not be confounded with the Uvinza through which we passed to the east of the Tanganyika.

Outside some of the villages there were large clay idols in different attitudes—sitting, standing erect, and recumbent—all being placed under small sheds with pots of pombé and heads of corn lying round them.

We camped on the banks of the Lulumbijé, which—after breaking through the narrow ridge we had just crossed—joins the Luwika. The united streams are known indifferently as the Lulumbijé or Luwika until the junction with the

June, 1874.

Lukuga. This exactly coincides with the information given me by the chief at the entrance of the Lukuga, of a stream falling into that river at a place one month's journey from the lake.

The Uvinza people displayed more skill in carving than any I had hitherto met, and many of their walking-sticks were very creditable specimens of the carver's art.

Several of both sexes wore pieces of cane or rings of beads through the centre cartilage of the nose, and their hair was tastefully worked into cones and ridges finished off by plaits.

The Lulumbijé was crossed the next day, and after a heavy and hilly march—during which several affluents of that river were met with—we arrived at the village of Kolomamba, situated on the top of a high range of hills whence we obtained a distant view of a large grove of oil-palms surrounding Rohombo, the first village in Manyuéma.

At Kolomamba the people were on the point of moving, having lately been worsted in one of those innumerable squabbles which are perpetually going on.

The arms of the people of Uhiya are light spears and large bows strung with strips of cane, throwing heavy arrows. Those of Manyuéma consist only of heavy spears and large wooden shields.

A harangue was now given by the kirangosi of the Arab caravan, to the effect that we were about to enter the dangerous country of Manyuéma, the natives of which were more cruel and treacherous than any with whom we had yet met. Consequently stragglers would most certainly be cut off, killed, and probably eaten.

June, 1874.

I consoled myself with the idea that I was so very thin that they would not consider me worth the trouble of eating, for there was hardly a meal for one man on my bones.

Although Rohombo could be seen from Kolomamba some hours' weary tramping were necessary to reach it.

Open grassy glades interspersed with thickets of jungle were on either side of us, and as we drew near crowds of people lined the road eager to have a stare at the caravan.

I arrived with the leading part and being shown the camping-place—an open space with three small stockaded villages—ordered my tent to be pitched under a large tree standing on one side.

Soon afterwards I found it moved into the full blaze of the sun; and on enquiring the cause was told that the Arabs' kirangosi had directed it as he wanted the place under the tree for himself.

I, of course, would not stand this treatment and had my tent put back again. Upon which the kirangosi declared he would not camp here unless he had the place he wanted, so to end the dispute I told him he could go to the devil if he liked. He then moved on a mile further with his people, while I remained with mine; and later the Arabs apologised for his impertinence.

These kirangosis give themselves airs and do much as they please with their own masters, and I suppose this fellow thought I should submit to the same.

The people here were rough and dirty-looking, and wore their mud-plastered hair in irregular masses.

Food was fairly plentiful—bananas, fowls, eggs, flour and palm wine being obtained.

The oil-palms are climbed by means of a piece of the mid-rib of the palm-frond, flattened and softened, and a rope of creepers, the mid-rib being passed round the tree and the rope behind the man's back, and tied together. The tree is then climbed in the same manner as cocoa-nut palms frequently are in the East Indies.

During our two days' stay one of the natives constituted himself my showman. To each visitor to the camp he would point out my books, boxes, &c., and on my meals being brought would raise a shout that instantly caused a large crowd to assemble to witness my feeding. And I may add that the performance seemed to give general satisfaction.

The tameness of the goat excited an intense amount of wonder here, as indeed she usually did elsewhere, the people evidently thinking me a great magician to make her come to me when called.

Leaving this, we passed through a large and well-watered valley with streams running into

Lake Lanji and commenced the ascent of the mountains of Bambarré.

June, 1874.

Hour after hour we toiled up their steep sides, having often to assist our feet by clutching at the trees and creepers growing on their well-wooded slopes; and in the evening we camped at the village Koana Mina, now deserted for another erected rather more than a mile further on.

Resuming our ascent in the early morning we followed for an hour the winding path and then turned into a dense mass of forest and immediately began to descend.

The northern side of the Bambarré mountains differs greatly from the southern, for instead of being a simple slope they are seamed into enormous gullies and ravines. Sometimes our path was at the very bottom of them, then again at the top, and at another time along their precipitous sides.

No sunlight or breeze ever penetrates into these dark depths, for a mass of monster trees with spreading heads shuts out the slightest glimpse of sky.

And what trees they were! Standing on the edge of a ravine a hundred and fifty feet deep these giants of the sylvan world were seen springing from its depths; and looking upwards their trunks were lost amongst their dense foliage at an equal height above our heads.

Magnificent creepers festooned the trees, and every here and there some dead monarch of the

June, 1874. wood was prevented from falling by the clinging embraces of these parasites which linked him to some of his surviving brothers.

The ground was damp and cool, and mosses and ferns grew luxuriantly. Still, notwithstanding the coolness of the temperature, the lack of circulation of the air caused a deadly oppressiveness, and it was with feelings of relief that I again saw blue sky and sunlight streaming between the tree-trunks as they grew fewer and smaller towards the bottom of the hills.

Emerging from this truly primeval forest, we entered upon a fair country with green plains, running streams, wooded knolls, much cultivation and many villages. The first we reached was half an hour's march from the jungle.

And here we seemed to be in an entirely new country, for though Rohombo may be, conventionally, the commencement of Manyuéma, there is no doubt that its proper boundary, both ethnologically and geographically, is the mountain range of Bambarré.

The huts were ranged in long streets, sometimes parallel and at others radiating from a large central space; their bright red walls and sloping roofs differing from those hitherto met with. And in the middle of the street were palaver huts, palm-trees, and granaries.

In their dress the people were different from any I had previously seen.

VILLAGE IN MANYÉUMA.

SCANTY COSTUMES.

June, 1874.

The men wore aprons of dressed deerskin about eight inches wide and reaching to their knees. They carried a single heavy spear and a small knife with which to eat their food.

Chiefs were armed with short two-edged swords with broadened crescent-shaped ends, the scabbards being ornamented with iron and copper bells; and

HEADS OF MEN OF MANYUÉMA.

instead of leather aprons they wore large kilts of gaily coloured grass cloth.

The heads of the males were generally plastered with clay so worked in with the hair as to form cones and plates. Occasionally long flakes, both flat and round, hung down on the neck, and in these holes were punched for the insertion of

June, 1874.

iron and copper rings. Between the clay patches the scalp was shaven perfectly bare.

The women, who were prevented by the men from crowding round us on our arrival, had better figures and were better-looking—with the excep-

PEOPLE OF MANYUÉMA.

tion of a hanging lower lip—than any I had seen for some time.

In many instances their hair was worked into the shape of an old-fashioned bonnet deeply shading the face, whilst long ringlets flowed down their backs. But some, despising the bonnet or more confident of their charms, drew their hair off their foreheads and tied it together at the nape of the neck, letting it fall behind in tresses.

Their dress was particularly simple, it consisted only of a cord round the waist—on which beads were strung by the richer ones—and two small grass-cloth aprons. The front one was about the size of a half-sheet of ordinary notepaper, and that behind just a trifle larger.

June, 1874.

Notwithstanding their small dimensions these aprons were often elaborately stitched and ornamented with beads and cowries; and when the women went working in the fields or fishing in the streams they took off these gay clothes for fear of spoiling them, and replaced them with a small bunch of leaves.

The goats and sheep, as well as the people, differed from those on the other side of the mountains, being precisely similar to those described by Dr. Schweinfurth in the Dinka country, and this breed also extends all through Manyuéma and Urua. The sheep when well fed put on fat, and the caponised goats are particularly large and good. The she goats are wonderfully prolific, constantly producing three at a birth. I have heard of instances in which five and six have been born at one time, and have witnessed several cases of four at a birth.

We soon came to a larger village, where we camped; and the people came in from the surrounding country to gaze at a white man, although they had seen Livingstone, who stayed for some months with a neighbouring chief, Moéné Kussu. He had died and had been succeeded by his sons Moéné Bugga and Moéné Gohé. The latter visited us, and offered—on the part of himself and brother—all hospitality to a countryman of Livingstone, whose peaceful and unoffending progress through this land had tended to make an Englishman respected by the natives.

July, 1874.

We were delayed here by the illness of Muinyi Bokhari, one of the small traders of the caravan, who, thinking himself too poor to afford proper food, had actually been endeavouring to subsist on grass and earth. Consequently and very naturally, something had gone wrong in his interior.

Marching again on July 1st through a populous and well-cultivated country with many streams of bright water all flowing to the Luama, we reached the village of Moéné Bugga, and were warmly welcomed by the chief, who is held in respect by the surrounding villages. There is not that incessant petty warring in this part of Manyuéma as in other districts, where every village is constantly at variance with its neighbours.

Moéné Bugga follows his father's policy of maintaining cordial relations with traders, and, indeed, wishes them to establish a regular settlement at his village.

He spoke very warmly of Livingstone, who was evidently much liked whilst here.

Many chiefs accompanied by their musicians and arm-bearers called on us, and two of them each

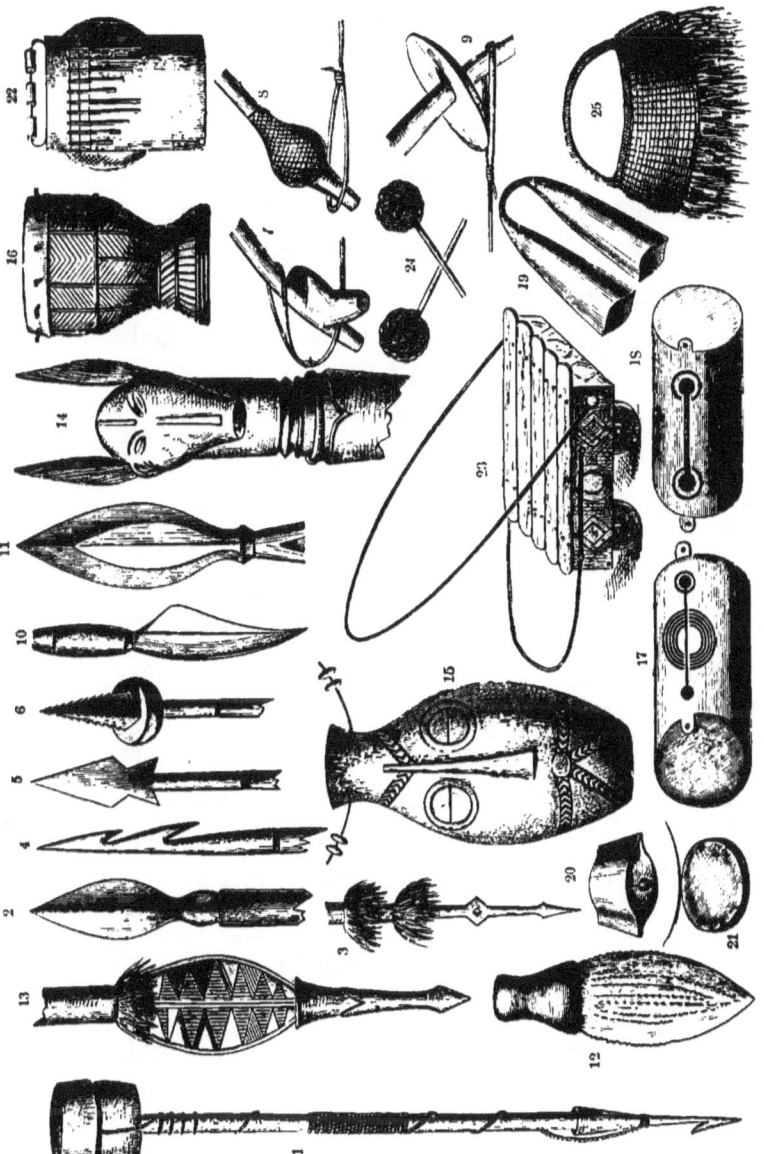

POT-POURRI.

1, Fish-spear. 2, 3, Spears. 4, 5, 6 Arrow-heads. 7, 8, 9, Modes of stringing bows. 10, 11, 12, Knives. 13, 14, Walking-sticks. 15, Charm. 16, 17, 18, Drums. 19, Iron gong. 20, 21, Iron bells. 22, Musical instrument. 23, Marimba. 24, Sticks for playing marimba. 25, Rattle.

[PAGE 357, Vol. I.

brought a dwarf who carried a rattle and shouted his master's name after this style, "Ohé Moéné Booté Ohé Ohé," and rattled the while.   July, 1874.

Moéné Booté's dwarf was covered with blotches and had a deformed knee, and was altogether a repulsive-looking object.

The musicians played an instrument called "Marimba," formed of two rows of gourds of different sizes fitted into a framework. Over each pair of gourds was a clef made of hard wood, which gave a metallic sound when struck with sticks having indiarubber heads. Of these sticks there were different sizes, the player dexterously changing one for another as a sharper or a duller sound was required.

Moéné Booté came shuffling up to me with a sort of sliding, half-dancing step, which did not get him ahead much more than a yard a minute; and every two or three minutes he halted whilst his marimba-player and dwarf extolled his greatness.

The people here seemed very affectionate among themselves and decidedly more prolific than any other race I had seen in Africa; but though endowed with many good qualities it cannot be denied that they are cannibals, and most filthy cannibals.

Not only do they eat the bodies of enemies killed in battle but also of people who die of disease. They prepare the corpses by leaving

July, 1874.

them in running water until they are nearly putrid, and then devour them without any further cooking. They also eat all sorts of carrion, and their odour is very foul and revolting.

I was entertained with a song setting forth the delights of cannibalism, in which the flesh of men was said to be good but that of women was bad and only to be eaten in time of scarcity; nevertheless, it was not to be despised when man meat was unobtainable.

Dancing in Manyuéma is the prerogative of the chiefs. When they feel inclined for a Terpsichorean performance they single out a good-looking woman from the crowd, and the two go through much wriggling and curious gesticulation opposite each other. The village drums are brought out and vigorously beaten, the drummers meanwhile shouting, "Gamello! Gamello!"

If the woman is unmarried the fact of a chief asking her to dance is equivalent to an offer of marriage, and many complications often occur in consequence.

At this place Muinyi Hassani thought himself unwell and detained us two days. Poor old Muinyi Bokhari was very ill and was informed that he would be left behind, unless he consented to part with some of his dearly hoarded cowries and beads to pay men to carry him. I tried to cure the old man, but my doctoring did not prove very successful.

Leaving Moéné Bugga's we passed villages

and cultivated land, and then through a gap in a low range of hills full of enormous trees like those on the northern slopes of the Bambarré mountains.

July, 1874.

Here I got into trouble for pigeon-shooting. I was walking along quietly in the middle of the caravan, and thought it as well to take the opportunity of shooting something for my supper.

WOMEN GOING FISHING.

Instantly there was a tremendous hullabaloo and every one rushed towards me both from the front and rear enquiring the reason a gun had been fired, saying that on the march in Manyuéma no gun should ever be discharged unless the caravan were attacked. My ignorance of this rule had given them a fright.

July, 1874.

After this we camped in a village belonging to another Moéné Booté, chief of the ferry across the Luama, and remained there two days chaffering about payment and because Muinyi Hassani was too lazy to continue the march.

SAMBO.

CHAPTER XIX.

THE LUAMA.—FISHERWOMEN.—SHOOTING HIPPOPOTAMI.—OPEN-AIR GRANARIES.—IRON.—A BURNING COUNTRY.—SHAMEFUL BEHAVIOUR OF TRADERS.—A SUSPENSION BRIDGE.—THE NATIVES TURN UPON THE TRADERS.—CONTEMPLATED ATTACK ON THE CARAVAN.—TWO CHIEFS TREACHEROUSLY SHOT.—VILLAGES BURNED.—WOMEN AND CHILDREN CAPTURED.—I PLEAD FOR PEACE.—INFLUENCE AS AN ENGLISHMAN.—A PALAVER.—THE CAPTIVES ARE LIBERATED.—MY VIEWS ARE NOT APPRECIATED.—FOUNDRIES.—SMITHIES.—MANYARA DRESS.—A DRUM-MAJOR.—THE SLAVING SYSTEM.—THE MIGHTY LUALABA.—GOING WITH THE STREAM.—NYANGWÉ IS REACHED.

July, 1874.

THE Luama is a large and important affluent of the Lualaba and rises in the mountains of Ugoma, a short distance from the Tanganyika and not far from the sources of the Lugumba and Lubumba. The latter, after a considerable détour, unites with the Luama about thirty miles above the point at which we crossed. The river has a very meandering course with many affluents and backwaters in which large numbers of fish are caught by the women.

At this time—in the middle of the dry season—it was perfectly navigable for large steam launches.

Across each small stream or backwater dams are built of hurdle-work with conical openings at intervals, something like the entrance to a wire rat-trap. When the waters begin to subside the fish endeavour to pass through these dams to the perennial streams.

The women then go fishing in the following manner. Doffing their grass-cloth aprons and replacing them with leaves, they take enormous baskets—some seven feet long, two feet six inches deep, and two feet wide in the middle—made of close mat-like work of split cane. These they set under the openings in the dams, which are then unfastened whilst some of the dark sportswomen go into the stream and drive the terrified fish towards the dam. The fish, seeing no chance of escape save by these holes, jump through into the baskets ready for their reception.

The fisherwomen seemed to think it great fun and enjoyed themselves immensely, shrieking, screaming and laughing the whole while.

Leaving the banks of the Luama we forded an affluent—the Lulwu, thirty yards in width and four feet in depth—and marching two miles further reached the bend of the Luama where we had arranged to cross it.

Canoes were here in readiness, but as there were only three the work of getting the caravan over occupied some time, for the river was fully a hundred yards in width and eight to ten feet deep in the middle and had steep banks.

Whilst we were thus engaged at 9h. 10m. local mean time, there was a slight shock of earthquake; a low rumbling sound and a faint though

CROSSING THE LUAMA RIVER.

distinctly perceptible tremor of the ground passing from E.N.E. to W.S.W.

July, 1874.

A large number of hippopotami were blowing in mid-stream on our reaching the river, so I occupied myself by firing at them. One, getting a bullet and shell in his head in rapid succession, sank, and the rest cleared out, which was a very desirable result since they often hog up underneath a canoe in deep water and heave it right out, capsizing all the occupants. The canoes bore marks of the tusks of these brutes, who look upon them as intruders and often attack them wantonly.

By the time the caravan had been ferried over the sun was very powerful and it was too late to proceed further, so we camped in a small scattered village about a mile from the river.

Although they afterwards became common, I here saw for the first time large platforms on which were stored huge bundles of grass ready for thatching the huts on the approach of the rainy season. The two centre poles of the platform, which were about twenty feet higher than the others, were connected with a square meshed net made of strips of bark. At each intersection of these strips bunches of matama and Indian corn were tied, the grain by these means being stored without a possibility of its heating as it sometimes does if placed in close granaries before it is perfectly ripe. But, *en revanche*, the birds carry off immense quantities from these open-air stores.

July, 1874.

Our next camp was at Kisimbika, the road to this place being along the right bank of the Luama, and across many dry beds of watercourses with sides and bottoms formed of very thin strata of a sort of shale with occasional outcrops of ironstone (hæmatite).

All the country around was either already burnt or burning, and at night the roar of the immense grass fires could be heard for a distance of three or four miles and the whole sky was lighted up by the blaze.

These huge fires often occasion slight partial showers of rain, the enormous up-draught causing the warm air to rush to a cooler level where the moisture is condensed and falls in the form of rain.

From Kisimbika we went forward until the 17th of July without any long halts. We camped nightly in the villages, much to the disgust of the natives, who were treated in an overbearing manner by the traders and their men.

Relying on their gunpowder-strength, the traders gave their men nothing with which to purchase food but told them to steal what they wanted themselves and also to bring in provisions for their masters.

The natives stood aloof or looked on sullenly whilst these blackguards robbed their granaries and their mortars and other articles of household furniture to make fires for cooking the stolen food. The only approach they made towards communicating with us was to propose that the caravan should join them in attacking other villages in order to obtain slaves.

July, 1874.

I gave my men extra rations to prevent their thieving, and in two or three cases paid natives who complained of them, and I treated the offenders to a sound flogging to show that I, as an Englishman, had no intention of making my way through the country by means of looting and force.

Yet I fear when my back was turned they were fully as bad as the others. Bombay always persisted that they never stole anything whatever, but I sometimes heard from Jumah that Bombay himself was not entirely guiltless.

On July the 18th we crossed the Lulindi, a broad stream which must be unfordable in flood.

At a height of twenty feet above the water there hung a very cleverly constructed suspension bridge. Four large cables of creepers were fastened to the trunks of trees, one pair about four feet higher than the other, and to these cables were secured other creepers from the tops of the loftiest trees on each side of the stream, while horizontal guys prevented the bridge from swaying about. Across the lower pair of cables sticks were laid to form a roadway. These were lashed in their places and wattled in with creepers, while a large network of the same connected the upper and lower cables on each side of the bridge.

July, 1874.

Altogether it was a very ingenious and effective structure and rather astonished me, more especially as I had never seen any similar construction in Africa, nor indeed did I meet with another.

Karungu, at which we camped, was a large town, or more properly group of villages lying on the slope of a hill, and it was arranged that we should

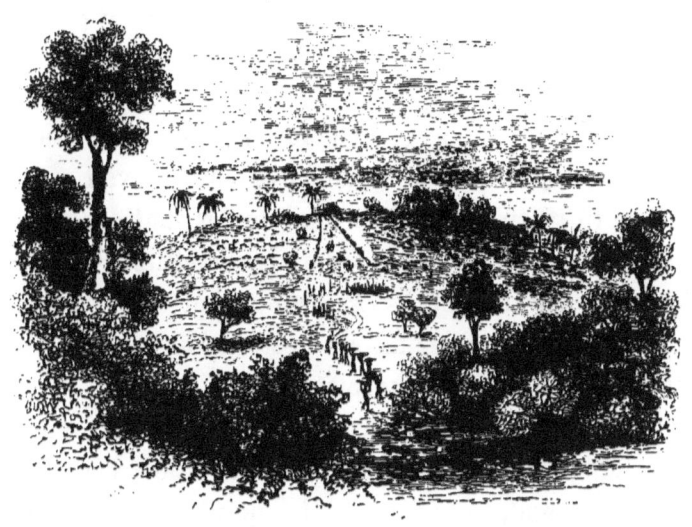

KARUNGU.

halt here for a day before starting straight away for Kwakasongo, an Arab settlement on the road to Nyangwé.

As I was sitting the next morning quietly reading and writing, I heard musketry-fire and a great disturbance in the Arab camp and saw the natives flying in every direction, pursued by the traders' men. Matters had evidently come to a crisis and I therefore collected all my men and ordered them, under pain of instant and severe punishment, neither to leave the camp nor to fire at the natives unless driven to do so in self-defence. I then went over to Muinyi Hassani to enquire the cause of the row, and found him all excitement and in a great fright. The story was this.

July, 1874.

The natives of villages at which we had camped since leaving the Luama had been following us with the hope of having an opportunity of attacking us in return for the injuries they had experienced at the hands of the caravan. In order to turn the tables and bring matters to a head, two chiefs had ordered something to be stolen from the Arabs, knowing that they would not hesitate to demand its restoration and that a palaver would then take place.

As anticipated, the Arabs sent some messages respecting the theft, whereupon the chiefs came to the camp and, confident in the numbers of natives lurking in ambush in the neighbouring woods, refused to restore the stolen property—a small bark box full of beads—unless payment was made for everything that had been stolen and destroyed in their villages.

Muinyi Hassani refused to accede to this and demanded that the box should be returned unconditionally. The chiefs replied that if Muinyi Hassani and his people wanted it they had better

July, 1874.

try to get it back by force. Then rising to go away, they were treacherously shot down by some armed Wanyamwési.

I told Muinyi Hassani I should defend myself if attacked, but since he was so entirely in the wrong I would not allow a single man to put his foot outside my camp to assist in any aggression against the natives.

By this time many surrounding villages were in flames and the pagazi were returning from the work of destruction, driving herds of goats and sheep before them and bringing in unfortunate women and children as captives; for the natives, notwithstanding their overwhelming numbers, would not face the Arabs' muskets.

In the afternoon however they began to assemble in greater numbers and I tried to persuade Muinyi Hassani to make peace; but the attempt only ended in another row. During the day, Kamwassa, son of Manyara, a chief who was friendly with the Arabs, came into our camp and I endeavoured to enlist his influence in inducing the natives to listen to overtures of peace. Still nothing could then be done to attain so desirable a result.

Many alarms were raised in the night and some guns were fired, but no fighting took place; and in the morning when crowds of people had gathered round the camp, shouting and yelling, Kamwassa urged them to listen to terms.

I believe the Arabs would have continued

fighting had I not been there; but they said, "We have an Englishman in the camp; he will give us a bad name to his consul at Zanzibar;" and as they all entertain a great respect for our consul—looking upon him as superior to every one but their own Sultan, with whom they deem him almost on an equality—my presence had some weight in checking further outrage and hostilities.

The palaver was opened by deputies from the natives and traders going to the opposite banks of a small stream near the camp, and then meeting in the middle and washing each other's faces. Then the natives came over to our side of the stream and some of the chiefs "made brothers" with people selected from amongst the caravan. The brotherhood business having been completed, some pen-and-ink marks were made on a piece of paper, which, together with a charge of powder, was put into a kettle full of water. All hands then drank of the decoction, the natives being told that it was a very great medicine.

Peace having been concluded, my next efforts were directed towards obtaining the release of the prisoners.

To this there was a very strong opposition; but I insisted on it and in the end it was arranged that ransom should be paid for them. Otherwise the natives might have thought we were afraid of them and would have attacked us further on the road.

July, 1874.

On leaving here we had a long and tiring march through many villages, and the caravan was much hampered by the goats—received as ransom for the unfortunate captives—constantly running off into the jungle.

When we camped I found some slaves captured at Karungu still in the caravan, upon which I demanded that they should be set at liberty.

HILLS ON ROAD TO MANYARA.

This led to a stormy discussion with Muinyi Hassani, who was not so anxious about the presence of my men now we had passed through the worst of Manyuéma. But I threatened him with all the terrors of the Sultan and English consul, and finally said I should set the captives free by force, if necessary. I told him plainly that I did not and could not interfere with the buying and selling of slaves by him and his friends, or with their seizing them by the strong arm when alone; but I was determined that the English colours, which had brought freedom to so many on both coasts of Africa, should not be disgraced in the centre of the continent.

July, 1874.

In the end the slaves were set at liberty and a hollow peace was patched up between us; but I decided to have nothing further to do with Muinyi Hassani on reaching Nyangwé.

The following day we arrived at the village of Manyara, standing amongst many others over which he was really though not nominally the chief.

All had two or three foundries in them, upwards of thirty feet long by twenty wide with low walls and an enormously high roof. In the centre was a pit, six feet wide, four deep, and twenty long, rather shallower at one end than the other. Across this, about six feet from the shallow end, was built a clay furnace four feet wide. The smaller of the two divisions of the pit was used as a stoke-hole, whilst the ore and slag ran into the other, and round the sides were small divisions containing charcoal and iron ore.

They sometimes use as many as a dozen pair of bellows at one time in order to make a sufficient blast. Their bellows are formed of two upright and parallel shallow wooden cylinders with vents leading into one nozzle, which is protected by clay from the effects of the fire. These cylinders are covered with grass cloth having a stick three feet long fastened into the centre, and are worked by holding one stick in each hand and moving them up and down alternately as fast as possible. By this means a good and continuous blast is produced.

After smelting, the iron is worked by smiths into small pieces weighing about two pounds and shaped like two cones joined together at the base, and a piece or rod the size of a large knitting needle projects from both ends. In this form the metal is hawked about for sale.

Small open sheds are used as smithies, and the anvils and larger hammers are made of stone, but small hammers are of iron. Those of stone are provided with two loops of rope to serve as handles, while the iron hammers are simply grasped in the hand and are without handles.

The dress of the people had now changed somewhat, the men mostly wearing kilts. Heads were still plastered with clay, but not so elaborately as amongst the first people I saw in Manyuéma.

The women wore round their waists a small strip of leather ornamented with iron and copper beads, and through this and between their legs a piece of rough bark cloth was passed, the ends being allowed to hang down before and behind.

They shaved the tops of their heads, leaving only a sort of trellis-pattern of very short hair, and a bunch of ringlets hung down the backs of their necks.

A friend of Syde's and some native chiefs met us here, and they treated us to so many extraordinary stories that it was impossible to rely upon anything they said.

July, 1874.

One of the chiefs was very elaborately adorned with kilt, cap, and scarf of variegated grass cloth, and was followed by men carrying shields and spears, whilst two others brought up the rear with an enormous drum slung on a pole. The hindmost one performed vigorously upon this instrument when approaching a village.

Two days' marching from Manyara brought us to Kwakasongo. On our way we passed a hill composed almost entirely of black speculum iron ore, and a curious mount with precipitous cliffs, which formed one side of it, rose sheer out of the plain.

At Kwakasongo there is an Arab settlement of some size, three white Arabs besides many half-castes and Wamerima being there. They have good houses and live comfortably, whilst they send out their caravans composed of slaves and Wanyamwési pagazi. One man alone employed six hundred Wanyamwési, all armed with guns.

These fellows get little or no pay, but are allowed to loot the country all round in search of subsistence and slaves. Some of the slaves they keep for themselves, giving their employers a sufficient number in return for the powder supplied to enable them to oppress the natives.

August, 1874.

The Arab who had six hundred Wanyamwési possessed upwards of fifteen tons of good ivory in his store-houses and was waiting for the road between Ujiji and Unyanyembé to be reported clear before sending it to the coast. Some others also had a good amount, but I found my friend (?) Syde was a needy beggar, and his stories about possessing great influence here were myths.

As usual, the Arabs were very civil and kind, and we could not tear ourselves away from their hospitalities under a week.

Muinyi Hassani meanwhile remained camped in a neighbouring village nursing himself through a bad attack of fever. I felt bound to doctor him notwithstanding our row about the slaves, and went two miles out and two back every morning and evening to look after him. But I never received so much as a word of thanks for my trouble, and I imagine my patient had neither forgotten nor forgiven my interference in the slave question.

We left Kwakasongo on the 1st of August, and after two marches came in sight of the mighty Lualaba.

From a bluff overhanging the river I obtained my first view of the stream—a strong and sweeping current of turbid yellow water fully a mile wide and flowing at the rate of three or four knots an hour, with many islands much like the eyots on the Thames lying in its course.

THE LUALABA.

The larger ones were well-wooded and inhabited by the Wagenya, a tribe holding all the islands and a long strip on the left bank, and as the sole proprietors of canoes having the whole carrying trade of the river in their hands.

August, 1874.

Canoes were numerous, and flocks of water-fowl winging their way from sand-bank to sand-bank in

COMING TO MARKET.

search of food gave life to the scene. To remind us of the dangers of the stream there were enormous herds of hippopotami blowing and snorting, and here and there the long scaly back of a crocodile floating almost flush with the water.

Just before coming upon the river we passed villages in which the huts had reverted to the shape of those in Uguhha and Ubûdjwa. Near

August, 1874.

them were regularly planted groves of oil-palms surrounded by hedges of prickly cactus, and at the entrance on each side huts were built for the guardians of the plantation. These groves were also protected from the attacks of elephants and other wild beasts by innumerable large pitfalls dug round about them, which rendered it necessary for the passer-by to be very wary in his walking.

On the evening of my arrival I entered into an agreement with some natives to convey me with a portion of my stores and men to Nyangwé by boat, whilst the remainder went by land.

Muinyi Bokhari, the poor grass-eating old man, died during the night and was at once buried by fire-light with very little ceremony.

When I went to the brink of the river early in the morning, not a canoe was to be seen. Shortly afterwards they began to pass from one island to another and to haul up and set fishing-traps. But not one came near us until about ten o'clock, when by dint of beckoning and shouting some men were induced to come across from an island in the middle of the stream and after a long palaver brought three canoes. These I hired and paid for on the spot and started at once for Nyangwé.

The passage down the river was rapid and pleasant owing to the swift current and the beauty of the scenery.

WAITING FOR CANOES.   [PAGE 376, Vol. I.

On the left bank the shore rose gradually till it culminated in a range of wooded hills ten or twelve miles distant; whilst the right bank rose abruptly in small cliffs crowned by hanging woods, and here and there broken by the embouchure of one of the numerous affluents of the giant stream. Islands, populous and wooded, were passed in constant succession.

August, 1874.

From flocks of duck feeding on the numerous sand-banks I managed to bag two or three couple, and found them almost precisely like an English wild duck, except in colour. The body was white speckled with brown; wings, head, and tail, black, shot with greenish blue.

In the afternoon the canoe-men put in at a fishing village on the right bank and declared their intention of halting. I told them they might stop if they pleased, but I and the canoes were going on to Nyangwé; for I well knew that if we camped neither canoes nor men would be forthcoming next morning. Seeing that I was determined, the men consented to go on.

At sunset I noticed some large huts on a bluff over the river. This was the commencement of the Arab settlement of Nyangwé, and a landing-place was just below.

Jumping ashore I went into the settlement, and my appearance rather astonished the people; for they had heard nothing of our approach and could not imagine where a solitary white man came from.

August, 1874.

The news of my arrival was at once communicated to Habed ibn Salim, a fine white-headed old Arab, commonly known as Tanganyika, and he came running out of his house, where he had been performing his evening devotions, to ascertain what it could mean.

A few words explained matters and we very shortly became great friends.

NYANGWÉ FROM THE RIVER.

My tent was pitched close to his house and the verandah of a large new building was placed at my service, and stowage for my stores and house-room for my followers were supplied without delay. A mess of smoking hot curry was also soon put before me; and very acceptable it was, for I had taken nothing that day excepting a cup of corn coffee before starting in the morning.

NYANGWÉ. [PAGE 378, Vol. I.

NYANGWÉ AT LAST!

At last, then, I was at Nyangwé! And now the question before me was, What success would attend the attempt at tracing the river to the sea?

August, 1874.

MARKET WOMEN. NYANGWÉ.

INDEX.

A.

Abdallah ibn Habib, i. 309.
Abdallah ibn Nassib, i. 154, 196.
Abdul Kader, i. 124.
Abdûllah Dina, i. 12, 14, 95.
Acacias, i. 52, 77, 85, 90, 99; ii. 287.
Accident, an, i. 321.
Aden, arrival at, i. 17.
Africa, formation of continent of, ii. 281.
Akalunga, i. 291.
Alexanderson, Captain Carl, ii. 275.
Alowy ibn Zain el Aidûs, letter of recommendation from, i. 7.
Alvez, José Antonio (Kendélé), ii. 57, 86, 117, 121, 135, 198; his settlement, ii. 201.
Ambriz, ii. 276.
American, an, ii. 269.
Ammunition, i. 320.
Andradé, Admiral, Governor-General of Angola, ii. 273.
Ants, a delicacy, ii. 29; hills, ii. 127.
Antelopes, i. 54, 90, 132, 135, 139, 140, 142, 199, 202, 213; ii. 150.
Apple, custard, ii. 287.
Arabs, extortions of, i. 9; defeat of an Arab expedition, i. 93; caravan, i. 132; kindness of, i. 163; slaves of, i. 212; old camp, i. 299; kirangosi, i. 349; settlement, i. 373.
Arms, carried by expedition, i. 72; by elephant-hunter, i. 82; native, at Mpwapwa, i. 88; Wadirigo, i. 88; Wagogo, i. 96; Wahumba, i. 121; at Hisinéné, i. 192; Wagara, i. 210; at Mikisungi, i. 279; Watuta, i. 285; Warua, i. 325; Wahiya, i. 348; Manyuéma, i. 353; Lovalé, ii. 165.
Arrows, poisoned, i. 82; ii. 9.
Askari, i. 20, 179, 208, 255.

Asmani, Bilâl Wadi, i. 170, 182, 195 199; ii. 13.
Asparagus, i. 13.
Atlantic, first sight of the, ii. 259.
Attacks, i. 145; ii. 34, 40.
Auction, an, i. 163.

B.

Badger, Dr., i. 7.
Bagamoyo, arrival at, i. 11; fire, i. 19; return to, i. 25.
Bailunda, country of, ii. 224, 318.
Baker, letter from Sir Samuel, i. 153.
Balomba, R., ii. 251.
Balooch'es, i. 151.
Bambarré (Kasongo's father), chief wife of, ii. 66.
Bambarré Mountains, i. 351.
Bamboo, i. 53, 236; ii. 152, 286.
Bananas, i. 245, 350.
Band, Kasongo's, ii. 93.
Bangwè, I. of, i. 248.
Banyan-tree, i. 201.
Baobab-trees, i. 49, 84; ii. 257.
Bark, boxes, i. 191; cloth, i. 192; sack, i. 198.
Basins, river, ii. 282.
Bastian, José Perez, ii. 132, 165.
Beans, i. 57, 224.
Bed-places, i. 191.
Bees, i. 213; ii. 152, 317.
Belgians, the King of the. ii. 331.
Belmont, settlement of Silva Porto, ii. 221.
Benguella, arrival at, ii. 267; the town of, ii. 269; leave, ii. 272.
Betsy, the, i. 248, 315.
Bihé, country of, ii. 196, 318.
Bilâl, i. 298, 308; ii. 62.
Bombay, i. 9, 20, 35, 102, 108, 155, 170, 196, 224, 236, 300, 309, 311; ii. 13, 62, 114, 268.

INDEX. 381

Books, box of, left at Ujiji by Dr. Livingstone, i. 168, 242.
Bowls, wooden, i. 329.
Bradshaw, Captain, R. N., ii. 279.
Bread-fruit trees, i. 13.
Bridges, natural, i. 222; a suspension, i. 365; fishing-weir, ii. 14, 34, 134; over the rivers Kukéwi and Kuléli, ii. 240.
Brother-making, i. 332, 369.
Buffaloes, i. 61, 132, 142, 202, 214, 220, 235, 327; ii. 222, 287.
Burghash, Syud, i. 150.
Burials, i. 120; ii. 110.
Burton, Captain, i. 108, 122, 149, 201; ii. 290.
Butterflies, i. 130.

C.

Cairo, i. 6.
Calasso, Dr., ii. 267.
Cameron, the *Frances*, ii. 275.
Camping, i, 38.
Camp at Rehenneko, i. 67; remains of Arab, i. 299.
Cannibals, i. 349, 357.
Canoes, at Malagarazi, i. 230; hiring at Ujiji, i. 246, 314; at R. Lulwu, i. 362; near Nyangwé, i. 376; at Nyangwé, ii. 6; on Lake Mohrya, ii. 65; at R. Kwanza, ii. 197.
Caravan, an Arab, i. 47, 51, 132; a Wanyamwési, i. 81; at Pakhûndi, i. 338; from Bihé, ii. 182; from West Coast, ii. 248, 251.
Carpentry, good, ii. 30.
Carving, i. 348.
Cassava, i. 41, 43, 323; ii. 241.
Castor-oil, ii. 285, 326.
Caterpillars, a delicacy, ii. 237.
Cattle, i. 94, 133; ii. 167, 184, 199.
Cauchoix, M., his great kindness, ii. 263, 267; news of his death, ii. 264.
Caves, i. 216.
Cemetery, a, ii. 211.
Chakuola, Ras and R., i. 273.
Chankoji, R., ii. 77.
Charlie, French, i. 23.
Chase, a, i. 214.
Chief, a young, i. 225; of Ujiji, i. 244; of Makukira, i. 276.
Chikumbi, ii. 184.
Children, mode of carrying, i. 89.
Christmas, a miserable, i. 188; another, ii. 92.
Chuma, i. 166.
Chunyo, i. 89.

Cinnabar, ii. 48, 330.
Claims, extortionate, i. 228.
Cloth, bark, i. 192; cotton, i. 276.
Clubs, village, i. 181.
Coal, i. 266, 329.
Coffee, ii. 325.
Coimbra, Lourenço da Souza (Kwarumba), ii. 95, 179.
Coneys at Usekhé, i. 117.
Congo, s.s., ii. 278.
Convolvuli, i. 50.
Copal, ii. 15, 287, 327.
Copper, i. 134, 319; ii. 149, 329.
Corn i. 57, 324; grinding, i. 193, 344; ii. 235, 327.
Corn, Indian, i. 44, 53; ii. 241, 285.
Corn, Kaffir or Matama, i. 53, 193, 285, 327.
Cotton, i. 278; ii. 325.
Cows in Lovalé, ii. 167.
Crane, a, i. 204.
Crew, hiring a, i. 249.
Crocodiles, in R. Kingani, i. 34; in the South Ngombé, i. 202; in Lake Tanganyika, i. 252; in R. Luguvu, i. 265; in R. Lualaba, i. 375.
Crystalline pebbles, i. 49.
Cucumbers, i. 150, 245.
Cultivation, i. 133, 297; instruments of, i. 325.
Currency, at Kawélé, i. 246; on Kongo, i. 310; at Nyangwé, ii. 3.
Customs, curious, i. 79, 95, 101, 120, 190, 333.
Cygnet, H.M.S., ii. 273.

D.

Daisy, yellow, i. 50.
Daiyi, ii. 79, 84.
Dance, native, i. 190, 258, 263, 358; ii. 91.
Daphne, H.M.S., i. 22, 30.
Darters, on Lake Tanganyika, i, 238.
Date, wild, ii. 288.
Dawson, Lieut. L. S., expedition of, i. 2.
Depredations, by Wadirigo, i. 83.
Deserts, ii. 282.
Desertions, i. 35, 47, 75, 95, 122, 135, 138, 152, 163, 172, 177, 179, 200, 315; ii. 13, 27, 108.
Destruction and desolation, i. 209.
Devils, sham, in Kibokwé, ii. 188.
Dillon, Mr. W. E., i. 5, 33, 35, 39, 43, 58, 63, 66, 152; letter from, i. 157; 160, 169, 171; his death, i. 174.
Dilolo, legend of Lake, ii. 171.

382 INDEX.

Dinah, my goat, i. 211, 350; ii. 39; Fort, ii. 44.
Disturbance, a, i. 128, 366.
Divers and darters, i. 238.
Donkeys, buying, i. 11; harness, i. 69; death of a, i. 85, 138; Muscat, i. 185; birth of a, i. 234, 309.
Dress, at Kawélé, i. 243; of Watuta, i. 285; of Warua, i. 325; at Ubûdjwa, i. 336; of Wahiya, i. 344; in Manyuéma, i. 353, 372; in Ulûnda, ii. 157; in Lovalé, ii. 165; in Kisanji, ii. 257.
Drum, wooden, i. 329.
Ducks, i. 377.
Duthumi, or Kungwa, Hills, i. 53; ii. 286.
Dwarfs, i. 357.
Dwellings, underground, ii. 89, 314.

E.

Earthquake, an, i. 362.
Ebony, i. 53.
Eclipse of the sun, i. 282; ii. 192.
Eggs, i. 57, 197.
Eland, i. 214; ii. 154.
Elephants, near the Makata, i. 61; hunter, i. 82; a herd, i. 135; tracks of, i. 114, 235, 290, 322; ii. 124, 154.
England, a work for, i. 209.
Expedition, *personnel* of, i. 170.

F.

Fauna, the, of Africa, ii. 288.
Ferry at R. Malagarazi, i. 225, 229; at R. Lulwu, i. 362.
Festival, Arab, i. 20.
Festivities, i. 130, 134; ii. 229.
Fetish, i. 101; man, i. 230, 304, 330, 336; ii. 67, 117, 159, 164, 168, 211, 218.
Fever, i. 32, 42, 152, 157, 249, 252, 322; ii, 14, 78.
Fire, at Bagamoyo, i. 19; at Kawélé, i. 312; of grass, i. 364; at Totéla, ii. 113; of country, ii, 134; of neighbouring camp, ii. 139.
Fireplaces, i. 191.
Fish, dried, i. 326, 361; in market at Nyangwé, ii. 5; in Lovalé, ii. 169.
Flogging, a, i. 241.
Forest, a, i. 351.
Fort Dinah, ii. 44.
Fortune-telling, ii. 219.
Foundries, iron, i. 338, 340, 371.

Fowl, Guinea, near Lake Ugombo, i. 82; near Simbo, i. 142; in Ulûnda, ii. 155.
Fowl, jungle, i. 142.
Fowl, water, on Lake Ugombo, i. 82.
Fowls, ii. 286.
Fracas, a, i. 26; ii. 15.
French beans, i. 13.
Frere, Sir Bartle, mission of, i. 6; comes to Bagamoyo, i. 32.
Frogs, i. 267.
Frost, ii. 161.
Fumé a Kenna, ii. 60, 115.
Fundalanga, ii. 152.

G.

Gags, for slaves, i. 341.
Game, mode of preserving, i. 192.
Garrison of Benguella, ii. 270.
Gateways, i. 141, 201.
Gazelles, i. 184, 188.
Geography, physical, ii. 285.
Germain, Père, i. 32.
Ghee, i. 89.
Giraffes, i. 61, 142, 199; ii. 287.
Gnu, or mimba, i. 139.
Goats, i. 41, 355; ii. 286.
Goître, ii. 315.
Gold, ii. 329.
Gonçalves, Senhor, ii. 204; settlement of, ii. 212.
Gorillas (Soko), i. 296.
Gourds, i. 191.
Granaries, i. 191, 199, 292, 346, 363; ii. 198.
Grandy, Lieutenant, i. 6.
Granite, i. 52, 84; rocks at Usekhé, i. 114; at Pururu, i. 130; near R. Ruguvu, on Lake Tanganyika, i. 296; near the West Coast, ii. 254, 294.
Grant, Col., i. 149.
Grapes, wild, i. 299.
Grass, tall, i. 340.
Graves, of chiefs, i. 49; of slaves, ii. 256.
Grinding corn, i. 193, 344; ii. 235.
Guava, ii. 205, 287.
Gulls, on Lake Tanganyika, i. 238.
Gum-copal, ii. 15, 287, 327.

H.

Habed ibn Salim, *alias* Tanganyika, i. 378.
Haméd ibn Haméd (Tipo-tipo), ii. 11, 20.

INDEX. 383

Hamees, i. 170.
Hamees ibn Salim, i. 51, 58.
Hanyoka, ii. 48.
Harmonium (?), Pakwanywa's, i. 333.
Hassan ibn Gharib, i. 310.
Hawks, fish, on Lake Tanganyika, i. 252.
Head-dress, of Wagogo, i. 96; of Wanyamwési, i. 194; of Wagaga, i. 227; of Wajiji, i. 244; at Kitata, i. 275; at Mikisungi, i. 279; of Watuta, i. 286; of Waguhha, i. 303; of Warua, i. 325; ii. 48, 73; of Mrs. Pakwanywa, i. 335; of Wahiya, i. 343; in Manyuóma, i. 353, 373; in Lovalé, ii. 165, 176; in Kimbandi, ii. 193; at Kapéka, ii. 199.
Heat, great, i. 330, 340; ii. 142.
Hemp, i. 245; ii. 328.
Henn, Lieut., i. 3.
Herons, at R. Kwanza, ii. 196.
Hides, ii. 328.
Hippopotami, in R. Kingani, i. 34; in Lake Ugombo, i. 82; in the South Ngombé, i. 202; in Lake Tanganyika, i. 252; in R. Luguvu, i. 265; in R. Lulwu, i. 363; in R. Lualaba, i. 375.
Hisinéné, i. 184.
Home, letters from, i. 308; ii. 272; safe, ii. 280.
Honey, i. 57, 101, 266.
Honey-birds, i. 54.
Hopkins, Consul, ii. 272.
Horner, Père, i. 12, 22.
Hospitality, Arab, i. 149.
Houses, thatched, at Khoko, i. 119; to be built for Kasongo, ii. 105.
Humbi, Hill of, ii. 241.
Huts, tembé, i. 87.
Huts, at Pururu, i. 129; at Jiwé la Singa, i. 133; at Hisinéné, i. 191; at Pakwanywa's, i. 332; in Uhiya, i. 345; near Nyangwé, i. 375; at Kifuma, ii. 30; in Ulûnda, ii. 159; in Lovalé, ii. 162; near R. Kwanza, ii. 198.
Hyænas, near Lake Ugombo, i. 83; at Kanyenyé, i. 113.

I.

Ice, ii. 161
Idols, i. 304, 330, 347; ii. 71.
Iki, L. (or L. Lincoln), ii. 12.
Illusion, an optical, i. 270.
Incident, an amusing, ii. 273.
Incivility, i. 343.

Indiarubber, vines, i. 329; ii. 288; export of, ii. 322.
Inspection, a minute, i. 226.
Iron, i. 245, 338, 340, 371; ii. 165, 181, 317, 328.
Islands, floating, i. 222, 256, 272; ii. 79, 84.
Issa, i. 35, 101, 128, 156, 170.
Itaga, i. 231.
Itambara, i. 223.
Itumvi, i. 173.
Ituru, i. 145.
Ivory, i. 124, 245, 374; trade in, ii. 321, 328.

J.

Jacko, i. 170, 229.
Jasmin, i. 185, 198, 217; death of, i. 219.
Jemadar Issa, i. 12, 13, 15, 27.
Jemadar Sabr, i. 15, 18, 28.
Jenjé (country of the Kaffirs), ii. 174.
Jiwé la Singa, i. 133; ii. 297.
João, ii. 174.
João, Baptista Ferreira, settlement of, ii. 216.
Jumah Merikani, i. 299; ii. 51, 54, 86, 107, 129.
Jumah Wadi Nassib, i. 315; ii. 40, 88, 113, 179.

K.

Kabba Rega, i. 154.
Kabengé, islands of, i. 315.
Kabogo, I. of, i. 216.
Kabogo, Ras, i. 253.
Kabongo, i. 252.
Kaça, R., i. 323.
Kadetamaré, i. 78.
Kafundango, ii. 162.
Kagnombé, town of, ii. 206; chief of, ii. 209.
Kamasanga, i. 272.
Kambala, village of, ii. 231.
Kambemba, Ras, i. 271.
Kamwassa, i. 368.
Kamwawi, ii. 37.
Kanyenyé, i. 104, 107; ii. 204.
Kanyumba, ii. 190.
Kaoli, i. 17.
Kapéka, ii. 198.
Karungu, i. 366.
Karyan Gwina, i. 262.
Kasékerah, i. 177.
Kasongé, i. 308.
Kasongo, ii. 20.

384 INDEX.

Kasongo, chief of Urua, ii. 69, 86; his return, ii. 92.
Kassabé, R., ii. 161.
Kassali, L., or Kikonja, ii. 26, 67, 78.
Kasuwa, i. 47.
Katamba, R., i. 338.
Katanki, Ras, i. 272.
Katendé, ii. 169.
Katimba, Ras, i. 260.
Katombéla, ii. 262.
Katupi, i. 296.
Kawala, ii. 143.
Kawélé, arrival at, i. 237; house at, i. 240; return to, i. 308; fire at, i. 312; second start from, i. 315.
Kawendi Mountains, ii. 300.
Kebwé, Ras, i. 253.
Kendélé. (See Alvez.)
Khedive, letter of recommendation from the, i. 6.
Khoko, i. 118; ii. 294.
Kibaiyéli, ii. 74.
Kibokwé, ii. 186, 317.
Kifuma, ii. 30.
Kigambwé Hills, i. 56.
Kigandah, i. 179.
Kihondo Hills, i. 58.
Kikoka, i. 32, 85.
Kikonja, ii. 83.
Kilemba, ii. 64, 65, 316.
Kilimachio Hills, ii. 313.
Kilolo, I. of, i. 260.
Kiluilui, R., ii. 123.
Kilwala Hills, ii. 51.
Kimbandi, ii. 190.
Kingani, R., i. 32, 34.
Kingfishers, i. 252.
Kinsembo, ii. 276.
Kinyari, i. 258.
Kipireh, i. 136.
Kirangosi, or guides, i. 349; ii. 26, 33.
Kirk, Dr., i. 24, 30.
Kiroka, i. 55.
Kirua, collecting a vocabulary of, ii. 110.
Kirumbu, i. 276.
Kisanji, country of, ii. 257, 319.
Ki Sara Sara, i. 137.
Kisémo, i. 49.
Kisenga, ii. 160.
Kisima, ii. 78.
Kisimbika, i. 364.
Kisokwch, i. 89.
Kitata, i. 275.
Kivira, I. of, i. 308, 315.
Kokéma, R., ii. 200.
Kolomamba, i. 348.
Kolqualls, i. 84.

Kombéhina, i. 66.
Kombo, i. 171.
Kongassa, i. 53.
Kongo, chief of Bailunda, ii. 231.
Kongo, R., i. 310; ii. 315.
Konongo, i. 175.
Kowamba, L., ii. 67.
Kowédi, ii. 78, 85.
Kowenga, I. of, i. 273.
Kukéwi, R, ii. 239.
Kungwa Hills, i. 53; ii. 286.
Kungwé, Ras, i. 254.
Kutato, the burst of the R., ii. 224.
Kwakasongo, i. 373.
Kwamrora Kaséa, i. 324.
Kwanza, R., ii. 191, 196.
Kwarumba, chief in Urua, ii. 37.
Kwarumba (Coimbra), ii 95.
Kwaséré, i. 339.
Kwatosi, i. 206.
Kwihuruh ("village of a chief"), i. 180, 197.
Kwikuruh, i. 147.
Kwinhata ("chief's residence"), in Urua, ii. 80.

L.

Lake dwellings, ii. 64.
"Lake Regions of Central Africa," ii. 290.
Lake-system of Africa, ii. 302.
Lanji, streams flowing to Lake, i. 251.
Lecture, a, i. 217, 348.
Lee, Mr. F., R.A., ii. 277.
Lemons, sweet, ii. 287.
Lemur, a, i. 135.
Leo, i. 73, 136, 200, 210; death of, i. 234.
Leopard, a, i. 78.
Lepidosiren, a, i. 270.
Leprosy, ii. 90.
Letters from home, i. 308; ii. 272.
Levée, a, ii. 102.
Lilies, i. 43, 50, 128, 133, 203, 262.
Lilwa, R., ii. 10.
Limes, i. 163; ii. 287.
Lindi, R., ii. 10.
Lindo (bark boxes), i. 191.
Lincoln, Lake (or Iki), ii. 12.
Lions, i. 44; ii. 87.
Liowa, chief of Western Ugara, i. 208, 211.
Livingstone, Dr., news of, i. 111; death of, 165; arrival of body, i. 167; particulars of death, i. 168; manner of transporting body, i. 181; his papers at Kawélé, i. 240, 311,

INDEX.   385

355; at Nyangwé, ii. 2; in Lovalé, ii. 170.
Livingstone, Oswell, i. 3.
Livingstone Search Expedition, first one, i. 2; second one, i. 5.
Loanda, arrival at San Paul de, ii. 272.
Locusts, ii. 243.
Lomâmi, R., ii. 11.
Longevity, instances of, i. 108, 109.
Lovalé, ii. 161, 317.
Lovoi, R., ii. 78, 138.
Lovuma, R., i. 299.
Lowa, R. (or Uellé ?), ii. 10.
Lualaba, R., i. 305; first sight of, i. 374; at Nyangwé, ii. 8; country near, ii. 312; affluents of, ii. 314.
Luama, R., ii. 152.
Lubiranzi, R., ii. 152.
Lufiji, R., i. 122.
Lufungu, R., i. 260.
Lugerengeri, R., i. 49; crossing it, i. 51.
Lugowa, i. 232.
Lugumba, R., i. 321.
Lugungwa, R., i. 327.
Luguvu, R., i. 265, 290.
Lukazi, R., ii. 34.
Lukoji, R., ii. 159.
Lukuga, R., i. 302, 305.
Lulindi, R., i. 365.
Lulu, Ras, ii. 10.
Lulumbijé, R., i. 347.
Lulumbiji, R., i. 305.
Lulwu, R., i. 362.
Lumeji, R., ii. 176, 184.
Lunga Mândi, ii. 127, 129, 316.
Lungi, ii. 225.
Lungu, i. 282.
Lupanda, ii. 145.
Luuluga, R., i. 258.
Luvijo, R., ii. 48.
Luwaziwa, R., i. 294.
Luwembi, R., ii. 12.
Luwika, R., i. 344.
Luxuries, ii. 202.

M.

Mabruki, i. 170; ii. 13.
Mabunguru Nullah, the, i. 131; ii. 296.
Machachézi, i. 253, 308.
Madété, village of, i. 82.
Magic, i. 116.
Magomba, grandson of, i. 104; great age of, i. 108; great grandson of, i. 111.

Majuto, ii. 243; death and burial, ii. 244.
Makakomo, islands of, i. 273.
Makanyazi, R., i. 266.
Makata Swamp, i. 48, 61; crossing it, i. 63.
Makukiza, i. 275.
Makurungwe, Ras, i. 273.
Malagarazi, R., i. 224, 230.
Mangos, i. 17; ii. 287.
Manioc, i. 17; ii. 286.
Mân Komo, i. 216.
Manoel, ii. 201.
Manyara, i. 371.
Manyuéma, country of, i. 352.
Mapalatta, i. 100, 183.
March, a desperate, ii. 247.
Marenga Mkali, the, i. 86, 90.
Marimba, a musical instrument, i. 357.
Market, at Kawélé, i. 244; at Nyangwé, ii. 3.
Markham, kind help of Mr. C., i. 5.
Marrows, vegetable, i. 57.
Marwa, i. 143.
Massanga, i. 272.
Massi Kambi, i. 269.
Masungwé, R., i. 235.
Matama, or Kaffir corn, i. 78, 85, 94, 224, 323; ii. 145, 293, 327.
Matomondo, i. 84.
Mata Yafa (chief in Lovalé), ii. 178.
Mata Yafa (Muato Yanvo, chief in Ulûnda), ii. 58, 148.
Mbumi, i. 79.
Mdaburu, i. 121; ii. 295.
"Medium," a, ii. 66.
Meginna, ii. 8.
Mékéto, i. 322.
Mello, Lieutenant, ii. 273.
Melons, water, i. 91.
Men, breakdown of my, ii. 241; relief sent to, ii. 266; arrival at Benguella, ii. 268; sent to Zanzibar, ii. 277.
Merikani, Jumah, i. 299; ii. 51, 54, 86, 107, 129.
Methusaleh, a veritable, i. 108.
Mfomdo Point, i. 251.
Mfuv, the, ii. 287.
Mganga, or medicine man, ii. 81, 118.
Mgunda Mkali, or Fiery Field, i. 125, 127; ii. 295.
Mhongo, i. 45, 49, 94, 100, 110, 118, 125, 206, 216, 224.
Mickikichi, or palm-oil tree, i. 285.
Miguu Mifupi, i. 118.
Milk-bush, the, i. 145.
Mimba, or gnu, i. 139.
Minstrels, Negro, i. 250.

VOL. I.   C C

Mirambo, i. 77, 124, 139, 150, 195, 227.
Miriro, chief of Akalunga, i. 292.
Mission, French, at Bagamoyo, i. 13; Scotch, on Lake Nyassa, ii. 330.
Mkombenga, i. 65.
Mkwembwé, i. 171.
M'Nchkulla, ii. 47.
Moéné Bugga and Gohé, i. 356.
Moéné Kula, ii. 158.
Moffat, Robert, i. 33, 43, 71.
Mohalé, R., and village, i. 56.
Mohammed ibn Gharib, i. 309.
Mohammed ibn Salim, i. 240, 309.
Mohammed Malim, i. 170, 188, 196, 315.
Mohrya, L., ii. 26, 62.
Mona Kasanga, ii. 26, 36, 49.
Mona Lamba, ii. 185.
Mona Pého, ii. 186.
Monkeys, i. 140, 253, 280.
Mpafu-tree, the, i. 326, 328; ii. 15, 113, 326.
Mpanga Sanga, i. 101.
Mpara Gwina, i. 277.
Mparamusi-tree, the, i. 77; ii. 288.
Mpeta, i. 230.
Mpimbwe, Ras, i. 270.
Mpwapwa, i. 83, 85.
Mrima Ngombé, chief of Ugunda, i. 180, 195.
Mshiri, chief of Katanga, ii. 140.
Msoa, ii. 139.
Msuwah, i. 44.
Mtamba, R., i. 213.
Mtésa, King, i. 153.
Mtonga, i. 46.
Muinyi Bokhara, i. 356.
Muinyi Dugumbi, ii. 2.
Muinyi Hassani, i. 367, 374.
Muinyi Useghura, i. 78.
Mukondokwa, R., i. 76, 82.
Mulattoes, ii. 249.
Mulongo, Ras, i. 308.
Munza, ii. 51.
Murphy, Lieutenant C., i. 8, 23, 32, 70, 152, 158, 168, 172, 178, 181, 198.
Musamwira, R., i. 268.
Music, i. 333, 356; ii. 93.
Mutilation, of women, i. 294; of men, ii. 98.
Mutiny, a, 156.
Mutwalé ("chief"), i. 224.
Mvumi, i. 94.
Mwéhu, ii. 77.
Mwéré Torrent, i. 57.
Myamburau, the, ii. 287.

N.

Nassibs, the ibn, i. 154, 167, 172.
Needlework, ii. 91.
New, Mr., death of, i. 3.
Ngombé Nullah, the South, i. 202.
Niamtaga, i. 236.
Nile, R., impossibility of identity with Lualaba, ii. 10.
Njivi Marsh, ii. 125.
Nullah, the, Mabunguru, i. 131.
Nuts, ground-, i. 324; ii. 285.
Nutmegs, in Uvinza, i. 236; at Russûna's, ii. 15, 326.
Nyangwé, arrival at, i. 378; ii. 1; departure from, ii. 13.
Nyanza, Lakes Albert and Victoria, ii. 303.
Nyassa, L., ii. 303.

O.

Oak, African, ii. 15.
Oil, palm, i. 245; ii. 4.
Omens, i. 150.
Ophthalmia, i. 159, 162, 171.
Oranges, i. 17, 214; ii. 287.
Ornaments, at Rehenneko, i. 66; Mpwapwa, i. 88; Wagogo, i. 95, 141; Wanyamwési, i. 194; Wagara, i. 210; Wagaga, i. 227; at Kuwélé, i. 243; Karyan Gwina, i. 264; Mikisungi, i. 279; Watuta, i. 285; Akalunga, i. 335; Waguhha, i. 304; Warua, i. 325; ii. 48; Mrs. Pakwanywa's, i. 325; Wabûdjwa, i. 366; Wavinza, i. 348; in Manyuéma, i. 335.
Outlet of Lake Tanganyika, i. 301.

P.

Pagazi, difficulty of procuring, i. 10, 25; death of a, i. 85; duties of, i. 107, 152, 177; an accident to a, i. 321; breakdown of the, ii. 241; death and burial of a, ii. 244.
Painting, oil, i. 332; face, ii. 48.
Pakhûadi, i. 337.
Pakwanywa, i. 327, 331; Mrs., i. 334.
Palaver, a, i. 369.
Palms, fan-, i. 62, 65, 262; -oil tree, i. 285; date-, i. 306; oil, i. 350; ii. 29, 138, 325; cocoa-, ii. 287.
Palmyras, i. 135.
Panic, a, i. 215, 220, 272.
Papaw, the, ii. 287.
Parks, public, i. 342.
Partridges, i. 142.

INDEX. 387

Payment, curious mode of, i. 246.
Pechel, Dr. Loesche, ii. 278.
Pembereh, great age of, i. 109.
Pepper, ii. 326.
Pickle, the, i. 248, 298, 315.
Pig, wild, i. 54.
Pigeon-shooting, i. 117, 359.
Point, highest reached, ii. 248.
Poisoned arrows, i. 82.
Polunga, I., i. 280.
Pombé, i. 130, 183, 190, 197, 245, 276; ii. 198.
Pombeiros, the, ii. 157.
Ponda, i. 262.
Poporla, chief of Kawala, ii. 143.
Porridge, i. 192.
Portuguese, the, i. 292; ii. 51, 66.
Pottery, i. 191, 245, 289; ii. 4.
Potatoes, sweet, i. 44, 53, 85, 191, 224, 245, 324.
Prerogative, a chief's, i. 358.
Primulas, i. 50.
Public-houses in Unyamwési, i. 181.
Pumpkins, i. 44, 57, 191; ii. 293.
Pururu, i. 128.

Q.

Quail, i. 202.
Quartz, i. 49, 52, 84; ii. 286.

R.

Rain, in Ugogo, i. 94; in Ugara, i. 208, 212; in Uvinza, i. 220, 235; on Tanganyika, i. 300; in Bihé, ii. 221; at Humbi, ii. 242.
Raphia, the, ii. 288.
Reception, a warm, ii. 202.
Rehenneko, arrival at, i. 66; stay at, i. 69; start from, i. 75.
Relief sent to men, ii. 266.
Rhinoceros, skull, i. 132; a white, i. 202, 214.
Rice, i. 53, 188; ii. 286, 327.
Rohombo, i. 349.
Rosako, village of, i. 38.
Rosin, i. 24.
Roses in Bihé, ii. 214.
Routes, trade, ii. 321.
Roubu, R., ii. 14.
Ruaha, R., i. 122.
Ruanda, i. 317.
Rubumba, i. 327.
Ruga-Ruga, i. 143, 145, 182.
Ruguvu, R., 235.
Rusugi, R., i. 234.
Russúna, ii. 12, 16.

S.

Sack, manufacture of a, i. 198.
Said ibn Salim al Lamki, i. 124, 147, 172, 182, 196.
Sail-making, i. 147.
Sale, a, i. 313.
Salt, i. 105, 134, 232, 245; ii. 4, 52, 330.
Salutations, i. 226, 342.
Samaritan, a good, ii. 263.
Sambo, i. 112, 170, 197, 231, 254; ii. 181.
Sandstone, i. 49.
Sankorra, L., ii. 12.
Scene, a lovely, i. 280.
Scheme, for exploration, i. 4; for commerce stations, ii. 331.
Scurvy, attacked by, ii. 260, 267.
Secretary-birds, i. 202.
Sem-sem, ii. 285.
Seruia, Mr., ii. 262.
Sesamum, ii. 326.
Sha Kélembé, ii. 175.
Shamba Gonèra, i. 26.
Shaykh ibn Nassib, i. 154.
Sheep, i. 355, ii. 286.
Showman, a, i. 350.
Signals, i. 194.
Silva Porto, settlement of, 220.
Silver, ii. 329.
Simbawéni, i. 56.
Simbo in Useghara, i. 58.
Simbo in Urguru, i. 142.
Sindy, R., i. 221, 222.
Sirius, H.M.S., ii. 277.
Skeletons of slaves, ii. 256.
Slaves, i. 164; of Arabs, i. 212, 373; ii. 27; of Portuguese, ii. 106; of Coimbra, ii. 136; of Alvez, ii. 147; escape of a gang, ii. 163; of Silva Porto, ii. 191; export of, ii. 246.
Slave-trade, the, i. 209, 246, 255, 257, 277, 324, 341; ii. 4, 141, 168, 217, 256, 321.
Small-pox in Kanyenyé, i. 106.
Smithies, i. 372; ii. 189.
Snakes, i. 135, 189; ii. 145; the supper of a, ii. 192; a trader in, ii. 269, 289.
Snipe, i. 188.
Snuff, liquid, i. 233.
Soap, ii. 24.
Soko (gorillas), i. 296.
Soorghi, i. 17.
Sona Bazh, ii. 161.
Speke, Captain, i. 149.
Spiders, i. 298; ii. 289.
Spinning, cotton, i. 278.

c c 2

Spiteful, H.M.S., ii. 274.
Springs, hot, i. 302, 337.
Stanley, Mr., news of success of his first expedition brought to Bagamoyo, i. 2 ; second expedition, i. 4.
Stores, i. 23, 163, 320.
Storms, i. 259.
Story, an improbable, i. 115; a curious, i. 204.
Strike, a, i. 68.
"Suahili Tales," i. 312.
Sugar-cane, i. 245 ; ii. 286, 325.
Superstitions, i. 144, 189, 253, 272, 302 ; ii. 83, 118, 188, 192.
Surgery, ii. 24.
Suspension bridge, a, i. 365.
Susi, i. 166.
Sycamores, i. 119, 262.
Syde ibn Habib, i. 246.
Syde ibn Omar, i. 80.
Syde Mezrui, i. 250, 310, 332 ; ii. 2.
Syud Burghash, i. 150.

T.

Taborah, i. 162.
Taka, chief of Eastern Ugara, i. 185, 205.
Tales, Suahili, i. 312 ; strange, ii. 87.
Tamarinds, i. 163 ; ii. 287.
Tanganyika, first sight of Lake, i. 237 ; start for circuit of, i. 250; enlargement of, i. 268; how fed, i. 295 ; leaving, i. 317 ; last sight of, i. 322 ; ii. 302.
Tanganyika, *alias* Habed ibn Salim, i. 378 ; ii. 2.
Tarya Topan, i. 23.
Tattooing, i. 193, 227, 336, 343.
Teak, ii. 15, 288.
Teal, bird like, near Mvumi, i. 98.
Teeth, chipping, i. 193, 286, 343.
Temba Lui ("Devil's Finger"), ii. 236.
Tembé huts first met with, i. 87.
Temé, i. 176.
Terekesa, a, i. 83.
Terraces, i. 297.
Téwéré, i. 205.
Thieving, i. 236, 241, 282, 298, 365 ; ii. 32.
Thrashing, a, ii. 34.
Thunderstorm, a, ii. 77.
Timber-trees, ii. 326.
Tingi-tingi, i. 285; ii. 84.
Tipo-tipo (Haméd ibn Haméd), ii. 11, 20.
Tobacco, i. 224, 245, 258; ii. 86, 205, 293, 325.

Tomatoes, i. 245.
Totéla, ii. 106.
Traders, at Kawélé, i. 242 ; at Karungu, i. 367 ; on Lake Sankorra, ii. 25 ; a Portuguese, ii. 228.
Trade, slave-, i. 209, 246, 255, 257, 277, 324, 341 ; ii. 41, 141, 168, 217, 256 ; various articles of, 321.
Traps, for game, i. 136 ; for fish, i. 269 ; 362 ; ii. 160.
Trees, giant, i. 351.
Tribal marks, i. 193, 286.
Turk, a, i. 177.

U.

Ubûdjwa, i. 327 ; ii. 311.
Uellé, R. (or Lowa ?), ii. 10.
Ufipa, i. 281.
Ugaga, i. 225.
Ugali, or porridge. i. 192.
Ugara, i. 185, 205 ; ii. 300.
Ugarowwa R. (same as Kongo and Lualaba), i. 310 ; ii. 10.
Ugogo, i. 91 ; ii. 292.
Ugoma, Mountains of, i. 307 : ii. 310.
Ugombo, R. and L., i. 82.
Uguhha, i. 317.
Ugunda, i. 179, 200 ; ii. 299.
Uhha, i. 225.
Uhiya, i. 343 ; ii. 312.
Ujiji, i. 237 ; return to, i. 308 ; second start from, i. 315.
Ukaranga, i. 236 ; ii. 301.
Ulegga, ii. 9.
Ulûnda, ii. 152, 317.
Ulungu, i. 281.
Umbrella, an, i. 207 ; gay, ii. 248.
Underground dwellings, ii. 89, 314 ; streams, ii. 318.
Unyanyembé, Arab governor of, i. 124, 147, 172, 182, 196.
Unyanyembé, arrival at, i. 145 ; departure from, i. 171 ; ii. 298.
Urguru, i. 140 ; ii. 297.
Urua, ii. 68.
Useghara, Muinyi, i. 78 ; ii. 285, 289.
Usekhé, i. 114 ; ii. 294.
Ussambi, ii. 138, 316.
Utendé, i. 207.
Uvinza, East, i. 217, 224 ; ii. 300.
Uvinza, West, i. 347 ; ii. 312.

V.

Village, of Msuwah, i. 45 ; stockaded, i. 145; ii. 139, 159; Kasékerah, i. 178 ; in Ugunda, i. 201 ; Téwéré, i.

206; Mân Komo, i. 216; destroyed by Mirambo, i. 228; deserted, i. 234, 340, 345; ii. 15; Kinyari, i. 258; Karyan Gwina, i. 263; in Manyuéma, i. 352; burning, i. 368; Russûna's, ii. 19; in Urua, ii. 36; Mussumba, ii. 60; in Lovalé, ii. 167; in Bihé, ii. 205.
Visits, a round of, i. 149; a state, ii. 21, 57, 60, 170, 207, 233.
Visitors, i. 69, 100, 123, 225, 255.

W.

Wadirigo, predatory tribe, i. 83, 88.
Wagenya, i. 375.
Wagogo, i. 92.
Waguhha, i. 245, 303.
Wahumba, i. 120.
Wainwright, letter from Jacob, i. 165.
Wakimbu, i. 127.
Wamerima, i. 9, 36, 119, 164.
Wanyamwési caravan, i. 81, 86.
Warori, i. 164.
Warua, i. 323.
Warundi, i. 245.

Wasuahili, i. 9, 164.
Water, lack of, i. 83, 127; contrivance for carrying, i. 87; green, ii. 48.
Watersheds, i. 133; ii. 283.
Watosi, i. 195.
Watuta, i. 285.
Wedding, a, ii. 76.
"Westward Ho!" i. 171.
Wheat, i. 150; ii. 327.
Whindé, i. 44.
Wine, palm, i. 245.
Women, mutilation of, i. 294; fisher-, i. 362.

Y.

Yacooti, ii. 229, 237.
Yamini, Ras, i. 283.
Yams, i. 16, 245.
Yellala Cataracts, i. 310; ii. 333.

Z.

Zambési, R., ii. 161.
Zanzibar, arrival at, i. 8; leave, i. 11.
Zebra, i. 90, 139, 188; ii. 161, 288.
Ziwa, or pond, i. 98, 104, 145; ii. 293.

THE END.

AND ITS RELATION TO THE ANTIQUITY OF MAN.

By JAMES GEIKIE, F.R.S., ETC.,
OF H.M. GEOLOGICAL SURVEY.

Second Edition, thoroughly Revised.

With much New Matter embodying the most Recent Discoveries, additional Maps and Illustrations, &c.

Demy 8vo, 24s.

"There is a great charm in the well-balanced union of cultivated powers of observation and analytical method, with considerable imagination and much poetical feeling, which runs through the pages of this volume. . . . . . We have indicated but imperfectly the philosophical spirit which marks every step of this inquiry into the wonders of 'The Great Ice Age,' and we strongly recommend the volume to all who are prepared to read thoughtfully, and weigh the evidence of truth carefully, in the assurance of finding that there are indeed 'Sermons in Stones.'"—*Athenæum.*

"Every step in the process is traced with admirable perspicuity and fulness by Mr. Geikie. . . . . This book will mark an epoch in the scientific study of the Ice Age."—*Saturday Review.*

"The book shows everywhere the marks of acute observation, wide research, and sound reasoning. It presents in a readable form the chief features of the great Ice Age, and illustrates them very amply from those great tracts of Scotland in which glaciation has left its most distinct and most enduring marks."—*Spectator.*

"No one can peruse this most interesting book without feeling grateful to Mr. Geikie for his masterly summing-up of the evidence, and appreciating the spirit of scientific candour with which he states his conclusions. At once in respect of its matter and its tone, the work forms a valuable contribution to our scientific literature."—*Scotsman.*

"By far the most important contribution to the chapter of Geological inquiry that has yet appeared. We can assure our readers that they will find in Mr. Geikie's book an admirable and satisfactory summary of the present condition of opinion on some of the most interesting of geological questions, which are here discussed in an agreeable and readable manner."—*Westminster Review.*

"This work, without any sacrifice of scientific accuracy and completeness, is so clear and so free from technicalities, as to be intelligible to any reader of ordinary education. For knowledge and command of his subject, for skill in the arrangement of his facts, and for the clearness with which he reasons out his conclusions, Mr. Geikie occupies a high place as a scientific writer."—*Academy.*

"Can be cordially recommended both to the geologist and the general reader. The explanations are so full, and the method of handling so free from technicality, that with a moderate amount of attention the book may be understood, and its reasoning followed, by those who had previously little or no geological knowledge."—*Nature.*

DALDY, ISBISTER & CO., 56, LUDGATE HILL, LONDON.

CLIMATE AND TIME
IN THEIR GEOLOGICAL RELATIONS:
A THEORY OF SECULAR CHANGES OF THE EARTH'S CLIMATE.

By JAMES CROLL, LL.D., F.R.S., of H.M. Geological Survey.

With Illustrations, demy 8vo, 24s.

"One of the most philosophical contributions to the science of geology within the last half-century. Every page is distinguished by close and earnest thought, and the conclusions arrived at, whether we accept them or not, are the result of striking powers of deductive analysis."—*Athenæum*.

"Whatever verdict may ultimately await the author, it will be readily conceded that he has shown himself master of a very wide range of knowledge, and that his pages are marked by unusual originality of thought and vigour of reasoning."—*Academy*.

"Admirable alike for its abundance of carefully-collected facts, and for the sobriety and force of its reasoning. Our readers must go to the book itself to judge of the capacity and patience with which Mr. Croll's thesis is argued out."—*Spectator*.

"Mr. Croll's work is everything which a scientific work should be that requires deep research and laborious thought, combined with the boldest generalisation. . . . . The theory is at once beautiful, simple, and complete."—*Quarterly Review*.

"Since Sir Charles Lyell sent forth his 'Principles of Geology,' we do not think we have had a work that is likely to be so influential on the future of the science as this."—*British Quarterly Review*.

"The publication of this volume marks one of the great eras in the progress of geological investigation. No greater clearing of ground, lengthening of cords, and strengthening of stakes in the fields of geology have taken place since the days of Hutton."—*Philosophical Magazine*.

"We are not saying too much when we affirm that in the department of geological philosophy which it discusses it will rank alongside Lyell's 'Principles,' and will secure the reputation of its author."—*Geographical Magazine*.

"This is the most important work that has appeared on geological events and changes for many years. We have no hesitation in saying that the author's reasoning must be conclusive to any unbiassed mind, and that he has established upon an incontrovertible basis his theory that the glacial epochs are primarily, although not directly, due to the eccentricity of the earth's orbit."—*Standard*.

"This is one of the most striking and original books published for many years. Not only can no student dispense with a thorough examination of its contents, but the clearness with which some of the most wonderful problems connected with the physical history of the world are stated, and the striking character of the methods by which their solution is attempted, will enlarge the range of thought of any reader, however unfamiliar with such investigations."—*Inquirer*.

"A great part of the volume is taken up with an able discussion of the heating powers of ocean-currents, and the physical cause of oceanic circulation. Mr. Croll then endeavours to show that ocean-currents are caused by the impulse of the prevailing winds of the globe, regarded as a general system. He stoutly attacks all other theories of oceanic circulation, reviewing Maury's and Dr. Carpenter's especially at great length. His examination of these two theories is, indeed, exceedingly acute and searching, and their overthrow is apparently complete."—*Scotsman*.

"A very important contribution to geological inquiry; and for a long time no work has appeared which in equal measure is so certain to exercise an influence on the future of the science."—*Magazin für die Literatur des Auslandes*.

DALDY, ISBISTER & CO., 56, LUDGATE HILL, LONDON.

𝔈𝔩𝔢𝔳𝔢𝔫𝔱𝔥 𝔗𝔥𝔬𝔲𝔰𝔞𝔫𝔡.

With Portraits and numerous Illustrations, 2 Vols. demy 8vo, 26s.

MEMOIR OF
NORMAN MACLEOD, D.D.
BY HIS BROTHER, DONALD MACLEOD, D.D.,
One of Her Majesty's Chaplains.

"We once more commend to our readers a work which is a fitting monument, erected with the true self-forgetfulness of a loving brother and a faithful biographer; and which will leave the abiding impression that in Norman Macleod all who knew him mourn a devoted, gallant and delightful friend, and his Church and country lost a magnificent champion of the good, the noble, and the true."—*Times.*

"The biographer's delicate duty has been performed with tact and good taste, and it is rare that one writing so soon after his hero's death is able to give so much completeness to his portrait."—*Daily News.*

"Mr. Donald Macleod has done his work of compiling this memoir of his justly-celebrated brother with care and good taste. The introductory chapters give an interesting glimpse of a state of life and manners that is now well-nigh forgotten."—*Pall Mall Gazette.*

"There is in this memoir a sense of vivid reality and of close personal contact, which is a rare quality in this branch of literature."—*Saturday Review.*

"A memoir worthy of the subject. It may well do for Scotland what Dr. Stanley's Life of Arnold did for England."—*Spectator.*

"There is throughout these volumes a freedom from cant and sentimentality that is rare in the biography of a popular divine."—*Athenæum.*

"The life of a good and honest man is here narrated with a simplicity and truthfulness which disarm criticism."—*Examiner.*

"This book is a portrait, and it is so well done that it may be taken as an example by writers who have such a delicate piece of work in hand. . . . That a man so free in thought, so bold in speech, so broad in charity, should be at the same time so simply devout, full of all the tremblings of the tenderest piety, is a lesson and example to us all."—*Blackwood's Magazine.*

"You could not say where he was greatest, but you felt that everywhere he was a streaming fountain of influence, and a man among a million men."—*Fraser's Magazine.*

"A really good book. . . . We would venture earnestly to commend it to the consideration of the English clergy. . . . Brave and tender, manful and simple, profoundly susceptible of enjoyment, but never preferring it to duty; overflowing with love, yet always chivalrous for truth; full of power, full of labour, full of honour, he has died, and has bequeathed to us, for a study which we hope will reach far beyond the bounds of his communion and denomination, the portrait of a great orator and pastor and a true and noble-hearted man."—*Church Quarterly Review.*

"A man of great faculty, whose genius was of the kind that would have justified itself in almost any direction. He might have been an artist, a great commander, an author of high rank. We think of him with an affection which increases in the light of more intimate knowledge, as a true worker for others, a devoted, self-denying man."—*British Quarterly Review.*

"A valuable and interesting book. It is the life of a thorough man . . . with boundless fun there is always strong sense and real earnestness."—*Westminster Review.*

"We have nothing but praise for these volumes. Inspired by deep affection, the author's work has been done with delicate skill, with perfect fairness, and with here and there a courageous word for 'freedom's holy law.'"—*Theological Review.*

DALDY, ISBISTER & CO., 56, LUDGATE HILL, LONDON.

Works by the late Norman Macleod, D.D.

Peeps at the Far East:
A Familiar Account of a Visit to India. With Illustrations. Small 4to, 21s.

Eastward:
Travels in Egypt, Palestine, and Syria. With Illustrations. Crown 8vo, 6s.

Character Sketches.
With Illustrations. Post 8vo, 10s. 6d.

The Starling.
With Illustrations. Crown 8vo, 6s.

The Old Lieutenant and his Son.
With Illustrations. Crown 8vo, 3s. 6d.

Reminiscences of a Highland Parish.
Crown 8vo, 6s.

The Earnest Student:
Memorials of John Mackintosh. Crown 8vo, 3s. 6d.

The Gold Thread.
With Illustrations. Square 8vo, 2s. 6d.

Wee Davie.
Sewed, 6d.

Parish Papers.
Crown 8vo, 3s. 6d.

Simple Truth spoken to Working People.
Small 8vo, 2s. 6d.

War and Judgment.
A Sermon preached before the Queen, and published by Her Majesty's Command. Sewed, 1s.

How can we best Relieve our Deserving Poor?
Sewed, 6d.

DALDY, ISBISTER & CO., 56, LUDGATE HILL, LONDON.

www.ingramcontent.com/pod-product-compliance
Lightning Source LLC
Chambersburg PA
CBHW020533300426
44111CB00008B/650